Singing in the Lower Secondary School

T0355472

Oxford Music Education Series

The Oxford Music Education Series was established with Janet Mills (1954–2007) as series editor to present concise, readable, and thought-provoking handbooks for all those involved in music education, including teachers, community musicians, researchers, policy-makers, and parents/carers. The series encompasses a wide range of topics and musical styles, and aims to provide 'food for thought' for all those looking to broaden their understanding and further develop their work. Written by acknowledged leaders of education who are passionate about their subject, the books present cutting-edge ideas and aim to stimulate good practice by showing the practical implications of research.

Other titles in the Oxford Music Education Series

Janet Mills: *Music in the School* (2005)

Janet Mills: *Instrumental Teaching* (2007)

Adam Ockelford: *Music for Children and Young People with Complex Needs* (2008)

John Paynter and Janet Mills (eds): *Thinking and Making: Selections from the writings of John Paynter on music in education* (2008)

David Bray: *Creating a Musical School* (2009)

Janet Mills: *Music in the Primary School*, 3rd edn (2009)

Martin Fautley: *Assessment in Music Education* (2010)

Singing in the Lower Secondary School

Martin Ashley

MUSIC DEPARTMENT

OXFORD
UNIVERSITY PRESS

OXFORD
UNIVERSITY PRESS

Great Clarendon Street, Oxford, OX2 6DP,
United Kingdom

Oxford University Press is a department of the University of Oxford.
It furthers the University's objective of excellence in research, scholarship,
and education by publishing worldwide. Oxford is a registered trade mark of
Oxford University Press in the UK and in certain other countries

First Edition published in 2015

Impression: 2

Library of Congress Control Number: 2015934488

ISBN 978-0-19-339900-6

Printed in Great Britain by
CPI Group (UK) Ltd, Croydon, CR0 4YY

Foreword

Few would question the importance and centrality of singing to the human species or its essential place in music education: 'men sang out their feelings long before they were able to speak their thoughts'.[1] John Paynter, in *Sound and Silence*, quotes Szabolsci: 'man was most strongly influenced by the natural sounds he experienced directly ... above all he had his own voice'.[2]

Fast forward to the twentieth century. Before England had a national curriculum requiring all pupils aged 5 to 14 to sing and use their voices, school inspectors referred to the importance of singing.[3] Recommended activities included performing a range of songs and imitating and recalling simple melodic vocal patterns, as well as improvising using the voice. In this Oxford Music Education Series, composer and broadcaster Howard Goodall, for a time the National Ambassador for Singing, provided a helpful foreword to David Bray's *Creating a Musical School* (2009), and in *Assessment in Music Education* (2010), Martin Fautley illustrates how 'singing features as a performing activity throughout music learning'.[4]

So why, you may well ask, do we need a book on singing in the lower secondary school, specifically? The sad truth is that singing in many, if not most, secondary schools remains a challenge. (The available data suggests that only about a quarter of English secondary schools boast singing that can be described as good or excellent). This is despite the success of the Sing Up campaign led by Goodall; despite the excellence achieved by cathedral choristers; despite the popularity of TV talent programmes such as *The Voice* and *The X Factor*; and despite Fautley's support for quality assessment of singing.

---

[1] Otto Jespersen, *Language, Its Nature, Development and Origin* (New York: Henry Holt and Company, 1922)

[2] Bence Szabolsci, *A History of Melody* (London: Barrie and Rockliff, 1965), quoted in John Paynter and Peter Aston, *Sound and Silence* (Cambridge: CUP, 1970)

[3] DES, *Music from 5 to 16: Curriculum Matters 4* (London: HMSO, 1985)

[4] Martin Fautley, *Assessment in Music Education*, Oxford Music Education Series (Oxford: OUP, 2010)

Drawing on his research and practical experiences, Martin Ashley helps the reader to find their own accessible solutions, particularly secondary school music specialists who do not consider themselves to be singing specialists. He teases out the differences of approach and outcome for 'Just singing', for Choral work and for Vocal work, and between music for leisure and music for learning. He distinguishes between the roles of curricular and extra-curricular music in schools and progression routes in and beyond schools, raising important considerations in respect of the role of English music education hubs in ensuring singing strategies as part of a national plan. Ashley explodes the myth about the voice 'break', pointing out that it is the consequence of poor vocal management and inappropriate repertoire. Handling voice 'change' for both boys and girls needs to be part of the professional toolkit of the secondary classroom teacher.

Ashley concludes that 'no singing at all is probably preferable to bad singing under the direction of an insensitive teacher who knows or cares little about adolescent voices.' This is probably true, but should any system be allowing such a teacher to continue to teach without being challenged and supported in finding an acceptable solution? For this reason alone, Ashley's book should be essential reading for all involved in the training, professional development, and inspection of music teachers, including, of course, the teachers themselves.

Richard J. Hallam MBE
Chair, Music Education Council 2013/16

About the author

Martin Ashley trained originally as a middle-school music specialist. He taught for 17 years in UK state and independent schools before moving into higher education at the University of the West of England, Bristol. There he led programmes of teacher development including the EdD and BA in educational studies. In 2007 he moved to Edge Hill University, where he was awarded a personal chair for his AHRC-funded post-doctoral work in young masculinity and vocal performance, and an institutional chair on appointment to the role of Head of Research. He retired from that role in April 2013 in order to concentrate more intensively on his research into young male singing and the promotion in the UK of the 'cambiata' singing concept for adolescent voices. He developed, in collaboration with the National Youth Choirs of Great Britain, and continues to promote through the Association of British Choral Directors, the cambiata based 'Boys Keep Singing' project.

Contents

Introduction

There are many fine musicians and dedicated music teachers working in our schools, but by no means all of them are singers or choral specialists. Teaching and directing the singing of lower secondary school children may never have been part of their musical experience or training. This book is written for quite a wide audience, but a key target group is those working in secondary schools that are music specialists but not singing specialists. Some teachers in that category may be content to run music departments where there is little or no singing. Others may feel that there ought to be more singing in their school than there perhaps is, but either lack confidence in tackling the problem or feel they could improve what they do. Yet others working in secondary schools may be from choral backgrounds. If they are organists or church musicians, choral singing by children of lower secondary age may be what they have lived for much of their lives. For the majority of secondary music specialists, the peculiar and intense emphasis on children's voices in ecclesiastical choral music may well be an entirely alien world.

Whatever the background and previous experience of the individual, all have something to learn that can only be learned within the context of the lower secondary school. Singing in the lower secondary school is not easy. If it were, it would be more widespread than is actually the case. Singing in the lower secondary school is actually a specialism within a specialism. It is not the same as choral singing and it requires a specialized knowledge of young adolescent voices peculiar to those that teach music at this level. It also requires particular knowledge of young adolescents and their music, underpinned by an unquenchable enthusiasm that is resilient enough to overcome the fact that school, and certainly school music, is irredeemably by definition 'not cool'.

As we shall see in Chapter 2, much is written about school singing as though it were such a 'good thing' that a school without singing is unthinkable. Yet schools without singing are common. The available data suggest that in just under half of English secondary schools, *there is no singing at all*. In only about a quarter of English secondary schools is the singing good or excellent. Chapters 2 and 3 deal with the policy issues. Chapter 2 paints a picture of advocacy groups demanding a level of singing that has never been achieved in English secondary schools, and a schools inspectorate highly critical of the failure of schools to achieve it. Chapter 3 extends this discussion to address the inequality of provision, grasping two particular nettles. First, the fact that good singing is significantly more likely to be found in private, fee-charging schools than in publicly funded schools. Second, the fact that there *is* good or excellent singing in a minority of publicly funded schools, and this has everything to do with the quality of senior leadership and music teaching. It has somewhat less to do with the socio-economic background of the pupils.

I was invited to write this book mainly on the strength of research and development I have been carrying out over the last two decades since leaving behind a 17-year career in schools for work in higher education and teacher training. A clue to the nature of this work is in the title of the first chapter—all can sing, even 13-year-old boys. My approach to singing is a democratic one powered by the conviction that singing is for all. This sets me at odds with a cultural trend that has seen less and less public choral singing and instead a focus on individual vocalists or small bands competing in popularized talent shows. Singing has become a spectator sport and much of its entertainment value seems to lie in the humiliation of contestants being given their marching order by the 'judges'.

Not content with fighting one battle though, I have also taken on the far older challenge of getting 13-year-old boys to sing. Earnest writing about the problem of so-called 'missing males' in singing dates back something like a century, so it is not a new one. Yet my own background in cathedral music has convinced me that this is a problem worth tackling. Not only can 13-year-old boys sing uniquely well, they can do so with a conviction for music that becomes lifelong. I had once thought that everybody knew and understood this, but was disabused of this notion by a piece of research I carried out for a project funded by the organization Youth Music. This was during the period when I managed the chorister outreach programme of Bristol Cathedral. The unique finding of that research, carried out across the primary schools of the Bristol area, was that children *and their teachers* believed that boys were incapable of singing well. Boys gave up singing, not because it was 'girly' but because the prevailing belief and expectation was that they *could not sing*, or could only sing in 'low, gruff voices'.

Another early piece of research that still remains seminal in my thinking was a detailed sociological study of the all-male choir of a large, nationally known city church. There I was disabused of my earlier false belief that boys sang in church choirs because they were bribed by camps, football games, swimming or bowling trips, and free pizza. They sang because they *loved singing* and *loved the music* they sang. This study also resulted in further revelations of the extent to which low expectations of boys with regard to singing in many schools really was a major issue. In 2003 I was awarded a fellowship by the Arts and Humanities Research Council (AHRC) that permitted a year's complete freedom to undertake a full-time post-doctoral study entitled 'Young masculinity and vocal performance'. The conditions of the award were that every genre and context of young male singing should be examined.

The study concentrated on the work of solo boy performers who had made commercial CDs, ranging from highbrow classical through pop–classical crossover to 'cheesy' pop and punk rock. The boy artists were interviewed and observed, but of far greater relevance to the present volume were the visits made to some 30 secondary schools around the country to play the work of these boys in lower secondary classes, assess reactions to it and discuss it with the pupils. The detailed study was published as a research monograph by the Edwin Mellen Press, entitled *Teaching singing to boys and teenagers* (Ashley 2008b). A revised and more accessible version was later published by Ashgate with the title *How high should boys sing?* (Ashley 2009a). Although there was some necessary examination of the physical nature of the adolescent boy voice, this was a sociological study that examined gender and social class. The entry point was the popular belief that boys consider singing 'sissy' or 'unmanly' and do not want to 'sound like girls'.

The exit point was a much deeper understanding and an appreciation that generation is probably more significant than gender. Music education in the UK has for some years now stressed the importance of the triumvirate of listening, composing and performing. What *How high should boys sing?* showed above all was that there is an almost complete disconnection between listener and performer in boys' singing. The clue is in the title, 'How high?' When boys of lower secondary age sing beautifully in a high voice, the audience is 'elderly people' or 'grannies and mothers'. Young adolescent boys do not often listen to age peers singing, though girls can think such boy singers 'cute'. If the same boys attempt to sing in a lower, more 'manly' voice, the audience of grannies and mothers is lost, but no new audience is gained. Boys are then simply compared with girls and it is possible to see where the belief that boys cannot sing, or sing only in a 'low, gruff voice' comes from. *How high should boys sing?* showed that boys can be damned if they do and damned if they don't. There is no universal answer to the 'how high?' question.

One chapter of the present volume owes much to this study. Chapter 6 deals with the vital issue of how adolescents, male and female, construct and manage their identity through music. It deals with the inevitable generation gap between teacher and pupils and proposes a version of school singing that is neutral ground or mutually acceptable territory. School singing is not 'cool', but it can be enjoyable for teacher and pupils. Importantly, it can be a *means of learning music*. I stress this point because, even in schools where the singing is strong, the full potential of voice-based music pedagogy is seldom realized. I say more about this shortly in the first chapter. The study also contributed to Chapter 9, which deals with the management of gender in the music class. This chapter, however, owes more to the largest research grant of my career.

Widening young male participation in chorus, also funded by the AHRC, was undertaken jointly with my colleague David Howard at the University of York in collaboration with the National Youth Choirs of Britain. The project became known by its popular title *Boys keep singing* (Ashley & Howard 2009), suggested by the professional media company that made the films that are still available as a free resource for schools. This project coincided with another major event in UK school singing, the rise and subsequent contraction to a sustainable business model of the Sing Up national singing programme for English primary schools. It became very clear to me that Sing Up had been given no brief to address the big issue revealed by *How high*? It is all very well enthusing primary school children about singing, but what happens when they move up to secondary school?

There is a wealth of research that looks at what I have called the 'great exodus'. It has been known for many years that large numbers of children, boys and girls, turn against singing on transfer to secondary school. I could never understand the logic of an intensive programme in primary schools with little real continuity, progression, or follow-through to secondary schools where the need is arguably greater. Hence the singular aptness and appeal of the 'keep' in boys *keep* singing. Unfortunately, I have subsequently learned the extent to which the title might have been 'boys *and girls* keep singing'. This book has been written largely because of the number of secondary schools where, in the words of one interviewee, 'nothing happens' after all the good work in primary schools. The theme dominates almost every chapter of the current volume.

It was through *Boys keep singing* that I became thoroughly acquainted with the work of the Cambiata Vocal Institute of America (CVIA), studying its principles and corresponding with its then director, Don Collins. CVIA sets out a systematic approach to keeping young adolescents singing, largely through drawing on the extensive research work undertaken on young adolescent voices, mostly in the United States. The possibility of cambiata in the UK as a systematic solution to the 'low, gruff voices' problem is belatedly attracting interest, not least from the publisher of the present volume. The nature of adolescent voice development in both boys and girls is explained in Chapter 5. The singularly important consequences of understanding this for the choice of repertoire is addressed in Chapter 7, and the cambiata system itself in Chapter 10.

The story could have ended there, but I have undertaken one more major study since *Boys keep singing*. The 'how high?' question continues to burn and further fuel has been added to this fire by quite widespread speculation in the popular press that young adolescents are reaching puberty sooner than in the past. If this is true, the consequences are significant. Not only will voices change earlier, but social and cognitive maturation will proceed differently. The timing of puberty is in fact a question of considerable significance for singing in the lower secondary school. Of particular relevance to the present volume is the interesting dynamic between biology, which we cannot control, and the organization of schooling which, in theory at least, we can. So I set out to determine whether the timing of puberty has changed and to reopen the whole question of where the singing range should be located for children of lower secondary age.

Over 1,000 boys' voices were recorded and systematically analysed. Boys were drawn from the National Youth Choir of Scotland, seven English cathedral choirs, one Australian cathedral choir, and ten secondary schools with patient music teachers across England. This was a physiological study that looked in depth at the acoustic properties of boys' voices as well as associated anthropometric data such as height, weight, lung volume, neck circumference, and the changes in such quantities during the growth period of puberty. This book has been able to draw, therefore, upon quite an extensive period of detailed study of both sociological and physiological aspects of young voices.

One important dimension, however, was still missing at the time the book was agreed with the publisher. What do practising secondary school teachers do with all this information? Why are 'keep singing' initiatives such as cambiata (described in Chapter 10) so little known-about, still less applied, in so many English secondary schools? How might this change and what are the obstacles to change? To address these questions I recruited another cohort of secondary schools, 20 in all, to visit, observe, and analyse. Some of these schools were ones I had been to before through *Young masculinity and vocal performance* (my first AHRC-funded project in 2008), others were ones I had come to know through my university-based teacher education work. Collectively, they are referred to in this book as the practitioner group. They represent an intentionally skewed sample because they are mostly schools where the singing is good or outstanding. A small number of schools otherwise good but undistinguished by their singing are also included by way of comparison or reality check. They are also all state-funded schools, because it is in that sector that the real challenges are found.

Members of the practitioner group completed an online survey based on some of the issues arising from the research I have described above. Also included in the survey were the issues arising through initiatives such as the National Music Plan and the constant outpouring of criticism by the schools inspectorate, addressed in Chapter 2. Some of these schools were then visited for lesson observation and interviews with teachers and pupils in order to elucidate and understand better the survey responses. Two of the schools were chosen to be observed over an extended period and filmed for the supporting website resources planned to accompany this book. In this way, I hope the book is not simply an indulgence in many years of research into children's singing, but also a useful and practical handbook that has credibility for 'real teachers'. The practitioner group and their responses to the survey are referred to regularly throughout the text.

Chapter 1

All can sing—even 13-year-old boys

'A schoolmaster must be able to sing; otherwise I won't acknowledge him'

Martin Luther

Introduction

In this chapter, I commence with some basic foundations. First, there is a fairly extended discussion of what the 'lower secondary school' actually is. Then there is a similar discussion of what 'singing' actually is. To problematize these everyday words is not to indulge in academic navel-gazing, as I hope the discussions will show. We need a particular understanding of what the lower secondary school actually is because regional or national variations in the age range considered to be 'lower secondary' can have a significant impact on the way we might go about singing. Similarly, there are many different kinds of singing and many different possible understandings of 'learning to sing'. Not all are appropriate to the context of the lower secondary school, and there are some particular understandings of 'singing' that are peculiar to that phase of education.

Having established a shared meaning of singing and the lower secondary school, we are then ready to explore and map out a clear philosophy for singing in the lower secondary school. I refer in Chapter 2 to a failure in much recent UK documentation to articulate a clear philosophy and rationale beyond a 'motherhood and apple pie' desire that children should sing. There is often too much angst-driven advocacy, and too little analysis with regard to whether or not there is much singing in the lower secondary school and to what real purpose.

Defining the lower secondary school

Thus far in the text, it has been taken for granted that there is a shared understanding of what is meant by 'lower secondary school'. A number of different understandings, however, are possible and the actual age range of children to be taught will vary according to local variations in the organization of schooling. Potentially this matters a lot, for the period of early adolescence is the most critical time for young people's singing. The relationships between chronological, biological, intellectual, and social maturity are significant and even a year's difference in the age at which students begin and end their lower secondary education can be decisive in determining how things are approached and what outcomes are achieved.

During the gestation period for this book, considerable thought was therefore given to the title. The publisher, not unreasonably, wanted a title that would market the book as widely as possible to an international audience. A parochial term such as the English 'Key Stage 3' was therefore considered unsuitable. The author had in mind a particular kind of school student, but to define this in a way meaningful in England, let alone the rest of the world, was not an easy task. 'Lower secondary school' implies learners who have progressed beyond the first or elementary phase of their education, but have not yet got that far with the next stage. Three ways of viewing the problem might be considered:

♦ The logistical (how schooling is organized and administered);
♦ The biological (how far the students have progressed to physical and mental maturity);
♦ The socio-cultural (the extent to which students have 'grown up' in the context of the society of which they are part).

The second and third of these will necessarily occupy substantial portions of later chapters. The first can be dealt with fairly succinctly.

Logistical considerations and definitions

In England, there have been and are a number of different ways of dividing schooling up into age phases. 'Lower secondary' implies an intermediate stage between elementary and high schooling, but the actual age boundaries of that are quite fluid. The most common system in England is the two-tier one of 5–11 primary schools and 11–16 or 11–18 secondary schools. Also influential in England is the system used in the fee-charging independent schools. Independent schools for senior students (13 and over) are often known as 'public schools', which is very confusing for non-English readers where the term 'public' usually means the opposite, i.e. available to anyone and not fee charging. The English term for this is 'state maintained', usually abbreviated in official documentation to 'maintained' but popularly referred to as 'state'. In the public school system, transfer is most commonly at age 13, the 14th birthday occurring during the first year at public school. The most common term for fee-paying schools educating students up to the age of 13 is 'preparatory school', usually abbreviated to 'prep' and meaning preparation for senior schooling (and not having to do your 'prep' or homework, as I once thought as a small boy). 'Junior school' is sometimes found as an alternative to 'prep school', though more often for schools that transfer at 11 or 12.

Finally, there is still a three-tier system operative in some parts of England, consisting of first schools, middle schools, and upper schools. The most common age range for middle schools is 9–13 (thus corresponding to the senior half of preparatory schools) but 8–12 middle schools are also found, which correspond to the Scottish system where primary schooling is up to age 12 rather than 11. The three-tier system in England has nosedived in popularity in recent years and is now found only in isolated pockets. A significant reason for this is cost. It costs somewhat more to educate an 11-year-old in a middle school than a primary school because middle schools generally have facilities more on a par with secondary schools and have staffing ratios that must take account of the need for subject specialists. Unsurprisingly, this is a significant consideration when it comes to music and singing.

Another reason, however, was the 1988 Education Act. This was a significant milestone in that it established what are generally referred to as 'National Curriculum Years'. Before 1988, UK school years were numbered according to progress in each phase. Thus 'infant schools' educated children up to 'junior age' who became first- to fourth-year juniors, becoming 'first years' again on transfer to secondary school at 11. The 1988 Education Act created 'key stages': Key Stage 1 (KS1) is Y1 and Y2 (formerly 'infants'), KS2 is Y3–Y6, KS3 is Y7–Y9, and KS4 is Y10–Y11. Critically, KS3 was allocated to secondary schooling and high-stakes tests known as 'SATs' (not to be confused with SATs for US university entry) were introduced at the end of KS2 and KS3. The KS2 SATs, taken at age 11, were a death blow to middle schools because what came to be seen as an important 'public examination' taken by 11-year-olds occurred at the end of primary schooling when children could be coached and taught to the test. The same SATs occurring halfway through the middle school curriculum did not offer such a neat opportunity and were quite disruptive of the work and concept of a 9–13 curriculum.

A further complication is that, for reasons best known to its creators, the English National Curriculum Year system is a year out of phase with the 'grade' system of most other countries including the United States and Germany. Thus US grade 6 is actually English Y7, and so on.

If the reader can bear with this protracted exposition a while longer, it does have a very important part to play in children's singing. Three-tier systems are generally the norm in the United States. Elementary schools cater for kindergarten to grade 5 and high schools cater for either grade 9 to grade 12 or grade 10 to grade 12. In between are variously found either middle schools or junior high schools. The actual interpretation varies from state to state, but a fair generalization might be that middle schools are for grades 6–8 and junior high schools for grades 7–9. As in England, local logistic and demographic factors may exert an influence, the need to maintain stable and viable school populations often determining the exact age range of the middle tier. Some understanding of the US system is necessary because nearly all the most important research on adolescent voices has been carried out in the United States with junior high schools much in mind (Cooksey, Swanson, Gackle, and Cooper are leading names; see the bibliography).

The working definition of 'lower secondary school' I use in this book is ages 11–13 or, more specifically Y7 and Y8 of the English system (i.e. grades 6 and 7 in most other places). This is the top two years of English middle school, the senior years of English 'prep' school, or the bottom two years of US junior high.

With the benefit of hindsight it has become increasingly clear that, for a number of reasons, the English reformers of the 1980s may not have achieved the optimum solution when they created KS3 (Y7–Y9), which does not comfortably define the 'lower secondary school'. Various reasons are given for this, the influence (or not) of public examinations being one of them. In this book the reason given is that Y7–Y9 is out of step with important changes in singing development. These are explained fully in Chapter 5. Admittedly this would be a very minor consideration for most school managements, but growing numbers of English schools are introducing some of the all-important work for 16+ examinations a year earlier, effectively extending KS4 (or upper school) to three years. This can motivate young people who might otherwise drift, seeing Y9 as a 'doss' year. Y9 (age 13–14) has always been the most difficult year, as most teachers who have to cope with a bottom Y9 set on a wet Friday afternoon will testify. On the other hand, Y9 can be an important year for young people to take time out to reflect and devote due consideration to their futures and the examination options that will partly determine these.

The first tacit admission of the uncertain status of Y9 by government was when the end of KS3 SATs disappeared in 2008 amidst massive criticism by both researchers and the public that the tests were unhelpful and disruptive. This was sealed by a debacle over the marking when a private firm brought in to 'modernize' the tests was guilty of considerable mismanagement. Music, as a subject, has felt keenly the effect of this process. Significant numbers of Y9s can present an increasing challenge to their music teachers because they have decided that music will not be an examination option for them. At the same time music can suffer from students increasingly outgrowing their willingness to defer to the process of class singing and the 'school song', begun in primary school. The subject is thus under pressure from two directions and many music departments see Y9 as a transitional year with its own particular problems and solutions.

Biological considerations

Why does this matter so much? The middle years of schooling broadly coincide with the transformation from childhood to adolescence. 'Child' and 'adolescent' are both vague terms with ill-defined meaning, but the difference between a young person who is clearly a child and a young person who is clearly an adolescent is both considerable and of fundamental importance to the way we might go about singing. By defining the lower secondary years as UK Y7 and Y8 (US grades 6 and 7) I have adopted an inevitable compromise between logistics and biology, or between physical, social, and chronological age. Some definitions of adolescence attempt to link the phenomenon to puberty. The physical changes of puberty are of the utmost importance to singing in the lower secondary school, with the emotional changes and changes in self-identity coming a very close second. These matters occupy much space later in the book.

It would be extremely convenient if we could hang our definition of 'lower secondary' upon the biological marker of puberty, but nature does not permit this. Puberty comes early for some young people and late for others, and the lower secondary years bisect puberty clumsily and imperfectly. There will never be a good match between an economic, legal, or logistical attempt to decide when childhood ends and adolescence begins and what happens for any given young person in terms of endocrine driven development. On average, and I stress quite emphatically *on average*, if we set the age at 11 we have set it too early. Most 11-year-olds belong physically more to the realm of childhood than adolescence. If we set the age at 13, we have almost certainly set it too late. Most 13-year-olds belong physically more to the realm of puberty-defined adolescence, though more so now than 50 years ago. Emotional and cultural orientation within these tempestuous waters I shall leave until later, but it will be a singularly important topic.

I am tempted to state after having taught a good number of years in both systems that although neither system is perfect, transfer at 13+ is a better system than transfer at 11+. Therefore I see the lower secondary years more in terms of the consummation of childhood than an inferior or undeveloped phase of adolescence. My recipe for singing in Y7 (grade 6) is one that sees it as the time when vocal and choral processes begun in childhood reach their apotheosis. My recipe for Y9 (grade 8) is one that sees a new start for young people that ideally ought to build upon a musical childhood. Y9, in this view, quite simply does not belong to lower secondary. It is better seen as the foundation year of upper school. Y8 (grade 7) is a transitional year that is not always easy to manage. For boys, I am inclined to suggest that the world would be as near perfect as possible if we all adopted the Scottish system of ending primary school at the end of Y7 (grade 6). This is perhaps less clearly the case for girls, though girls seem more tolerant and adaptable in the face of an imperfect system than boys.

I did come across this rather interesting definition of biological adolescence in the *Encyclopaedia Britannica*:

From a biological perspective, adolescence should be the best time of life. Most physical and mental functions, such as speed, strength, reaction time, and memory, are at their peak during the teenage years. It is the time when foods taste best, appetite is heartiest, sleep is sweetest, and *music is most seductive*. The impact is not purely physical, for it is also in adolescence that new, radical, and divergent ideas can make the most profound impact on the imagination.

The emphasis on 'music is most seductive' is mine.

Socio-cultural considerations

Biology and singing are relatively easy to deal with because there are clearly defined events in physical development that are objective and measurable. We examine these in detail in Chapter 5. The socio-cultural dimension is harder because so much depends on the social world in which children are immersed. Eleven-year-olds in a primary school are looked to as the 'seniors' who represent the culmination of the school's work and the role models and examples for younger children. The same 11-year-olds in a secondary school might be looked down upon as insignificant little kids. Very probably many of these 11-year-olds will feel their smallness and look to the cultural practices of the older students in the school. Adult authority will tend to act against this process in most cases. Few people want 11-year-olds swearing or boasting about sex as 16-year-olds might.

The way this is managed through the pastoral organization of the school can affect the kinds of cultural identity assumed by students in Y7 and Y8. The attitude of the music teacher may well be critical in determining the attitude of the children to singing with regard to this. The very act of singing together in class has strong connotations of childhood that can conflict with the foundations of youth music in adolescent rebellion. If the teacher acts with confidence in treating the lower secondary classes as the culmination of childhood and the *preparation* for adolescence, the students are less likely to have inhibitions about the 'school song' and singing together. If the teacher has little understanding of childhood or lacks empathy for that phase of life, the result may be an insecurity of identity in which many students become lost in a nihilistic world that is neither that of the child nor the adolescent. Such conditions are not conducive to class singing. We address the issue in more depth in Chapter 6.

The matter is further complicated by the way identities are managed in the primary school. Where there is strong leadership of singing right up to the end of primary schooling there is unlikely to be a problem. Weak leadership in the primary school, however, can result in a contagion through which end-of-childhood nihilism can affect Y6 (grade 5) or even the year below. Musical identity can be an early casualty of this. Y7s may arrive from some primary schools with the idea already formed that singing together in class is 'babyish'. One of the most important points that needs to be appreciated, in the UK at least, is that two-thirds of a child's compulsory music education takes place in the primary school (music in England is compulsory in KS1, KS2, and KS3, the first two of these key stages being primary).

The degree to which secondary music teachers fully appreciate this and perceive importance in working with primary schools to ensure continuity and progression from age 5 to age 13 is again critical for singing in Y7 and Y8. More than this, it is crucial to the entire way in which young people move on from eight years of compulsory music education either to study music further or to grow up as adults possessing a foundation of musical literacy adequate to serve them as culturally literate citizens. The problem does not exist, or is at least of a somewhat different order, in 13+ transfer systems. In 11+ transfer systems, however, there is rather too much evidence that at least some secondary music teachers are disconnected from primary music and see the teaching of Y7 and Y8 more as a distracting chore than one of the most important parts of their role.

This problematic divide between childhood and adolescence is also manifest in differing pedagogic approaches that have been brought into growing prominence through the important work of Lucy Green. Green's seminal work *How Popular Musicians Learn* (2002) has highlighted a fundamental difference between traditional, teacher-centred didactic methods that might be used to teach a whole class song and the informal, learner-centred, discovery-based ways through which popular musicians teach themselves (now irrevocably associated with Apple's 'Garage Band'). A project increasingly well-known in England by the name of 'Musical Futures' is based on a system of informal pedagogy that contrasts strongly with the formal pedagogy of choral teaching. We will need to look at Musical Futures and what it means for singing in the lower secondary school in later chapters. The crucial point at this juncture is that Musical Futures was begun with Y9 students as the initial target. Arguably the downward extension of the Musical Futures approach into Y7 and Y8 represents an incursion into childhood.

Defining singing

For better or for worse, we have established that this book is about teaching singing to students in early adolescence, aged between 11 and 13, wherever and however they might be located within the logistics of schooling. What, though, is meant by 'singing'? This is no more straightforward a question than what is meant by 'lower secondary'. Hitherto, singing in the lower secondary school has been referred to principally as though it were synonymous with whole class singing. An important text from an earlier age that I shall refer to from time to time is Herbert Wiseman's *The Singing Class*, published in 1967. Wiseman takes it for granted that the job of the music teacher is simply to rehearse a class much in the way one would rehearse a choir. He was an early exponent of the fact that voices do not 'break'. A good many years before John Cooksey published his studies, Wiseman was showing how both boys' and girls' voices changed gradually during adolescence, and how these changes should be accommodated in the singing class.

He deserves far more recognition for this pioneering work than history has granted. It is depressing for anybody who has been involved in education over decades to see potential progress revealed by research that is then forgotten, only to be 'invented' many years later by somebody else, but never synthesized into general practice. Wiseman's book also contains a wealth of practical detail on how to produce good singing from young adolescents in the singing class. Were more of his technical advice to be followed, I am confident that the standard of school singing would be a great deal better than it is currently in many schools. Nevertheless, the world is now a more complicated place than it was in 1967 and we need something more than a manual on how to rehearse a choir. We need to know how to cope with the gulf that has grown between youth music and choral music that Wiseman did not appear to have to contend with. There are of course at least three main contexts for school singing:

- Singing by all during timetabled music lessons;
- Elective singing in a diversity of extracurricular music-making;
- Individual singing lessons where the voice, effectively, is the instrument.

I am going to suggest also that there are broadly three categories of 'singing' that are appropriate in different ways in these different contexts:

- 'Just singing';
- Choral work;
- Vocal work.

I use these terms throughout the book in connection with the type of pedagogy that is appropriate in the different contexts.

'Just singing'

Many years ago when I was only just beginning my research into boys' voices, I became involved in a small difference of opinion with a producer working in the commercial music industry. I had stated the mantra that 'boys don't sing' and was taken to task by this individual. 'Boys sing all the time,' he said. His more or less exact words were, 'stand on a tube station platform and you will see them with their iPods plugged in, singing along'. I was taken a little aback at the time. Did he really think this was *singing*? There is truth in what he said, however. Singing is a natural human activity and people have no need of a singing teacher or choir director to teach them how to join in—in earlier times perhaps with the radio or round a campfire, in our own time with the iPod. Moreover, there are several references later in this book to interviews with boys in school where the boys do indeed confirm that they sing all the time— *provided they think no one can hear them.*

I have evolved the term 'just singing' to describe this inherent ability possessed by the majority of people to join in a simple song. There is no formal instruction beyond the minimum required to pick up the words and melody if not already known. This might be through following a vocal leader employing the call and response method, or singing along with a downloadable backing track. It may be nothing more than singing in the bathroom or singing along quietly with the iPod. Importantly, it is unlikely to involve much in the way of evaluation, either in the form of the assessment of learning outcomes or any judgement of the singer's performance. There is a direct relationship here with anxiety that may arise when the singers are aware that they are being listened to. Boys may well cease 'just singing' if they think someone can hear them. This is discussed in more depth in Chapter 8. There is also an important relationship between the extent to which singing is part of a pedagogical strategy for learning music or merely an activity undertaken for light relief. This is a theme that dominates much of the book. Important questions arise when what is sanctioned as acceptable for the music class is in reality little more than 'just singing'.

Choral work

At the other end of the spectrum from 'just singing' is choral work. Choral work, in simple terms, is what goes into the creation and rehearsal of a choir. It is characterized above all by blend and unanimity. Individuals must subordinate themselves to the group and must work together as a dedicated team. Choral work demands sustained concentration, high accuracy, and a strong commitment to a shared objective. Most important of all, when young people are involved, it demands a high level of instruction and learning. This is likely to include learning to sight-read staff notation; to hear, pitch, and describe intervals accurately; to respond with precision to pulse, metre, and accurate counting; to control breathing and posture; to understand voice production and management; and to follow accurately the gestures of a conductor who requires careful interpretation of dynamics and tempo. Commonly, such matters are associated with so-called 'classical' music (a most unsatisfactory term), but whenever the above are observed, the work can be called choral whatever the genre.

Practice differs considerably between the UK and the US with regard to choral work. In many US schools, elective choral programmes are available. These are formal, assessed programmes of instruction that take place as timetabled curriculum lessons. They are likely to be taught by well-qualified specialist teachers possessing at least a master's degree in choral conducting and not uncommonly a high level professional qualification such as the DMA (Doctorate in Musical Arts). There really is no equivalent to this in the UK. In spite of the so-called 'English choral tradition', outside the choir schools and musically orientated fee-charging schools, choral work in publicly funded schools is really quite rare. When it does occur, it is usually as an extracurricular activity and children must forfeit break times or remain behind after school if they wish to participate. This impacts particularly on boys' participation levels, as clashes with sports practices are hard to avoid. I say more about this large inequality of provision in Chapter 3.

For whatever reasons, 'choir' has ceased to be a safe word to use in most English schools. In spite of the efforts of a certain young, populist conductor of 'workplace choirs', for most young people, 'choir' conjures up three key images: 'elderly', 'posh', and 'church'. All three have become fairly instant turn-offs for the majority of young people, in the UK at least. Most members of the practitioner group, though they ran what were effectively choirs in their school, were highly circumspect and cautious about using the word 'choir'. I have explained elsewhere the reasoning behind the choice of title 'Widening Young Male Participation in Chorus' for the project I undertook with the National Youth Choirs of Great Britain. The aim was not to prop up the 'elderly' and 'posh' elements of *choral singing*, but to help rediscover the positivity of *singing in chorus* for a generation (and gender) that is in danger of losing it.

Vocal work

'Vocal work' is a term that I use in this book to mean something that is more than 'just singing' but not choral work. The term 'vocal work' should cover the majority of contexts when young people's voices are used as an integral part of a pedagogical strategy for learning music. Vocal work might include individual instruction by a peripatetic teacher when the student has chosen the voice as his or her 'instrument'. Rehearsing the school musical or preparing a small vocal band for a performance could qualify as vocal work rather than 'just singing' provided it can be clearly shown that students have progressed in their under-standing and skill level within music as an outcome. In the context of the present volume that is concerned with the musical learning of all children aged between 11 and 13, what I will refer to as the 'class chorus' is a key vehicle for vocal work.

The class chorus, simply defined, is where democratic vocal work takes place with a class of 30 or so, only a small minority of whom would elect to join a choir. Although few children, boys in particular, will willingly join a choir, it would indeed be a disastrous loss if no child experienced singing in chorus. A great deal can be learned about music through careful, purposeful, and well-prepared work with the class chorus. There is very little doubt in my mind that learning is at its most intense and musical attainments highest when the method of instruction with the class chorus is based up the pedagogy of Zoltán Kodály (see Houlahan & Tacka, 2008). If proof is needed of this, the reader should perhaps look at the Kodály-based system that underpins the work of the National Youth Choir of Scotland.

Youth singing in Scotland has been revolutionized since the introduction of systematic progression from universal primary provision through area choirs to the national choirs. Kodály pedagogy is behind this undoubted success story.

For a whole variety of reasons, of which lack of initial training is probably the single most significant, the Kodály system is little used in English schools. The Voices Foundation has adapted its own version of Kodály pedagogy for use in primary schools with often good results in those primary schools willing to buy into it, but this is only a relatively small minority. The Foundation has the laudable ambition of extending its provision to cover the whole years of compulsory music education. It will be a long time, if ever, before this has a significant impact upon the lower secondary scene and there are, of course, many alternatives promoted, both Kodály and non-Kodály based.

Another major issue with vocal work concerns whether or not the child's so-called 'singing voice' should be developed. There is vague talk in much official UK documentation about children 'learning to sing' but what this means is never clearly defined. Most of the singing I have observed in English lower secondary schools does not use the 'singing voice'. The students use for singing the same vocal production that is used for speaking. This confines their singing to a narrow range at the lower end of the voice and results in a forced tone, often inaccurate intonation, and a degree of vocal strain that would horrify many singing teachers. Such poor use of the voice would not pass muster for choral work in the US and it is a moot point as to how far vocal work should go in correcting it. The issue is complicated by two factors. First, many 'popular' vocalists also use only their speech voice for singing. Second, the 'singing voice' in any case changes quite dramatically during the lower secondary years as boys and girls go through puberty. This may well lead to contraction of the range and raises many questions about keys and singing tessitura that are seldom addressed. Discussion of these singularly important matters is developed in Chapters 4 and 5.

Towards a clear philosophy

I recall fairly vividly (though it is 36 years after the event) my teaching practice in the Willowford South Lower Boys' School (pseudonym used, though I doubt the school still exists). The 'lower school' consisted of what is now Y7 and Y8 and I remember my tutor saying 'I want to see how you cope with teaching those boys some traditional folk songs'. My main method of coping, I recall, was to bash out 'The Lincolnshire Poacher' very loudly on the piano and yell at any boy who looked as though he wasn't singing it. As far as I can recall, that was largely what music lessons consisted of for those boys. Everything I know now about teaching music in the lower secondary school I have learned *since* gaining QTS, through bitter experience in the earlier part of my career, and through much observation and analysis of the practice of others in the most recent.

Why should 12-year-old boys have to sing the 'The Lincolnshire Poacher'? I cannot recall that rather fundamental question being on the curriculum of my initial training. It was simply assumed to be a good thing and what one did in those days. I do recall learning that Ralph Vaughan Williams and Gustav Holst spent many weeks tramping across moor and fenland collecting English folk song in order to 'add a little rustic appeal' to their compositions. Rather more than this, there was a longstanding belief that

In true folk-songs there is no sham, no got-up glitter, and no vulgarity . . . and the pity of it is that these treasures are getting rare, for they are written in characters the most evanescent you can imagine, upon the sensitive brain fibres of those who learn them, and have but little idea of their value. Moreover, there is an enemy at the doors of folk-music which is driving it out, namely the common popular songs of the day; and this enemy is one of the most repulsive and insidious.

The above words are those of Sir Hubert Parry from 1899 and are indicative of what the Harvard psychologist Stephen Pinker might refer to as a belief in the noble savage. 'Classical' music tended to adopt, in somewhat paternalistic fashion, the folk song of the peasantry. Folk song was both romanticized and nationalized and proclaimed to be preferable to the vulgarity of 'common popular songs'. In Parry's day the music hall was the enemy. In Wiseman's day, the enemy was the 'crooner'. Today it would be presumably *The X Factor* if not the entire contemporary commercial music (CCM) industry. There thus evolved for use in schools the concept of a suitably rustic national song book. An early version of this was the one published in 1905 by Boosey & Co, edited by Sir Charles Stanford and subtitled '*A Complete Collection of the Folk-songs, Carols, and Rounds Suggested by the Board of Education*'.

My experiences as a young teacher with 12-year-old boys and 'The Lincolnshire Poacher' have much to do with this alliance between folk song and the classical choral tradition, brokered by members of the 'great and good' such as Sir Charles Villiers Stanford (1852–1924). The implicit deference to such authorities was why such practices were 'a good thing and what one did in those days'. It might be thought to be now only of academic or historical interest, but this is not so. There was, in 2008, something of a spat between the compilers of what was to become the Sing Up song bank for primary schools and rightward leaning politicians who had been appalled to learn that the whole-school renditions of 'When a Knight Won his Spurs' that they had grown up on had largely disappeared from school assemblies. Here was a chance for revival of the old *National Song Book* of their youth. The *Daily Telegraph* reported that:

Ministers wanted a definitive list of 30 songs that every 11-year-old should know. But that has now been rejected as too 'culturally imperialist'. Instead a 'national song bank' is to be created containing 600 songs.

The Secretary of State incumbent at the time of writing this book amply demonstrated his political credentials in his role as shadow education secretary of the day. The *Telegraph* continued:

Michael Gove, the shadow education secretary, criticized the decision to abandon the original songbook project. 'This Government is so paralysed by political correctness and terminally afflicted by dithering that it cannot even decide on a simple thing like the songs children should learn,' he said. 'This Government has given us a history curriculum which makes it impossible for children to take pride in our country's past and now they have come up with an approach to music which is like iTunes without the style.' (*Daily Telegraph* 2008)

A simple thing? I was a member of Howard Goodall's advisory committee for the Sing Up national song bank, and I can assure the reader that it was not a simple thing! The line I take in this book is that the selection of repertoire should be guided neither by simplistic, nostalgia-based nationalism nor by the compulsion to second guess what children will think is 'cool' on iTunes. It must be guided by sound pedagogic principles and a clear rationale or philosophy. I am going to suggest three foundation stones upon which this must be built:

♦ Singing material must be of high musical quality;
♦ Singing material must be appropriate to the vocal development of the students;
♦ There needs to be a pedagogical purpose beyond 'just singing'.

There is nothing here about 'classical' or 'popular', or the way these terms are commonly understood and (mis)used. There is a lot, though, to position school repertoire within education as opposed to entertainment or leisure. This will be one of my main themes. We almost certainly need to add that the repertoire must be inclusive, representative of multicultural Britain and, at risk of sounding political, Britain's current postcolonial position in the world. The statement 'high musical quality' embodies a significant degree of subjectivity. The task of expounding and justifying it, which is attempted in Chapter 7, is not easy. Slightly easier is the task of explaining what is meant by appropriate to the vocal development of the students. This is begun in Chapter 5 and continued in Chapters 6 and 7.

The result of getting the underlying philosophy right will not be 'youth music', it will be 'school music'. 'School', as I have said, 'is not cool'. 'Uncool' does not have to mean boring or irrelevant. Most children accept that they come to school to work and learn and that this is a necessary part of their life. The best teachers of any subject make it interesting and relevant. A certain degree of conviction and clarity of purpose is required of music teachers if children are to accept that this outlook applies to music as well as to mathematics and English. Without a clear focus on teaching and learning, continuity, progression and development ('school music' in other words), the music department will look very weak when the senior management comes looking to prune 'frivolous' areas of the curriculum. A better answer is required to the next question than the one I was supplied with as a trainee teacher.

What is the point of lower secondary music?

There are books on the philosophy of education that go into great depth about aims and purposes. Judging by a lengthy series of posts on the UK's *Teaching Music* website (Teaching Music 2014) I analysed recently, there does not seem to have been that much discussion of such texts in the training and development of secondary music teachers. Although they might give braver answers to their students, discussion on the forum appeared to reveal quite a high level of angst with regard to the 'why are we doing it?' of KS3 music. Whatever high ideals we might hold about the intrinsic value of education, the lower secondary years are the time when many students transform from doing things 'because teacher says' to a phase highly characterized by instrumentality. Twelve-year-olds are by no means incapable of deep reflection on value, meaning, and purpose but the majority of students who have not already discovered that they have a deep love for music will begin to want to know 'why are we doing this?' They will want to know 'will it get me a good job?' By the time they have reached Y9, many will be quite turned off by a subject where the teacher is unable to give a good answer to either of these questions.

The school curriculum is a crowded place. In addition to the 10 or so traditional academic subjects, there is constant pressure to respond to advocacy groups demanding a place in the curriculum. Citizenship education, environmental education, education for sustainability, health education, sex and relationships education, global education, development education, gender education, healthy eating education, economic education, industrial understanding, online safeguarding education ... All these things have their advocates and the list continues almost ad infinitum. The naivety of the more peripheral pressure groups that think there must be space for their pet 'ism' somewhere in the school day is breathtaking. Nevertheless, the more loudly such groups shout, the more likely they are to succeed in pushing out unimportant 'frill' subjects. Could music be vulnerable to this?

There has been a National Curriculum in the UK since 1988 and this has always included music. Singing has always been a prescribed part of this for 5–14-year-olds. In theory, then, government has sanctioned the view that singing is important enough to be included in the statutory curriculum. Nevertheless, a huge panic spread throughout the music industry and amongst music educationists when the UK education secretary (at the time of writing) Michael Gove announced plans for his 'Ebac' that would not include music. Why was this? A possible answer has come to light in the most recent of several severe and damning critiques of music education by the English schools inspectorate, OFSTED (Office for Standards in Education). Music, it seems, is not considered by most school managements to be an 'academic' subject. It is not therefore 'serious' or of any real importance. It is somewhere on the periphery of the curriculum along with other 'frills'.

It must make uncomfortable reading for many in the music teaching profession to be confronted with statistics about the ongoing decline in the number of young people choosing to study music as a 16+ public examination subject (currently 'GCSE' in the UK). OFSTED attribute this in part to the poor quality of lower secondary work. In too many schools what they experience in the first two or three years fails to convince students that the subject is worth a GCSE. It can also sometimes let down some of the few who do choose music GCSE, only to find that they were poorly prepared in the lower school. It is not pleasant to be the subject of OFSTED criticism, but inasmuch as OFSTED argue that music is a 'proper' academic subject that requires the same rigorous teaching and learning strategies as other academic subjects, the inspectorate ought to be seen as a good ally of music departments.

The real point of lower secondary music, then, is that it must be a 'proper' subject taught with the same academic rigour as other 'proper' subjects. Perhaps my own background owes something to a classical, liberal education harking back to the ideals of Plato. Plato set music and sport firmly as second only to what are now so tiresomely referred to as the 'basics'.

Children enter school at six where they first learn the three Rs (reading, writing and counting) and then engage with music and sports. At eighteen they are to undergo military and physical training; at 21 they enter higher studies; at 30 they begin to study philosophy and serve the *polis* in the army or civil service. At 50 they are ready to rule (*The Republic*, transl. H. P. D. Lee, 1955).

Music and sports—two subjects I used to teach and regard as quite fundamental to the development of the young people I taught! So deeply engrained was this order of priorities that I have had to come to terms with the apparent fact that a large number of school managers, in the publicly funded sector at least, do not share them as a matter of course. Earlier, I had prided myself in the rigorous academic examinations I took in music and it never occurred to me that anybody might not consider music a serious, academic subject. Why, though?

I have written at length elsewhere of my research into how boys come to value choral singing. That research discovered that in an as yet unquantified, but perhaps quite large number of boys, there is a hidden love for singing. Here, from an earlier book, are what some boys of lower secondary age said about choral singing and what it did for them:

It's deep down inside. It's a feeling you can't put into words.

The first time I heard the choir, it just sounded so amazing, you wouldn't believe what it sounds like.

It was when I discovered that I could fill that place with sound, that it made my voice so big.

Any one of those boys could have been me. On the basis of those feelings, I knew that I wanted to study and practise music as some kind of profession. One thing I shared with those boys was exposure at a young age to choral singing in cathedrals. This, in the UK, has come to be a privilege associated with high degrees of cultural capital. It is not the life experience of the vast majority of children who will attend publicly funded schools. A contention that often runs near the surface of my thinking is that those who, like myself, have always assumed music to be a 'proper' and rigorous academic subject are often cocooned in their own worlds. If lower secondary music is to have any clear point, its advocates need to step outside their own world of values and assumptions and justify the subject by the same criteria that any other subject is justified. The process might look something like this:

- The cognitive elements that are *unique to the subject*—sometimes called, after Howard Gardner, 'intelligences'. Musical intelligence has several of these such as the ability to process sound, identify, and respond to components of sound such as rhythm and timbre, and make links between feeling and sound.
- The unique language and literacy of the subject. Next to the actual languages themselves, *the staff notation system of music is a key literacy*, fluency in which defines the extent to which one has undergone a rigorous academic training.

- The intrinsic worth of the subject—*how important is the subject in the cultural life of the nation*? Music figures very highly here—but what kind of music? The musically educated will have a well-informed critical approach.
- The vocational potential of the subject—how large and diverse are the employment opportunities within the industries that recruit graduates in the subject and what is the economic contribution of these industries? The cultural and creative industries claim to be of some importance in advanced Western economies.

In Chapter 2, I develop this theme further in a more extended discussion of the nature of advocacy for music.

What is the point of KS3 (lower secondary) singing?

As we shall see in the next chapter, there is no shortage of documentation from official and quasi-official sources proclaiming that all children *should* be taught to sing throughout the lower secondary years (including Y9). As we have said, rarely does this documentation elaborate on what it means by singing or how it should be taught. Still less is there any consideration of *why* it should be taught. Issues such as the fundamental difference between 'choral work' and 'vocal work' and associated pedagogies seem not to be appreciated at all. So let us not beat about the bush. Let us give the answer that Kodály gave. Kodály did not develop his principles because he wished to colonize the world with Hungarian folk song. He aimed for a universal musical literacy (a forgotten socialist ideal?) and above all, he aimed for a better understanding of music by those training as orchestral musicians.

There is simply no better way, according to Kodály, of achieving both these objectives than through linking the ear and voice through the medium of singing. OFSTED never tire of reiterating the importance of an aural/vocal approach to internalizing musical concepts (the process known as *audiation*). They give somewhat less attention to the ideal of a universal musical literacy, every child learning to read and write music. Given the extreme importance that is attached to learning to read and write the English language, this is very revealing. The relevant statement of subject content in the new UK National Curriculum is inexplicit and nebulous:

…use staff and other relevant notations appropriately and accurately in a range of musical styles, genres and traditions.

It is difficult to identify anywhere what is precisely meant by 'accurately', still less how 'accuracy' may differ as children progress from one level of learning to another. Expectations for the reading and writing of the English language in the equivalent section of the English curriculum is tellingly more explicit:

Reading at key stage 3 should be wide, varied and challenging. Pupils should be expected to read whole books, to read in depth and to read for pleasure and information … They should be taught to write formal and academic essays as well as writing imaginatively … This requires an increasingly wide knowledge of vocabulary and grammar.

It is, of course, assumed that by the end of primary schooling, nearly all students will have attained a basic fluency in the reading and writing of the English language and there is, to borrow from the vernacular, all hell to pay if they have not. In one fell swoop, music is kicked to the touchline of the curriculum periphery. It has a system of reading and writing as fundamental as print is to the English language, but fluency in this is not the absolute prerequisite for all else that it is in the 'important', 'basic', and 'core' subject of English.

This is not a book about music and music education. It is a book about singing within music education. A whole book could be written about musical literacy, but that is not the objective or brief here. It is simply to comment on the contribution of singing to music education as a whole. The question therefore arises as to whether singing contributes to students learning to read and write music. Although the practitioner group saw singing as an important part of their pedagogy, the majority view was that it was one of only several strategies. Only a small minority saw it as the key pedagogical principle, as in the Kodály system. Music education has a lot more to do than just teach students to sing, and there are more ways than singing of developing both the cognitive elements of music and the notation system of music. Figure 1.1 shows the percentages of the practitioner group choosing each of the possible options.

In developing a pedagogical strategy we need to distinguish between learning *to* sing and learning *through* singing. The former might be of some importance, the latter, vital. I was recently working with a Y7 (11- and 12-year-old) class and I asked them to give me their memories and impressions of primary school music, comparing it with their new experience of secondary school music. Many talked about activities such as sitting in a circle playing percussion instruments. None mentioned singing. Incredulously, I asked them whether there had been any singing at primary school. Almost all said yes. The issue appeared to be that they had not associated singing with learning music. This was very revealing.

It is also, perhaps, our starting point. A much stronger case clearly needs to be made for learning music and musical skills *through* singing. When it

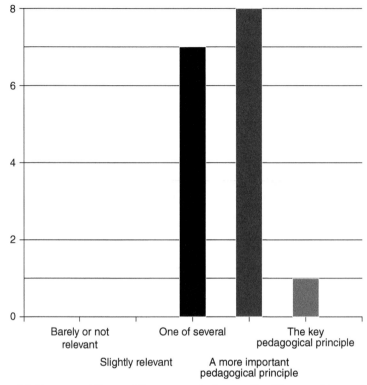

Figure 1.1 Response of the practitioner group to the question 'How would you rate the purpose of singing in KS3 curriculum music lessons relative to other methods of instruction?'

comes to acquiring fluency in reading and writing notation, I am not convinced that the case actually is that strong—unless one develops a system of instruction that is uniquely and intensively focused on singing. Much the same applies to the other claim made for singing, that it develops aural acuity and the inner ear. In keeping with the practitioner group, I am inclined toward a blended approach in which singing is used in conjunction with other forms of instruction, including information technology (IT) and the digital keyboards that have largely replaced percussion instruments. I develop discussion of this in Chapter 8. I also revisit the question of singing and musical literacy in a different way in Chapters 3 and 6. These address potentially divisive and controversial elements of equality and identity where singing plays a significant role.

Summary and conclusions

♦ There is, in almost any advanced education system, a phase between the elementary, or primary school, and the upper, or high school. This phase, ideally, should be the best possible fit with the beginning of adolescence and onset of puberty.

♦ The beginning of adolescence (rather than a bureaucratically derived chronological age span) is a unique period of life and a critical phase in the development of music and singing.

♦ School music needs to make a real contribution to a rigorous education, and the core role of music in the development of intelligence needs to be understood. There is little point in creating curriculum space that represents little more than an intrusion of young people's leisure time into the school day.

♦ There needs to be a clear pedagogical strategy for vocal work that is a lot more than 'just singing'.

♦ A pedagogical strategy for vocal work needs to address the following issues:
  - The development of aural acuity, musical intelligence and the inner ear
  - The development of fluency in reading and writing music
  - Cultural awareness of a range of vocal and choral material
  - Enjoyment and positive disposition to the subject
  - Critical awareness of different genres of vocal and choral music and the way these are exploited in society.

Further reading

Alexiadou, N. & Brock, C. (2013) *Education around the world: a comparative introduction*. London: Bloomsbury.

Houlahan, M. & Tacka, P. (2008) *Kodály today: a cognitive approach to elementary music education*. Oxford: Oxford University Press.

Mills, J. (2005) *Music in the school*. Oxford: Oxford University Press.

Pitts, S. (2012) *Chances and choices: exploring the impact of music education*. Oxford: Oxford University Press.

Chapter 2

The Sing Up legacy, the National Music Plan, and OFSTED

Two things above all characterize the singing scene: policy and rhetoric. This chapter looks carefully at some of the key happenings with Sing Up and what OFSTED have been saying. It provides a very sober analysis of the rhetoric embedded in documents such as the Henley Report and the subsequent National Music Plan.

Introduction

In Chapter 1, I outlined a somewhat perilous situation riven by contradiction and rhetoric. On the one hand, there are advocates of singing and music education who assure us that all children in the lower secondary school should be singing. On the other hand, there is ample evidence that in almost half of all UK state-funded secondary schools, there is little or no singing. Only in the top quarter (musically) can the situation be said to be good. This fact is remarked on constantly and unrelentingly by the UK schools inspectorate, OFSTED. In this chapter I look in detail at this situation. It seems to me that the entire situation lacks a certain degree of credibility. Is it really possible to have such a wide gap between rhetoric and reality? Does it really mean anything when a national inspectorate is so consistently critical of a situation that seems never to improve? Has the inspectorate overplayed its hand? What is going wrong and is the dream attainable?

Advocacy dependency

Music needed no advocacy when it was a core subject within a classical, liberal system, but the ideals of Plato have long ceased to underpin the school curriculum. The result is that music is now forced to justify itself and turns largely to extrinsic benefits in doing so. Singing, we are assured, helps with literacy, numeracy, social development, happiness, and many more doubtless worthy goals. Much more rarely do we hear that it actually helps with learning music and that learning music needs no more justification than learning mathematics.

Music and singing are not short of passionate and eloquent advocates. Occasionally these *are* heard. The Sing Up National Singing Programme for English primary schools that we shall look at in this chapter was one of the most significant examples of recent times. Sing Up, however, as a national project with core government funding, has come and gone. The ending of core government funding for this programme largely coincided with a panic about the status of music in the new EBac qualifications framework and the big economic downturn following the global banking crisis of 2008. This is a problem that commonly besets the arts subjects. To some extent they ebb and flow in synchronization with national and global economic tides. They also experience a significant chance effect as projects such as a community opera scheme receive time-limited funding grants. This is not the way to build sustained development, nor is it the way to convince hard-nosed politicians and economists that the 'frill' subjects are not, in fact, 'frills'. I have coined a phrase for this: it is *advocacy dependency*. Subjects that are dependent on the advocacy of supporters, friends, and enthusiasts will always find it difficult to achieve an unassailable position of necessity in the curriculum. They will constantly be vulnerable to budget cuts and the marginalization of vital infrastructure such as initial teacher training.

This is exactly what has happened to school singing. Subject advocates bemoan endlessly the fact that trainee primary school teachers may receive as little as six hours' music during a three-year degree course. The lack of choral training for secondary music specialists elicits similar despair. I have sat through many meetings, both formal and informal, over many years hearing the same thing again and again. One reason this happens is because the advocacy of music education concentrates on peripherals. The case for singing as part of a rigorous, worthwhile academic programme that will convince hard-nosed economists as well school managements is clearly not being made. If it were, there would be more singing in the lower secondary school.

The following all contain at least a grain of truth, sometimes more than a grain. Only the last makes the core point that is so often missed:

+ Singing is a natural human activity;
+ Singing has intrinsic value and needs no other justification;
+ Singing brings demonstrable health benefits;
+ Singing contributes to general wellbeing and happiness within a school;
+ Singing brings demonstrable improvements in other areas of learning, including numeracy;

♦ Every child should have the opportunity to discover whether singing is an activity they might like to take further;
♦ Singing is a particularly effective pedagogical strategy in a rigorous approach to music learning.

With all the pressures young people face, we have to consider also how we justify singing to them. 'Because the national curriculum says you must' is absolutely not the way to do this! A teacher who resorted to such a strategy would be one who had not him or herself come to appreciate how much singing can help children learn music. In Chapter 1, I introduced the 'school is not cool' idea. It is another paradox that while music and fashion are the two most important means through which young people construct their identities, school managements have come down really hard on the latter but not the former. English schools now have some of the most rigorously enforced dress codes in the Western world.

At a personal level, I have always doubted the link between what students wear and how much and how well they learn. Nevertheless, powerful senior managements now completely override students' dress sense. The fact that they do not do so for music is another demonstration that music is not 'serious'. School dress codes do not mean that many young people elect to wear school shirts and blazers for their out-of-school social life. I have seen how students, even if they object to constant nagging about shirt tucking, come to accept that there is a difference between work and leisure, sometimes even with pride. The lesson that might be learned from this is that all but a few students will come to respect that singing can be part of their learning at school, and it can become so without infringing on the way they use their own music in their leisure time. This requires strong leadership and a clear pedagogic purpose for singing that is shared with understanding between the music department and the senior management team. Senior managements should not need to be convinced by extrinsic advocacy, however well-meaning this may be.

I have long believed that education is not and cannot simply be about providing children with what they want. That is the role of entertainment. Education is about choice and empowerment and those two key criteria are embedded in the statement 'every child should have the opportunity to discover whether singing is an activity they might like to take further'. Quite possibly, they may decide they do not want to take singing further. That is their prerogative and it is fine if it is a well-informed choice. They might equally well decide that they do not wish to take the study of history or geography further. These subjects, though, will usually have been taught with some rigour in the years leading up to the choice of options. Students will reject them because they do not form part of their career plans, not because they have formed the opinion that they are 'frills' or 'entertainments' that have no value to anybody with a serious mind to future prospects.

The school is failing, in my view, if it does not give the child the opportunity to make a well-informed choice. This means that a high quality and reasonably wide-ranging experience needs to be provided for all children in the early stages, with the opportunity for progression for those who desire it. Crucially, this 'high quality and wide-ranging experience' needs to be for *all* children and it needs to be a serious experience of proper learning. The only time and place that this is going to happen is during the timetabled curriculum music lesson. What is needed to convince children during this vital time is not a competition to outdo popular TV talent shows. It is a clear demonstration of educational professionalism in which the children can see that they are learning many things that would never be learned through watching TV talent shows. We disrespect our students if we do not credit them with the ability to perceive this.

Let us see what our practitioner group thought. They were asked about the contribution KS3 curriculum singing makes to students' progress and development through rating key items on a four-point scale from 'not very important' to 'indispensable'. A score of 3.73 thus indicates that a majority of the practitioners though the contribution indispensable (Figure 2.1).

The use of the singing voice is seen by these practitioners as all but indispensable to *the development of aural acuity, the internal ear, and musical memory.* Almost as highly rated was *a means of developing a sense of musicality.* The practitioners also thought it, on average, 'one of the best methods' to *identify musical students who will benefit from extracurricular activities.* In other words, students on entry to the secondary school need to learn vital musical skills through singing, and there is also something of an expectation that some students will progress further after identification of aptitude through singing. This largely accords with my own view as expressed in the last two of the above bullet points. The practitioners also indicate that enjoyment is important. Singing, in other words, is a natural human activity that needs no extrinsic justification.

The Sing Up legacy

The fortunes of the arts subjects ebb and flow with the economic fortunes of the nation. One of the most spectacular demonstrations of this claim in recent times has been Sing Up, the National Singing Programme for primary schools. Sing Up was established in 2007 as an outcome of an earlier initiative under the

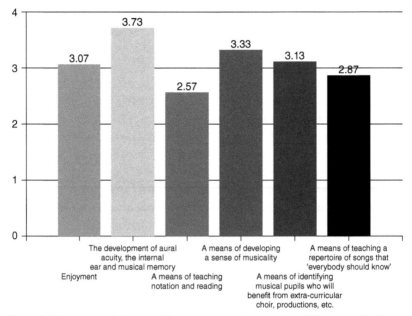

Figure 2.1 Response of the practitioner group to the question 'What contribution do you think KS3 curriculum singing makes to pupils' progress and development?'

auspices of the 1997–2010 New Labour government. Funding to make this programme available free of charge to every primary school ended in 2011, a year after the new coalition government took office. To be fair, the coalition funded Sing Up quite generously during its first year in government, and Sing Up has continued to operate in reduced circumstances since then under a self-funding business model. The earlier initiative that gave birth to Sing Up was the National Music Manifesto, launched in 2004. Between the years 2007 and 2011, Sing Up received £40 million of core government funding to achieve its stated aim to 'raise the status of singing and increase opportunities for school children throughout the country to enjoy singing as part of their everyday lives, and to support all primary schools to become "singing schools".'

There is little doubt that Sing Up was largely successful in its stated aims of raising status and promoting enjoyment. The organization has been careful to commission high-quality evaluative research from respected institutions with the capability to carry it out. The various reports produced have shown that there was a significant increase in primary school singing and that many children who might not otherwise have done so came to enjoy singing as part of their everyday lives. This emphasis on participation and enjoyment is only a first step, however. OFSTED continue to raise concerns about the *quality* of vocal work in primary schools and still further its pedagogical purpose. Is a 'singing school' one that draws on the voice to teach musical literacy and musical understanding with standards of rigour similar to those expected for literacy and numeracy, or is it 'just singing'?

For me, the most convincing evidence of a positive impact was the study undertaken by Graham Welch and his colleagues, based on established scales of singing development (Welch *et al.* 2009a). This showed that children inside the programme left primary school on average two years ahead of their peers in non-Sing Up schools, in terms of singing development. This is undoubtedly a result of considerable significance, though questions remain about the *quality* as well as *quantity* of vocal work. There are some painfully poor examples of primary school singing on YouTube and it is a matter of concern that anybody thinks they are suitable for sharing, let alone celebrating. The need to educate primary school teachers about what counts for quality in children's singing remains, as does the need to develop a better understanding of how children develop musical skill and learn about music *through* singing.

With considerations about music pedagogy and singing in mind, it could also be argued that Sing Up concentrated too much on advocacy that stressed extrinsic benefits. It did not sufficiently make the case for music as a fundamental element of the curriculum and singing as the key pedagogic strategy. If singing (and music) needs such intense advocacy by enthusiastic supporters, this is almost akin to saying that it does not really have an indispensable role to play in the development of a full profile of intelligence. Sing Up rhetoric is riven with statements such as

93% of respondents agreed with the statement 'singing supports children's development of speech, language and communication' and 90% of respondents said that singing 'supports curriculum learning'. Benefits were also noted for *social and emotional development* for children with special educational needs, improvements in learning Primary Languages and for children with English as a second language.

<http://www.singup.org/news-local-events/news-article/view/888-we-love-a-little-research-dont-you/>

This is very worthy and probably true, but there are other ways of supporting children's development of speech, language, and communication: for example, drama or an early start to the learning of two modern foreign languages as in the Steiner schools. The statement misses the fundamental point that must come first. Music is a key part of the curriculum and aural/vocal work is a (or the) key pedagogical strategy in music.

It is not hard to understand the reasons why if one goes back to the original Music Manifesto that was, by its very title, an advocacy project. Lest this be doubted, the Manifesto's own documentation described it as an initiative that is:

now led by a voluntary, apolitical 13-strong Partnership and *Advocacy Group* (MMPAG), chaired by Darren Henley, managing director of Classic FM. The MMPAG team work closely with the DCSF and DCMS but remain independent of the government (my emphasis).

<http://www.netsoundsproject.eu/node/386>

One has to ask why such advocacy was thought necessary in 2004. My own recollection of that year was that it was a time in which music education and singing had reached a particularly low ebb in primary schools. Most were coming to terms with endless government edicts about literacy and numeracy, including national strategies that prescribed in considerable detail by means of a graphic clock how teachers would spend each minute of their 'literacy hour'. Perhaps somebody thought life needed lightening up with a little 'frill'.

There is little in the advocacy approach that actually makes the case for a sound pedagogy of music education. The benefits of singing that are stressed seldom include *the development of aural acuity, the internal ear,* and *musical memory.* It is *singing* itself that is advocated, not the more fundamental task of developing in all school students a critical understanding of how music works and a personal toolkit of basic musical skills. Nowhere is this more obvious than in the conception of Sing Up as an initiative for primary schools only. The vital 11–14 years of KS3 received minimal attention, with the result that for many children everything stops at the end of Y6. This is not necessarily a reflection on how Sing Up's planners saw the world. They were simply carrying out their instructions to develop a programme for primary schools.

For reasons such as this and in spite therefore of its undoubted successes, I have tended to view the Sing Up programme as concerned more with participation than with pedagogy. The holy grail of primary school teachers with adequate training in music and music pedagogy remains as far out of reach as ever. Although Sing Up money funded some very good initiatives, such as training by the Voices Foundation and the highly successful Chorister Outreach Programme, Sing Up was in my view over-dependent on download-able backing tracks. In order to develop aural acuity and the inner ear, a properly trained music specialist should be able to play or sing live to the students exactly what they need at any given moment in a lesson, and this has to come from the resource of the teacher's own subject knowledge and musicianship. It is simply not realistic to imagine that such specialist ability is ever going to reach many primary school classes, let alone every one. I feel confident in stating that this will never happen. Our attention needs to be focused, therefore on two questions that need answering:

♦ Will every Y7 student be taught by a music specialist who can sing or play to them at any given instant what they need to develop their aural acuity and inner ear?

♦ Is it too late to start this process with the 11-year-olds of Y7?

What did the practitioner group think?

They were first asked how satisfied they were with the level of progress achieved by primary school students on entry to their school in Y7 at age 11 (Figure 2.2). Almost three-quarters felt that it was hard to say as there was so much variation between primary schools. This is an old chestnut that is supposed to have been addressed over the years by a common national curriculum, end of key stage testing and reporting, and ongoing initiatives to develop Y6–Y7 continuity. Secondary schools have been criticized in the past for taking insufficient note of what had been done in primary school. At worst, unprofessional attitudes such as 'you're starting proper school now' could be found and the

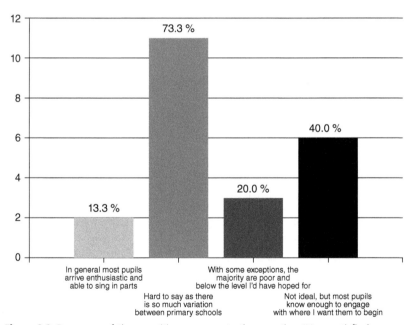

Figure 2.2 Response of the practitioner group to the question 'How satisfied are you with the level achieved by pupils on entry to Y7?'

careful work of primary schools was dismissed. This actually showed up in research as a dip in progress during Y7, a matter that ought to embarrass the secondary schools concerned. I am not inclined in this instance, however, to suspect my colleagues in the practitioner group to be guilty of this. The continuing position of music as a 'frill' subject dependent upon advocacy in many primary schools probably justifies the perception that serious music education begins in Y7.

On a slightly more positive note, 40% of the practitioner group feels at least that most students know enough to engage with where they want to start. The practitioner group was then asked specifically about Sing Up (Figure 2.3). Just under half felt that in recent years, Y7 had been much more ready to sing than in the past. This is, on balance, a good result, but slightly over half the practitioners seem untouched by it and around a quarter have reservations. Although some believe that the new Y7s sing more in tune, an equal number feel that bad habits have been learned through, for example, too much 'just singing' with backing tracks.

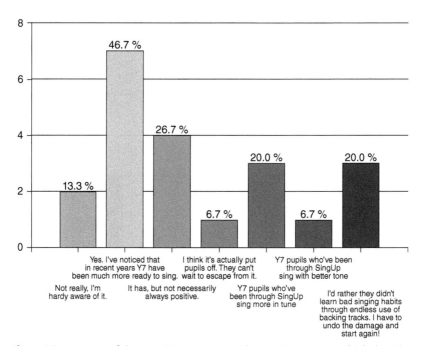

Figure 2.3 Response of the practitioner group to the question 'Do you think that Sing Up, the National Singing Programme in primary schools, has made a difference?'

The national scene

It is this question of precisely where to start that occupies us now. The secondary school music teacher will be faced each September with bright (hopefully eager) new faces representing a range of experience and attitudes to singing. According to Figure 2.3, just under half of our practitioner group have noticed that these new Y7s have, in recent years, been much more ready to sing. We may reasonably attribute this perception to the work of Sing Up. Over the next few years, this position will need to be revisited as the number of schools continuing to use Sing Up perhaps inevitably diminishes. There will be polarization between schools that remain enthusiastic and continue to subscribe to Sing Up, and schools that saw 'value' only when Sing Up was free. The teacher of the new Y7 class will need to make decisions about what to do with those of his or her new charges who come from either kind of school.

Y7, of course, is a time for fresh starts and new, clean slates. Fresh starts in what, though? Are the students simply to have more of the same kind of singing, or are they to experience something more akin to an aural/vocal approach where the voice is actually used as a pedagogical strategy to develop audiation and musical sense? Buried within the various documents of recent times, there is the hint of a pedagogical strategy in which the singing voice might play an important part in the teaching and learning of music at KS3. This is potentially about a good deal more than 'just singing', but unless we are prepared to delve fairly deeply, analyse the issues and supply substance that is missing from the documents, we shall be operating at a superficial level that goes little further than 'just singing'.

The National Music Plan

The National Music Plan was preceded by the Henley Report (DCMS 2011). This was written at the behest of incoming education secretary, Michael Gove, by Darren Henley, managing director of the Classic FM radio station and chair of the Music Manifesto Partnership and Advocacy Group. It reflected the then new government's stated belief that 'every child should receive a strong, knowledge based cultural education and should have the opportunity to learn and play a musical instrument and to sing'. 'Knowledge' and 'culture' might be picked out as key words by anyone familiar with the thrust of UK education policy since 2010. 'How to sing' is identified as 'an important area of knowledge that needs to be learnt'. The crowning statement in the document is its second key recommendation: '*Singing should be an important part of every child's school life from Early Years through until at least Key Stage 3.*'

In other words, all children, girls *and* boys, should be singing in school up to the age of 14. As we shall see shortly, this is an exceptionally optimistic example of rhetorical aspiration. There is little else of substance in the document that addresses such key questions as:

- *Why* should all 11–14-year-olds be singing?
- What should they be singing?
- What will they learn from this?
- How should teachers go about it and what sorts of standard should be expected?
- What should teachers do when confronted by students apathetic or hostile to being made to sing?

Henley offers little in the way of answers to these questions and the remainder of the references to singing in the document do little else than highlight the existence of Sing Up. One can be forgiven for wondering whether the document's author has ever actually been left in charge of a Y9 class on a wet Friday afternoon. Nevertheless, it is a splendid aspiration in the true tradition of advocacy.

The National Music Plan puts a little more flesh on the aspirational bones. Without saying why it is needed in any pedagogical sense, it calls for a singing strategy to ensure that every child sings regularly. This might be because children could be learning quite a lot about music, but the Plan falls back on the old advocacy chestnut of 'improve students' learning, confidence, health and social development.' Nevertheless, it is reasonably clear that what is envisioned is a strategy that operates 'in and beyond schools'. The need for progression is recognized and implicitly the need for empowerment and choice. Some children, for whom it is appropriate, should be able to progress to chorister schemes, to area or county youth choirs, and even to the National Youth Choir. There is also a recognition that while a small minority of students will progress in their singing to county or even professional level, a larger number should engage in amateur or semi-professional singing for the 'rest of their lives'. This I wholeheartedly support, and of course it has been going on for many decades.

The aspiration for progression to county and national choirs sounds good on paper, but in practice for reasons I explain in Chapter 3 it can be regarded as remaining, at the time of writing, firmly in the domain of the aspirational. The reality is that there is a long way to go before any child in an English primary school has a realistic route through area and county choirs to the National Youth Choir. A great deal more progress has been made with this in Scotland than in England. The 'National' Music Plan neatly sidesteps the fact that there is a National Youth Choir of Scotland and National Youth Choirs of Great Britain, which in reality might be more suitably named the National Youth Choir of England. I shall need to tackle these politics in later chapters, though the irony that at the time of writing a referendum for Scottish independence is in near prospect cannot pass unnoticed.

Much store was set by the National Music Plan on the creation of new 'music hubs'. The hubs were to be responsible for a singing strategy in their area. Local authority music services have had a long-standing role in supporting schools through such means as the provision of peripatetic instrumental (and vocal) teaching, or the recognition that certain activities need to take place at county rather than school level. The better music services often provided excellent singing opportunities, but as with so much in music education, this tended to be patchy and students were victims of a 'postcode lottery'. A hoped-for outcome of the creation of music hubs was an end to this patchiness. Reorganization, it was hoped, would offer the chance to improve or replace the less good music services. The inclusion of the voluntary and professional music sectors within hubs was an interesting idea. At the time of writing it is too early to say whether this is leading ultimately to greater or reduced patchiness. Early signs indicate potential differences between hubs based in dispersed rural counties and hubs based in large, metropolitan centres of music-making.

The English National Curriculum

On the subject of curriculum provision, the Music Plan was very short on detail, preferring the fallback position of 'Schools make their own decisions about how they teach music, based on the statutory National Curriculum (subject to outcome of the National Curriculum review).' At KS2 (primary ages 7–11) all students will have 'opportunities for increasing their knowledge and understanding and developing their skills, confidence and expression in music through singing...' Interestingly, specific mention of singing has disappeared from the corresponding section for KS3 (11–14) though no explanation for the apparent change of emphasis is given. The National Curriculum review has now taken place and the new 2014 curriculum is similarly short on detail. This reflects a process that has been ongoing since the first big slim-down by Sir Ron Dearing in 1994 of the impossibly overprescribed original 1988 version of the National Curriculum.

The 2014 National Curriculum, which applies only to those schools that have not opted out of direct LA control by becoming academies, states simply that students must 'learn to sing and use their voices' and should be taught to '... perform confidently in a range of solo and ensemble contexts using their voice...' The lack of detail is understandable as a reaction to earlier over-provision of detail and a political direction towards restoration of autonomy for schools and professionalism for teachers. However, its blandness and unwillingness to elaborate on what it means by 'learn to sing and use their voices' may not be that helpful. Some may see it as little more than a banal statement of the obvious. At least the statement has the status of a statutory requirement, meaning that the extent to which students are learning to sing and use their voices can be inspected and reported on. Perhaps it is intended that books such as this will fill in the detail.

The practitioner group was asked on a four-point scale from *not at all* to *entirely* where they gained their ideas of what and how to teach from (Figure 2.4). The National Curriculum (pre-2014 version) was clearly of some importance, if only because it would be unwise to ignore a statutory document. However, the source the practitioners relied upon most was 'my own ideas', while music hubs made the least contribution. 'Other ideas through networking' was of some importance, but this is presumably informal net-working akin to the sharing of 'my own ideas' amongst colleagues rather than the organized leadership of music hubs. This is of some significance given criticisms made by OFSTED that secondary music teachers work too much in isolation and music hubs have made little progress in addressing this problem. We shall need to explore this very important topic in dialogue with the practitioners as the book progresses.

There is little else in the Plan about singing, other than an uncritical endorsement of the Sing Up song bank as an illustration of the use of technology, and an appendix of case studies, including one about boys' singing of which I was the author! My critique of the lack of pedagogic vision or substance in the documents make depressing reading, but should be familiar to anyone who has studied the work of Robin Alexander (see for example Alexander 2004). Building on earlier expositions of the same critique by authors such as Brian Simon, Alexander has made quite a good academic living out of the 'wot, no pedagogy?' theme across large swathes of educational endeavour. Without a clear pedagogy, we will end up with 'just singing'. If we have little more than 'just singing', then we are on a hiding to nothing convincing school managers that 'just singing' results in the long list of benefits claimed by the advocates who stress them.

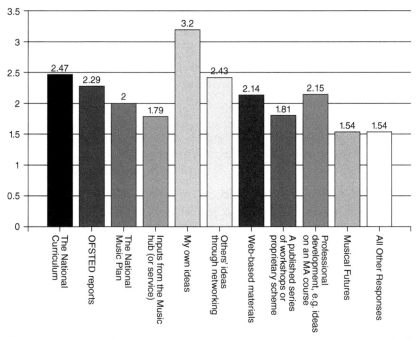

Figure 2.4 Response of the practitioner group to the question 'To what extent to each of the following contribute to the design of your KS3 curriculum?'

OFSTED

OFSTED provide what has become popularly termed a 'reality check' on this excess of aspiration, rhetoric and uncritical endorsement. It is left to OFSTED reports to comment indirectly on the inadequacy of documents such as the Music Plan and tease out the real detail. The inspectors are, for example, quick to spot that there can be a problem with backing tracks:

the use of a backing track in rehearsal was sometimes a hindrance rather than a help because it could not react to the conductor's direction or the singers' responses. As one experienced music coordinator commented, 'It's so much better to use live accompaniment—backing tracks don't have ears.' (OFSTED 2012: 55)

It is unfortunate, in my view, that comment on the inadequacy of pedagogic strategies that might be taught to new teachers emerges as criticism of existing teachers. If the problem really is as serious as OFSTED appear to suggest, matters need putting right at the stage of selection and initial training. Perhaps the design of the curriculum is at fault at least as much as its teaching or interpretation. When we consider the way singing is actually taught, as opposed to being used to teach other aspects of music, there is clear evidence that an information-poor curriculum has misled many teachers.

Critique of existing teaching, however, seems to be the way things are done when it comes to defining pedagogical principles. OFSTED's overall assessment of the position in 2009 comes across as a profound indictment of the situation they found:

Singing was an area of relative weakness. It was good or outstanding in only two in 10 schools and was inadequate in over three in 10. In the latter, it was not that the quality of the students' singing was poor but, rather, that no singing took place at all...

(OFSTED 2009, *Making More of Music*)

Perhaps we are used to such criticisms. In order to appreciate them fully, I usually ask students to substitute 'mathematics' or 'English grammar' for 'singing'. The newspaper headlines can only be imagined. University education faculties would be closed down and the Secretary of State might be forced to resign.

Two years is not a long time to change things. OFSTED's next subject report, nevertheless, makes it clear that they have seen little progress:

♦ By some way, secondary school students' musical achievement was weakest in Key Stage 3. This was a direct consequence of weak teaching and poor curriculum provision.

♦ One of inspectors' biggest concerns over the three-year reporting period was about the paucity of singing observed in secondary schools. Singing was inadequate—or simply not happening at all—in 41 of the 90 schools inspected.

♦ Students were performing songs from notated scores with good attention being paid to improving diction and tone quality. Of the 25 students present, just two were boys and these were from Years 7 and 8. The girls were from all year groups, including the sixth form.

(*Music in Schools: wider still and wider*. OFSTED 110158, March 2012)

A key point to note here is that, though primary school singing is by no means universally good, it is KS3, the lower secondary school, that is singled out for weak teaching and poor curriculum provision. It was pointed out not that many years ago by a delegate to a training day I was speaking at that two-thirds of a student's compulsory music education takes place in primary schools (i.e. KS1 and 2). The lower secondary school, which ought to provide a fitting and demanding climax to this compulsory experience for every child, lets down many children. The 'paucity' and 'inadequacy' of singing is part of that failing. Boys, it should be obvious by now, are more disadvantaged than girls by this weakness.

This requires explanation. For two-thirds of their compulsory music education, most students are taught by generalist teachers with little or no musical training. In theory, the final third, when the students are at their most mature and specialist music teachers take over, ought to be the best. Incredibly, however, OFSTED report that:

Even though all the lessons seen in the secondary schools visited were taught by specialist music teachers, the students in these lessons made less progress overall in Key Stage 3 than in any of the other key stages. (OFSTED 2009: 68)

Generalist primary teachers often have to rely on external input and support from initiatives such as Sing Up. Backing tracks have to substitute for teachers' inability or unwillingness to sing or play. Whatever the shortcomings of backing tracks may be, a good many of the students arrive in secondary schools at the age of 11 at least willing to sing. There they meet teachers with specialist musical training who at least in theory can sing or play to them, yet instead of building upon the students' willingness and improved singing competency identified in research, nothing happens. There is 'weak teaching, 'poor curriculum provision' and a 'paucity of singing'.

One clue as to why this might be is that OFSTED consistently report more favourably on KS4, sixth form and extracurricular music. This hints at the possibility that a number of teachers only enjoy working with older students who elect to study music. This is a situation that needs to be addressed early on in the selection of potential future music teachers. What would be the situation if teachers of maths or English decided that they only like to teach bright and compliant students who had chosen their subjects?

I am going to offer four headline explanations that we will explore in detail in the remainder of the book. In doing this, I am saying nothing that has not already been identified by OFSTED.

1. The fundamental place of singing in a foundational music pedagogy for *all* students is not clearly articulated.
2. There is confusion between 'just singing', singing by *all* students to develop core musical skills, and singing by *some* students who have chosen voice or choir as a performance option.
3. There is insufficient understanding of the technicalities of developing the singing voice, particularly during the lower secondary years when the voices of both girls and boys change in quality and functioning as a result of puberty.
4. There is, amongst many teachers, a fear of singing with young adolescents fuelled by popular beliefs about what is 'cool'.

It is left to OFSTED to offer the necessary clarification that is lacking in the rhetorical advocacy documents. Here In *Music in schools: wider still, and wider* (OFSTED 2012) it is spelt out:

Priority: improve pupils' internalization of music through high-quality singing and listening

The most effective music teaching recognized a key requirement of the National Curriculum programmes of study, that pupils should be taught: To listen with concentration, and to internalize and recall sounds with increasing aural memory. Developing pupils' intrinsic musical understanding—an understanding that goes beyond words and which is expressed through the quality of their musical responses—has at its heart the development of listening skills. These skills do not develop primarily on paper or in words—they develop in musical sounds, inside the head. In turn, the development of another internal musical process—singing, where the sound comes from within the body—links inextricably to the development of listening with musical understanding. Singing and listening are natural partners in musical learning, in the same way that speaking and listening underpin verbal language learning.

The objective is straightforward and the principle upon which it is founded is clear. Singing is not a 'frill' to gain light relief. It is, in partnership with listening, the way musical intelligence is developed. The development of musical intelligence is part of the total development process of the young person. If it is as straightforward as this, we are going to need to devote the rest of the book to exploring why it is apparently so impossibly difficult for just under half of all schools (46%, OFSTED figures). Before we do that, though, we need to pause to consider why it is that this appears to be a matter of so little concern to many school managements. Why is there not a national panic in schools to improve singing before the next OFSTED inspection?

I struggled for some time during the preparation of this book to understand why there is a hierarchy within a hierarchy. This is the hierarchy of how much notice anybody takes of what the school inspectorate actually says. If OFSTED inspectors announce a crisis in literacy or numeracy, all hell breaks loose in parliament and across the media. The education profession is severely censured from top to bottom and with unfailing predictability, and industry and business leaders are given their cue to state how ill-prepared young people are for work. If the inspectorates announce a crisis in school singing (as they do with clear and unfailing regularity), not that many people actually take much notice. To their credit, OFSTED have recently answered my question. They have identified the problem described above. They have identified that school leaders do not know enough about music to judge whether their music teachers are good enough. The school leaders do not see this as a particular problem because they do not see music as a serious, academic subject.

With this in mind, OFSTED have begun to produce documents to assist senior staff who do not have specific knowledge of music and music teaching in the observation of lessons. This is important, because most of the available evidence suggests that when an aspect of teaching and learning is observed or inspected, the importance attached to it rises. The thrust of OFSTED's documentation and guidance in this field is clear. Senior leaders are overestimating the quality of music teaching in their schools because they are not concentrating on musical learning objectives and outcomes. The teacher must be seen to be engaging in music making, not talking or the students spending time writing at the expense of musical activity:

There should be no doubt that you are in a musical lesson. Pupils should be given every opportunity to experience, listen, engage, explore, respond to and work creatively with the language of musical sound. Teaching should listen carefully and strive consistently to improve the quality of pupils' musical understanding and response.

How robustly is singing taught—with good attention to diction, singing in tune, phrasing and posture? How effectively is the voice and physical movement used to help pupils internalize and understand music?

(OFSTED, *Music in Schools: promoting good practice*)

Hopefully, when faced with such a demand, senior leaders may begin to appreciate their own needs for understanding more about music and music teaching. Why do school leaders not know much about music? Presumably because when *they* were at school, music was not a serious academic subject. The problem is deep rooted and is going, literally, to take generations to solve. However, the situation may not be totally desperate. I recently asked a secondary head teacher, not that long in post, the very question—do you take any notice of OFSTED music reports and if not, why not? Her initial answer was that she is extremely busy and relies, in addition to the *Times Educational Supplement*, on a smartphone app that pushes out the most important education news of the week. What OFSTED say about music is seldom or never featured on that smartphone app.

However, to my surprise she then went on to explain how she had recently replaced her music teacher. The previous one had been retired on competency grounds. Apparently, her senior team had visited his lessons and found that, in her words, 'The KS3 students were just playing on the Apple Macs and the KS4 students were just jamming on their guitars'. Needless to say, there was no singing anywhere in the school. The head had been keen to reintroduce singing in the whole-school assembly, so this troubled her. When asked to show his lesson objectives and assessment records, this teacher was apparently unable to do so. He has been replaced and when I was taken to the new music teacher's

Y7 class I found all the children, boys and girls equally, singing! I think the point to be made here is that although school senior leaders do not necessarily understand music in any depth, they do understand good teaching and learning. The problem is simply to convince them that music is as much about good, rigorous academic teaching and learning as any other subject.

OFSTED seem to have gone slightly overboard in creating a new role for music hubs with regard to this. They are no longer to be service providers that schools buy into. They are to become a quasi-inspection/advisory service to track and chase recalcitrant schools. The irony of conflict with current neo-liberal policy that devolves decisions about training to senior managements who know nothing about music seems to have escaped attention. Nevertheless, here are examples of what OFSTED say 'music hubs must do':

A secondary school head of music considered there was a strong culture of singing in the school, because the quality of singing in Year 7 lessons was good, there were some choirs and older students took part in an annual show. However, the repertoire of the Year 7 students was very limited. Singing was used for performance, *but not to promote learning or explore musical ideas.* (OFSTED 2013, *What Music Hubs Must Do*, p. 13, my emphasis)

In a successful comprehensive school, students taking the GCSE course said that the Key Stage 3 music curriculum they had taken *had not given them the theoretical and conceptual understanding they needed for GCSE.* (ibid., p. 13)

Year 8 class music lesson was the culmination of a unit of work on chord sequences and layers in pop music. Students had to perform a recurring chord sequence on keyboards. Most were unable to do this accurately and many gave up. Furthermore, the students showed little understanding of the purpose of this chord sequence in the music or how it connected to the tune, as this was not taught. The lesson was slow-paced and did not achieve its objectives. *The school senior leader who observed the lesson, a non-specialist, over-graded the lesson for non-musical reasons.* (ibid., pp. 9–10)

Summary and conclusion

The key points to emerge from this chapter include:

- ◆ A need to rediscover and articulate boldly the core purpose of music education in making a unique contribution to the development of a young person's intelligence and sensibility;
- ◆ A need for senior leaders to take music seriously as an academic subject, and to understand it better;
- ◆ A need for a realistic and contextually workable pedagogic strategy with the role of singing clearly defined;

♦ The need for a significant number of schools to 'raise their game' considerably if the expectations of the schools inspectorate are to be met.

Further reading

Gordon, E. (2007) *Learning sequences in music: a contemporary music learning theory.* Chicago, IL: GIA Publications.

OFSTED (2009) *Making more of music: an evaluation of music in schools, 2005–2008.* Reference 080235. London: Office for Standards in Education.

OFSTED (2012) *Music in schools, wider still and wider: quality and inequality in music education, 2008–2011.* Reference 110158. Manchester: Office for Standards in Education.

Chapter 3

Expectations, equality, and diversity

Low expectations rank very highly amongst the reasons for the paucity of singing reported by OFSTED. Unfortunately, expectations are not evenly distributed and the singing scene for 11–14-year-olds is characterized by inequality. The chapter has little alternative but to report that singing is significantly more likely to be found in independent than maintained schools. Across this general picture there are significant exceptions and neither sector is found to be applying important research findings in any significant way (see Chapter 5 below).

Introduction

Chapter 2 may have been daunting reading for any new entrant to the profession of secondary school music teaching. I am aware of that. It may also be disturbing reading for long-established members of the profession, particularly those working in schools where there is either no singing at all, or singing only as a showpiece extracurricular activity. Not all of these colleagues will share my views on the importance of singing and neither, therefore, will they be in agreement with some of the position taken by OFSTED. I am aware of that too. I am not particularly comfortable in supporting OFSTED in their criticism of many teachers who undoubtedly work hard to give their students the best they can with the level of support and resource available to them.

Unfortunately, nevertheless, this chapter has one more task of critique to undertake before the serious work of putting things right can begin. It is a large one with deep roots. Equality and diversity ought to be the main theme of the chapter, but these cannot be addressed until the issue of expectations has been dealt with. OFSTED are in no doubt that there is, in general, insufficient equality in music education. It is in fact the first of their seven priorities in *Wider still and wider*:

Priority: challenge inequalities among pupils and between schools

125 As well as wide differences in the quality of teaching and curriculum provision, survey evidence revealed considerable inequities in the way in which different groups of pupils, different schools and different local authorities were benefiting from additional provision in music.

126 Not enough of the schools surveyed had acted to improve participation in musical activities by under-represented groups. While most were aware, for example, that many more girls than boys participated in choirs, far fewer could provide evidence of concerted action that they had taken to overcome these differences.

Equally, OFSTED are in no doubt that this is down to the low expectations of school leaders:

The root of the problem lay in a lack of understanding, and low expectations in music, among the schools' senior leaders and their consequent inability to challenge their own staff, and visiting teachers, to bring about improvement.

One of the problems with equality is that it can become 'motherhood and apple pie'. Most if not all teachers are in passive agreement that it is a 'good thing' but, as *Wider still and wider* points out, 'far fewer could provide evidence of concerted action' to achieve it. This chapter needs to examine why so few could provide evidence of concerted action to achieve equality. Gender inequality in singing participation is a well-known phenomenon and is expanded further in Chapter 9. The concern in the present chapter is more with inequalities in the use of the singing voice as part of a strategy for a rigorous and serious musical education during KS1–3 (i.e. primary and lower secondary). Often overlooked is the need to equip students adequately for the demands of academic study of music in 16+ examinations and beyond, and to encourage more students to choose this option.

Inequality

The postcode lottery

Singing in the lower secondary school is one of the greatest areas of inequality. In some schools, it is excellent and truly inspirational. In others it is simply non-existent. In the case of primary schools Graham Welch has demonstrated that such inequality has little to do with the location of the school or the nature of its intake (Welch *et al.* 2009a). Too often, a 'challenging intake' of students from relatively deprived areas is used as an excuse that the 'kids won't sing' without even trying. The students do not have to be from challenging areas for this to happen. Merely being boys is sufficient for some teachers in some schools to say 'they can't or won't do that' or 'our kids wouldn't be capable of that'. I have encountered such dismal attitudes with a depressing regularity during my career.

Of course, children will never acquire any cultural capital if it is assumed that they are incapable of doing so. I once worked closely with a remarkable individual who had brought boys' dance to a secondary school in classic circumstances of deprivation and low expectation. The Ballet Rambert had visited the school and the PE teacher had not even given boys the option of attending the session because 'boys won't dance'. Some boys complained about this, with the consequence that a dance teacher was brought in to work with them. The boys' dance company that was started as a result subsequently went on tour and achieved national recognition. The attitude of the individual who inspired them was instructive. The phrase he repeated to me several times during the course of that particular study was 'We don't teach Mozart to stop kids shoplifting, we teach Mozart because he's one step below God'.

This highlights the importance of intrinsic value, the attitude of the teacher, and the fearless determination to confront low expectations and stereotyping. The evidence is quite clear that the social background of the students is less relevant than the attitude of their teachers. I have certainly worked with teachers in challenging schools whose commitment to the students astounds and inspires me and, yes, their students sing. I use the term 'postcode lottery' to describe the situation long prevalent in music education and particularly access to good singing. The subject is far too dependent upon children by chance attending a primary school where there is the 'dream ticket' of an inspirational teacher skilled in music, passionate about children's singing, and supported by a head teacher who places high value in the arts. As Welch's work suggests, this can occur anywhere. Equally it is possible for it to *fail to occur* anywhere. A school popular with aspirational middle-class parents and in receipt of good reports for most of its teaching is no guarantee of a good musical education and certainly no guarantee of good singing. For anyone who values fairness and equality of opportunity, this situation is just not acceptable. So entrenched is it, though, that I have written elsewhere with resignation that it is a *fact* that only a small proportion of boys will ever develop a capability in singing and enjoy participating in a good choir (Ashley 2013).

Cost and access

One of the more unfortunate features of music education is that it is relatively expensive. Advocacy schemes regularly call for all children to learn a musical instrument and schemes such as *Wider Opportunities* for KS2 have been introduced to overcome the otherwise prohibitive expense of such an ambition for schools or less-wealthy parents. The value and effectiveness of such schemes continues to be debated. Interestingly, *Wider Opportunities* was a political initiative introduced by New Labour's David Blunkett, though enthusiastically backed by the music industry.

OFSTED, in *Wider still and wider*, reserved heavy levels of criticism for the way the funds were being distributed. Inconsistency and mismanagement were said to have led to a failure of the scheme to achieve one of its core objectives, greater equality of access to instrumental tuition and the possibility of children from impoverished homes learning an instrument and continuing to learn it at secondary school. In *Music in schools: what the hubs must do*, the level of criticism is stepped up. Too many music hubs have failed in their core purpose of implementing the National Music Plan, including its requirement for a singing strategy. The reason OFSTED give for this is that many music hubs retain the ethos of the old local authority music services out of which they evolved. These services are primarily oriented to seeing their schools as 'customers', largely for the provision of instrumental tuition for those children that want it.

As 'customers' of such a service, many school managements (it is said) do not know enough to make the right selections. As we saw in Chapter 2, OFSTED would apparently prefer to see the music hubs driving music education forwards, more in the mould of the old inspection services that held schools to account for shortcomings and provided training and support so that the curriculum could be adequately delivered. They express their vision in this manner:

Hubs, therefore, should not be simply asking schools what they need, or offering services that schools can take or leave. They must act as champions, leaders and expert partners, who can arrange systematic, helpful and challenging conversations with each school about the quality of the music education and how the school and hub can work together to improve it.

The fact that so many hubs have hitherto failed to do this is perhaps met with some degree of resignation by those who could see foresee things developing in such a way and none more so than those energetic music leaders who had hoped that hubs would be a way of ridding the nation of lethargic music services. Perhaps OFSTED have failed to take account of the neo-liberal market context of education where the 'customer' is indeed king (or queen)? The impending funding cuts and redundancies in hubs are hardly likely to inspire the kind of staff morale that will lead to proactive championing, but this is unlikely to be recognized in an official report.

State and independent

In theory, the relatively unrealistic and prohibitive cost of music education ought to be far less of a problem with singing, since the voice is a free instrument owned by everybody. In practice, though, my own research repeatedly demonstrates the extent to which singing in the lower secondary school remains deeply divided between the independent, fee-charging sector of education and the state-maintained schools. The graph in Figure 3.1 is taken from a paper of mine published in the *British Journal of Music Education* (Ashley 2013) and sets out the position quite starkly. It reflects what I found when visiting schools during the research fellowship described in the introduction. The schools represented are not those of the practitioner group but those that agreed to take part in this previous project.

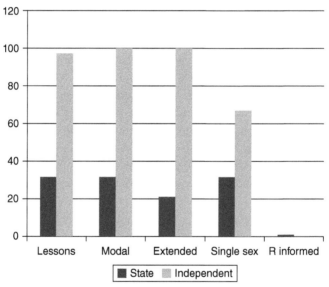

Figure 3.1 Boys' singing in 25 state maintained and independent UK secondary schools. The categories represented are whether or not class singing is a regular (weekly) feature of the Key Stage 3 music curriculum (lessons), whether or not boys aged between 11 and 14 were regularly engaged in extracurricular singing activities in the modal voice (modal), whether or not boys of that age regularly used their full extended singing range (extended), whether or not single-sex singing opportunities were provided for 11–14-year-olds, and finally, whether or not the teachers had heard of research such as John Cooksey's and used it deliberately to inform their practice.

From Ashley, M. (2013) 'Broken voices or a broken curriculum? the impact of research on UK school choral practice with boys', *British Journal of Music Education*, 30 (3): 311–27, with permission from Cambridge University Press.

The graph shows that in only one of the 25 schools in which the research took place was singing 'research informed'. I shall address this issue in Chapter 5. For the present, the obvious point to be gleaned is the great disparity between the state and independent sectors. All the independent schools, without exception, offered 11–14-year-old boys the opportunity to participate in a wide range of singing activities, including choral singing where the whole compass of the treble voice from A3 to G5 or above was employed. In five out of the six independent schools visited, regular curriculum singing by lower secondary-aged boys was observed. In stark contrast, in 8 out of the 19 state schools, there was *no singing at all*. Only 6 of the 19 state secondary schools had class singing comparable to the independent schools. This might be set alongside OFSTED's larger sample of 95 schools in which 29% had *no singing at all* and only 20% had singing that was good or outstanding. The picture can be said to be general and the research likely to be fairly reliable.

The figures are not explained by disparity in wealth or the supposed advantage of attending a fee-paying school. We need to look more deeply than that. The fact remains that in around 25% of the state-maintained schools there *was* good singing and, in line with Welch's work on primary schools (Welch *et al.* 2009a), this did not particularly correlate with the extent to which the school was in an affluent neighbourhood. Indeed, the one school where the boys' singing was both outstanding and research informed was located in an area of industrial decline and unemployment in the north of England.

Most of the schools visited for this book were state-maintained ones. In most cases, these were ones where the singing was either outstanding or at least actually taking place constructively in lower secondary curriculum lessons with opportunities for students to develop their whole singing voice in extracurricular work. The practitioner group sample, in that sense, is unlike the previous one displayed in Figure 3.1. It is a skewed one, disproportionately representative of state-maintained schools with good singing. It is representative of those teachers working in state-maintained schools who *are* successful with singing. These are the ones, I suspect, that it is most useful to learn from.

I have attempted to analyse from my admittedly small sample what is common across teachers working in state-maintained secondary schools where the singing is strong. The most common factor appeared to be that the teacher responsible had undertaken a fairly traditional, academic, undergraduate musical training. Close behind this in importance was that at least one teacher in the school had a significant degree of choral singing experience either as a child or as a student, or both. Importantly, this did not mean the music curriculum they taught was particularly traditional, academic, or 'classical'. These teachers often used 'popular music', such as pop songs or show tunes more likely to be familiar to the children, but were able to manage children's singing of these songs with a good understanding of vocal and choral technique.

In the majority, though not all cases, the teacher's choral experience had taken place within the context of a church choir or similar. The latter point is bothersome for two reasons. First, I do not wish in any way to be forced into the position of advocating a religious solution to the lack of singing problem. This is unlikely to be the way forward for many state-maintained schools. Second, though I have written much about the decline of religion and singing, the extent to which it still appears to be a surprisingly significant factor in whether or not singing is a strength in state-maintained schools is disturbing. Either singing declines with religion, religion is revived, or new ways are found of promoting good singing without religion. This is a big question that requires specific, statistically based research with a large sample.

For their report *Wider still and wider* OFSTED created a series of six best-practice videos. The school chosen to represent 'excellence in singing' was the London Oratory School. I have nothing against this school, indeed I celebrate the excellence of its choral work. Nevertheless it is a former grant-maintained grammar school with a strong choral tradition rooted in the Catholic liturgy. According to its website, it has its own junior house that admits '20 seven-year-old boys . . . for a specialist music education, with a strong emphasis on Catholic liturgical music'. Within the senior school is the Schola Cantorum which 'was established as a means of providing Catholic boys from the age of seven a rigorous choral education within the maintained system, something hitherto only available in the independent system'.

This rather illustrates exactly the point I am making. Behind the excellence in singing is a whole musical infrastructure based upon choral singing and the Christian liturgy. The school is now an academy and does not charge fees. That may be one reason OFSTED selected it, but one has to ask whether it was a wise choice and how much credibility it will have with teachers and school managers working in socially challenging, secular schools. One has to ask whether the London Oratory is the right template for the aspiration of diversity in singing. It is certainly possible to make a direct link between the London Oratory and the independent schools where 100% of boys sing in both modal and extended voice. The common factors are:

♦ Teachers with a traditional, academic musical training that included a significant amount of choral work;

♦ A school chapel (or equivalent) in which the whole school sings traditional Christian hymns, supported by a choir that rehearses and performs 'high art' sacred choral music.

Such a vision might appeal to certain right-leaning government ministers who may even see in the academy programme a means of promoting such values. I cannot be convinced, however, that it is the right template for improving singing in the lower secondary school across the board.

Pop versus classical

The popular media

The climate for school singing is not set by government ministers with a nostalgic yearning for the hymn-singing of their school assemblies. If it is set by anything or anybody, the popular media and the TV talent show genre must rank highly. The popular media have created a current view of singing that is dominated by the road to stardom for individual vocalists. Also lucrative has been the cultivation of beliefs such as 'boys don't sing'. This has led to an entirely new reality TV genre, currently capitalizing on workplace choirs. Choral singing, particularly when performed by static, ecclesiastical choirs that do not sway about or compete in 'last choir standing' contests, is portrayed as 'stuffy' and the sad remnant of an earlier era of establishment colonialism and religious imperialism. This is certainly the way such singing is viewed by the many boys and girls who have described it as the preserve of 'the elderly'.

The fact that the popular media portray things in such a way does not necessarily mean that young people uncritically absorb the values of popular TV entertainment. This is evident in this focus-group extract from a state-maintained comprehensive school where the music is strong and large numbers of boys as well as girls participate in extracurricular choral singing:

Y9: I watch *The X Factor*, just for the auditions, to see people sweat.

Y8a: You know, the way to find talent is to get rid of all the reality TV shows.

Y11: There are so many people at this school who are better than anyone of *The X Factor*.

Y8b: It's also so frustrating for a state school to be put down because we're not a private school. I came second in a public speaking contest but the main joy for me was beating <N> High School.

Teacher: It's more than that though. It makes me really angry. People only expect pop to come out of a state school (she imitates a lah-de-dah private school teacher who had put her down).

This extract takes us right to the core of the independent/state school divide over singing. This is a successful state school with a strong music department, but the students and their music teacher are made to feel inferior by students and teachers from independent schools who 'only expect pop to come out of a state school'. For the record, the above data were taken from a visit I made to this school in connection with my first research council fellowship. The school was selected as a member of the practitioner group and revisited several years later when a new generation of students had come through. Quite without knowledge of what any of his predecessors had said, this Y10 boy made the following observation of TV 'talent' shows such as *The X Factor*:

It's based on exterior rather singing, looking for things that will sell, rather than talent. It's about entertainment not music. People just go on it to get on telly. I know a lot of people that just like watching it at the audition stages because they like laughing at people.

Given the consistency over a number of years, I think it reasonable to take this as representative of the judgments of young people attending a publicly funded school who have been fortunate enough to receive a good musical education.

This does not necessarily mean that the independent schools have got everything right. The task of a school is to provide an education that results in well-informed, critical citizens. Knowing only about 'classical' music does not define being a well-informed critical citizen any more than knowing only 'pop' does. Judgement and taste in music is a far more complex field than such a simplistic view of things might suggest. The real difference is not between classical and popular but between entertainment and learning.

The students above have grasped that much of the entertainment value inherent in popular TV shows lies in 'seeing people sweat' or the humiliation of wannabes. The fact that the students are able to perceive this is indicative of operation at a level some way beyond the stereotype of mindless fodder for passive entertainment. Evidence of the impact of popular TV entertainment, nevertheless, can be found in this focus group of Y6 boys. They had been asked about whether they would willingly join in singing activities if these were introduced to their school. The responses below are representative:

♦ If you can sing solo, but not in a choir.
♦ If you can make money.
♦ A choir might be churchy.
♦ I get stage fright and I'd be embarrassed.
♦ If I was good at singing, I would want to sing solo and not in a choir anyway.

Here we can see the tendency to perceive singing as the road to stardom for vocalists. It is something that might be worth doing if it makes you rich but it is not something for the probable majority of young boys who do not aspire to show off as stage performers. Choirs are to be avoided because of their association with church. Here lay the seeds of the difference between many of the independent schools, with their intense focus on chapel and choral music, and the situation confronting the majority of teachers in the majority of schools. Nevertheless, those teachers working in schools without such advantage but determined to substitute musical education for the superficiality of popular TV entertainment can succeed and will be thanked by many of their students.

Education and entertainment

This is not just a difference between popular and classical music. It is to a somewhat greater degree a question of cultural capital and the value of music as a means of attaining cultural capital. Those who have analysed in depth the relationship between social class and musical taste generally conclude that the consumption of music cannot be equated in a simple way with such matters as visits to art galleries. Music is a far more popular cultural activity and enjoyed by many more people in much greater diversity than any other art form. It is also far more of a business and commercial undertaking than are art forms such as literature. For reasons such as this, there is no direct comparison between the specification of a canon of writers and artists that should be known and a canon of composers. Music elicits far stronger reactions of identity in young people than does literature or art. Music education shares with media studies the need for a critical deconstruction of the commercial music industry and its values but this is seldom fully appreciated.

Musical consumption ranges from fodder for 'cheesy pop' or *X Factor* style entertainment to Stockhausen or Cage. Such a range does not, however, delineate a straightforward continuum of social class. Omnivorous musical tastes are often to be found among those enjoying higher degrees of education and cultural capital. When such matters are considered it is easy to see that the terms 'popular' and 'classical' are amongst the most unsatisfactory that might be devised in making sense of the field of diversity, culture and musical taste. The term 'classical' is commonly but erroneously equated with anything perceived as 'highbrow', though strictly it refers to the late-eighteenth-century output of such composers as Haydn or Mozart. In reality, according to Pierre Bourdieu, highbrow consumers of Schoenberg might be more disdainful of lower-brow consumers of Vivaldi's *Four Seasons* than of consumers of highbrow jazz.

The term 'popular' is even less satisfactory. An analysis by Mike Savage of the *Cultural Capital and Social Exclusion* (CCSE) survey data (Savage 2006) makes the point that, if the criterion is the percentage professing enthusiasm for a specific genre, then 'popular' is actually less popular than 'classical': 55.7% of respondents 'liked and listened to' the *Four Seasons* as against 46.6% who 'liked and listened to' *Wonderwall* by Oasis, and 16.1% of listeners ranked 'classical' (meaning everything not 'popular') as their first-choice genre as against 14.9% listing rock (meaning rock as a specific genre within the generic 'popular'). The Brit awards now list over 80 genres that might loosely be labelled popular, but any one taken on its own does not remotely qualify for such an appellation. Young people of lower secondary age are bound to be more fluid in their tastes than adults with a confirmed musical identity. A key task of education is surely to engage critically with this fluidity.

Such engagement can only take place in the context of knowledge development. What probably matters the most is not whether the genre is 'classical' or 'popular' but whether the young people have felt challenged to learn something or accomplish something they feel to be worthwhile. This is the fundamental difference between education and entertainment. Singing needs to be evaluated principally by means of this criterion. In the field of popular entertainment, vocal music is the dominant form across almost every genre. It is a given, taken for granted in a world where the personality and performance style of the vocalists matters more than musical content. In what is called the serious or classical field, instrumental music is dominant. A tendency in classical circles to prioritize learning an instrument or playing in an orchestra does little to help with the general perception that 'vocals' are mere 'popular entertainment'. I have heard of children attending music schools to play their instrument and participate in orchestra being unceremoniously dumped in 'choir' for 40 minutes with little real thought given the case for singing as a key part of the training of any musician.

There is, or should be, a considerable difference between singalong karaoke and using the voice to grasp a point of learning or accomplish something new in music. In theory, the genre should not be relevant to this. However, I have sat through lessons based on clips from popular TV talent shows where the children learn nothing because the judges either have no real in-depth knowledge of singing, or it is considered by the producers of the programme that such knowledge has no place in an entertainment show. This is the actual feedback given by the judges in one clip that was used to introduce vocal work to a Y7 class:

I loved it. I think the industry's missing a boy band. You're cute. It's missing a harmony part maybe. There were too many high voices…

I like your personalities I think you're really well rehearsed. I like you a lot.

I really loved it. Nothing was contrived.

I thought that was terrific. I agree with the girls. You've all got great individual voices. I loved it.

It is hard to see how children can learn much of depth or value from an approach by judges that amounts to little more than 'I don't know anything about music but I know what I like'. The issue here is again less one of popular versus classical than one of entertainment versus education. Needless to say the above example was taken from a state-maintained school, though one in quite an affluent area. There is research that demonstrates that it is in this matter that some schools, including the independent ones that teach 'classical', may score over others. A study by Kathleen Scott-Bennetts (2013) has tackled inequality in musical provision and attainment in Australia. The issue that emerged was less that of popular versus classical than entertainment and frivolity versus serious academic learning. In schools where rock music dominated the curriculum, students saw music as a low-value 'frill' subject. At the school where there was a rigorous focus on academic learning in music a high proportion of boys participated in choral work, comparable to an English independent school. Rigorous learning in music was seen as part of the process of acquiring cultural capital. Students and parents were prepared to take music seriously because it was perceived as a 'proper subject'.

As opposed to viewing music as a 'frill' subject, merely light entertainment to provide relief from the more serious subjects, Balton students appear to regard music as occupying a significant position in their school lives, and in life generally (Scott-Bennetts 2013).

The 'position in life generally' included critical appraisal of how students constructed their own musical identity, and critiques of the values inherent in different forms of music-making. Some students at this school did complain about what they perceived as an excessive dominance of 'classical' music in lessons, wishing for more 'contemporary' music. Others recognized however, that 'you get all that at home, on the radio, everywhere'. If music is to be taken seriously, the expectations for learning have to be at least as high as for any 'serious' subject. The expectations for participation have to be equally high. Children of lower secondary school age are quite capable of evaluating whether or not they have learned anything worthwhile at school that they would not learn elsewhere, and they vote with their feet when 16+ examination options are chosen.

Walking a tricky tightrope

The right level of challenge

The best results in singing, then, are associated with the treatment of music as a serious academic subject. One has equally, though, to realize that one is dealing with children. If the expectation is that Y7 or Y8 will walk quietly and obediently into the music class to wait in silent expectation for whatever erudite discourse is to be dispensed by the learned pedagogue, one has of course made a big mistake. It is as big a mistake as the teacher with the low expectation that 'our children won't be able to do that'. Children new to the singing class will very likely be nervous or fearful of potential embarrassment (see Chapter 8). The last thing that is needed is a dry academic approach that will place them under stress. Their first experience of singing undoubtedly needs to be fun. Amusing warm-ups with actions are a good way of doing this. There are examples on the supporting website (<http://www.martin-ashley.com/teacher-pages>) where it is quite clear that the children are having great fun.

The earliest repertoire for new Y7 classes probably needs to be learned through call and response. Simple gospel songs with a limited range that can be instantly transposed to fit the available voices are good here. Such songs may soon result in children swaying about or clicking their fingers. Boys are more likely to do this than girls. Let them! This, however, is all groundwork. If the foundations are properly laid and singing is a continuous part of the curriculum, progress to real learning and higher expectations will be quick. It needs to be remembered at all times that music is a practical subject and that by far the larger part of any music lesson should be devoted to music-making, not teacher talk. *Academic can still be practical.* Talking by the teacher and writing by the students is not what makes things 'academic'. It is the ability to listen critically, analyse, and provide concise but accurate explanations of why something is not good enough, and identify in a clear instruction what must be done to effect the desired improvement. If the reader finds this hard to accept, perhaps he or she will be more convinced by the words of a 12-year-old boy in Y8:

They [teachers] probably want to know what a boy wants to get out of singing. They [boys] don't want to *just sing* songs and the teachers tell them they're good when they're not. They need to know the truth, they probably want to get toward the truth so they can practice at it. (My emphasis).

Once the serious learning begins, it is highly desirable that it is based on what the children are actually singing themselves. Rather than sit them down and lecture them on an extract sung by somebody else, get them singing straightaway.

They can be recorded and the learning developed through a critique of the playback of their own singing.

Children or older teens?

In such a way, there is a good chance of a good match between singing repertoire and learning needs. At lower secondary level, though, this can still be quite difficult. From nursery rhymes to the Sing Up song bank, there is a vast wealth of music that would be considered 'children's'. Interestingly, this all largely disappears at around the lower secondary age. The exceedingly challenging question of repertoire is addressed in Chapter 7. Here I want to extend a little further my critique of the TV talent show approach from a pedagogical point of view. One definition of 'children's music' is simply 'music written by children'. Students learning English study the works of high-quality authors for young people as well as some of the classics of literature. They also spend a considerable amount of time on writing and critiquing their own material.

One of the strengths of music education in recent decades has been the emphasis on listening, composing, and performing. I am frequently impressed by the level of composition I see produced by lower secondary students using software such as Sibelius. This is more commonly instrumental music, but much is to be learned about the voice and singing through writing songs. Indeed, if children have to sing what they have just written, they will soon learn about the compass of the voice, how far it can be extended, what other voices might be needed to realize what is in the mind, what makes a good vocal line and what does not. The attentive teacher who is knowledgeable about such matters can scaffold children's learning to a level significantly higher than is possible through spectating TV talent shows—or even analysing 'classical' CDs. Children can and should be encouraged to sing what they have written rather than use the playback facility of the notation software. All this is part of using the voice as an active aid to musical learning.

At one school visited in researching for this book, Y7 and Y8 students had been given the task of writing a carol for the Christmas concert. The concert was an annual event that took place in the city's well-known concert hall before an audience of up to 1000. Some of the compositions were of at least as good a standard as those that win events such as carol competitions organized by local newspapers. More to the point, they were sung with interest and enthusiasm by other students in the school because what had been achieved was, in an entirely literal sense, 'children's music'.

When it comes to finding authentic children's music within what is so loosely defined as the 'popular' field, the lower secondary age group really is quite hard to cater for. The various specific pre-teen and early teen genres that have come and gone since the 'bubblegum' pop era have usually been well outgrown by the age of 11 or 12. In my own research I found that children of primary age would make comments about teen pop such as 'It's my kind of music and I really like it'. Only one or two years later when these children had progressed to lower secondary age, the language applied to the same music had changed to such an extent that the comment 'that was pop!' was uttered with disgust. Teen idol singers are often 'adored' by hysterical pre-teen and early teen girls and held in utter contempt by secondary school students keen to demonstrate sophistication in equal measure. Most 12- and 13-year-olds in my own research were keen to demonstrate their new post-primary status by a rejection of the 'cheesy' and approval of what they generally referred to as 'rock'.

Meta-analytical studies such as Roberts & Christenson (1997), however, reveal that students of lower secondary age are seldom in tune with the real meaning of rock. It is more a desire to appear grown-up and an attraction to the general soundscape. Lyrics are not appreciated, or are appreciated differently by different children in ways unintended by the songwriter, perhaps fortunately in view of some of the subjects covered. With obvious exceptions such as the perennially popular *Joseph and the Amazing Technicolour Dreamcoat*, rock is not really children's music; and 11- and 12-year-olds, for all their champing at the bit of adolescence, are still essentially children. Newspaper stories of premature sexualization, while containing a grain of truth, also contain a bushel of sensationalism and exaggeration.

Nowhere are the difficulties discussed above more apparent than when it comes to the way the commercial music industry treats children of lower secondary age. On the one hand, they are bombarded with material that they themselves cannot sing authentically because they do not yet have the voices of older adolescents who can 'shout and snarl' aggressive rock vocals or belt out the emotional lead of Broadway. On the other hand, when the commercial music industry *does* turn its attention to children, it is usually to commodify and market them as satisfaction for adult fantasies of childhood and 'cuteness'. There are many commercial CDs and professional video-clips of talented children in the lower secondary age singing beautifully in the whole voice. Few of these are really suitable for use in the classroom because they are blatantly targeted at and imaged for 'grannies and nans' (or in the words of one 14-year-old, 'menopausal women who want to trade in their teenage son').

When children do appear on TV talent shows, it is often under circumstances of freakish precocity that have little connection with the real world of the lower secondary school child.

Musical Futures

Informal pedagogy

It is not possible to close a chapter on expectations, equality, and diversity without mention of the significant secondary music project funded by the Paul Hamlyn Foundation and known as Musical Futures. In the strictest sense, Musical Futures is not about genre or musical paradigm. It is about pedagogy. Contrary to the general trend towards teacher-centred, didactic methods taken by the pedagogy of most subjects over the last decade, Musical Futures has moved in the opposite direction of informal learning. The reason for this is its roots in Lucy Green's seminal text *How Popular Musicians Learn* (Green 2002). Green has deduced five key pedagogical principles through her studies of the informal musical learning of popular musicians:

1. *Learning music that students choose, like and identify with*, as opposed to being introduced to music which is often new and unfamiliar, and chosen by a teacher.
2. *Learning by listening and copying recordings*, as opposed to learning through notation or other written/verbal instructions.
3. *Learning alongside friends*, instead of learning through instruction with continuous adult guidance.
4. *Assimilating skills and knowledge in personal ways* according to musical preferences, starting with whole 'real world' pieces of music, as opposed to following a designated progression from simple to complex, involving specially-composed music, a curriculum or a graded syllabus.
5. *Maintaining a close integration of listening, performing, improvising, and composing* throughout the learning process, as opposed to gradually specializing and differentiating between listening, performing, improvising, and composing skills.

These are pedagogical principles, not a prescription for any particular paradigm or genre. In that they do indeed describe how popular musicians learn while running contrary to the way 'classical' musicians are generally trained through formal, graded examinations, Musical Futures is inevitably associated with popular music. When it comes to singing, the orientation towards popular music is very clear in the use of the terminology 'vocals' rather than 'choral'.

This is particularly the case in the recently introduced units on 'Exploring Vocals' and, for Y7, 'Singing and Music Technology'.

There have been well-intentioned attempts to introduce children to classical music through *Musical Futures*. Indeed, units on 'classical' are part of the suggested scheme and, importantly, endorsed by the Hamlyn Foundation. The divide between popular and classical is, however, potentially exacerbated rather than reduced by an emphasis upon pedagogy over genre. Where there is strong choral singing, teacher-centred pedagogies are almost invariably to be found. Indeed, the music teacher who is also a successful choir director may be amongst the most didactic and teacher-centred of all the staff members of a school. Much of what is involved in choral pedagogy involves a performance routine by the teacher that students must follow absolutely.

Musical Futures was adopted with some enthusiasm by the former Hertfordshire Music Service. John Witchell, the senior adviser, wrote this:

For most of the time young people accept the school curriculum. They may not necessarily like all subjects, but they recognize some sort of value in what they do and, given some reasonable teaching, get down to the business of learning. I appreciate that this is an over-simplification. However in music a cultural barrier seems to emerge and it is often only removed by exceptionally inspirational teaching. It is recognized that most young people are passionate and knowledgeable about their music that they experience in their own time. But, because of this emotional ownership, teenagers do not readily accept the music that the school provides (preface in Green & Walmsley, 2006).

This is very close to the 'school is not cool' argument that was presented in Chapter 1. Students will accept mathematics teaching though many may not like it, but this is, perhaps uniquely, a bridge too far for music. Witchell's claim that musical barriers are often removed only by exceptionally inspirational teaching is all but impossible to refute. Does Witchell's view then amount to a capitulation to an inevitability; only highly exceptional teachers will succeed with a formal 'choral' approach whilst the informal 'vocals and technology' approach is appropriate for the majority?

Pitfalls

Musical Futures is a powerful strategy with potentially far-reaching consequences for singing. It can easily be misconstrued by teachers who may not have really understood the philosophy and pedagogy behind it. OFSTED, for example, found that:

There were, however, schools where a Musical Futures approach—as defined by the school, and not through endorsement by the Paul Hamlyn Foundation—resulted in poor progress because teachers did not demonstrate that they still had a key role to play and that the principles of good musical teaching and learning still applied (OFSTED, *Wider still and wider*: 41.

The same might be said of any pedagogical system devised to overcome difficulties in music learning. The Kodály system can produce superb results in the hands of an inspirational teacher who really understands it. It can equally result in dull, dry routines and a bunker mentality in which everything must be done exactly the way it was done in Hungary 50 years ago.

It is the pedagogy of informal learning that is primarily endorsed by the Paul Hamlyn Foundation. The inevitable drawback is spotted by OFSTED when they report that:

... At no stage did the teacher promote good musical learning, or support and challenge the students sufficiently. Significantly, she did not play or sing a single note herself during the entire lesson. (OFSTED, *Wider still and wider*: 41)

This observation may be part of a struggle at conceptual level where questions may need to remain open and possibilities be explored and evaluated. The 'key role' that teachers may have to play is defined by Lucy Green in this way:

The role of the teacher is different. It involves standing back, observing, and attempting to empathize with the goals that the pupils are setting for themselves, and then at that point diagnosing their needs and then acting as a guide. (Green, n.d.)

Does this 'acting as a guide' legitimate the teacher singing or playing herself? It may do if the teacher goes about it in a democratic way as a co-creator of the music with the students. Such an approach would come perilously close to the educational philosophy of John Dewey. This has been highly influential in the development of educational thought over decades but is hardly popular with current administrations that are sanctioning returns to more traditional curricula, teaching methods, and examinations.

Of some significance is the fact that none of the teachers in the practitioner group was an enthusiastic advocate of Musical Futures, and 62% did not use it at all (Figure 3.2). It needs to be remembered that the practitioner group sample is one that is skewed toward traditionally trained teachers who feel comfortable with the didactic pedagogies of choral instruction. The inevitable question of cultural capital surfaces through the reasons given. Schools and teachers selected on the grounds that the singing was known to be a strength of the school generally expressed little need of Musical Futures. The feeling was that they were achieving the results they wanted without it. This does not mean that they were right or that it is right to deny students, or some students, the potential benefits of a Musical Futures approach. Questions such as cultural capital and its association with music as a 'serious' academic subject,

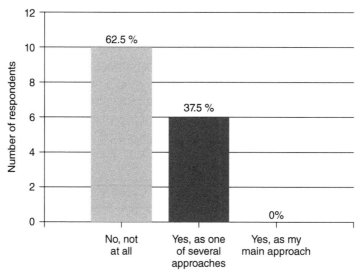

Figure 3.2 Response of the practitioner group to the question 'Do you use Musical Futures in KS3?'

the marginalization of music to 'frills' status, and the ability of senior managements to understand and evaluate music pedagogy though remain there in the background.

Though informal pedagogies with links to the philosophy of John Dewey are currently unpopular with those advocating strict discipline and teacher-centred instruction, it is essential that healthy, open, and critical discourse about pedagogy be maintained. In an effort to do this, I reflected for another volume on how boys do learn choral singing in some of the best choirs (Ashley, 2014). I concluded that learning takes place, not in a fragmented, graded, wait-until-you-know-enough fashion, but in a community of practice where boy singers are expected to be every bit as competent as the adults in the community. The following features loosely shared with the informal learning of Musical Futures might be identified:

♦ The boys like and identify with music that has become part of their life and familiar to them from the age of 8 upwards.
♦ The boys learn by listening, observing, and copying the performance of the choir and the older boys and men in it.
♦ The boys learn alongside friends within a protective cocoon of solidarity.

- The boys assimilate skills and knowledge in a personal way that research demonstrates to be sometimes quite different to the way the choir director imagines he or she is teaching.
- With the exception of improvising, which is somewhat discouraged, the boys closely integrate their listening and performing. They may also have a go at composing, though the attitudes they may encounter if they do can sometimes be patronizing.

Conclusion

Equality and diversity are necessary parts of any music education strategy. Unlike other subjects perceived to be 'core', 'essential', or 'basic', music is subject to widespread variation with regard to what is expected of students. It is a given that music is hugely important in young people's lives, in significant measure as a leisure activity. The relevant boundaries between education and entertainment, though, are articulated more clearly in some schools than others. Although it might be conceived as a simplistic 'classical' versus 'popular' polarity, it is more helpful to see things in terms of a capitulation to entertainment as opposed to a determination to pursue music with academic rigour. The latter is demonstrably more likely in independent schools than in state-maintained schools. It is instructive, though, that that there are problems with equitable distribution of available funds for expensive instrumental tuition in the areas of some music hubs. Given that the voice is a free instrument, it would not appear to be the cost of instruments that gives the independent schools their advantage. The disparity is better explained by expectations and the seriousness and rigour of the approach to music. A similar divide in the quantity and quality of singing can be found between those state schools that appear to treat music seriously and those that do not. It is likely that singing will improve if more teachers are prepared to set musical standards that demand more than the level of spectating popular entertainment, but the drive for this needs to come from better informed and more supportive senior managements. Whether it is appropriate to expect music hubs in turn to drive senior managements is an interesting political question raised by OFSTED.

- There is unacceptably wide variation in the provision of good singing, amounting to a 'postcode lottery'.
- This does not necessarily correlate with the social background of the school district. Inspirational and committed teaching (or the lack of it) is a key factor of variance that sometimes transcends socio-economic capital.

♦ The most important divide is not between 'popular' and 'classical' but between entertainment and education.

♦ In spite of the fact that the voice is a 'free instrument owned by everybody' there is in general more and better singing in independent, fee-charging schools that in publicly funded schools. It is not therefore a simple question of ability to purchase instruments and pay for instrumental tuition.

Further reading

Bourdieu, P. (1984) *Distinction: a social critique of the judgment of taste.* London: RKP.

Green, L. (2008) *Music, informal learning and the school: a new classroom pedagogy.* Aldershot: Ashgate.

McPhersen, G. (2006) *The child as musician: a handbook of musical development.* Oxford: Oxford University Press.

Roberts, R. & Christenson, P. (1997) *It's not only rock and roll: popular music in the lives of adolescents.* Cresskill, NJ: Hampton Press.

Rudolph, T. & Frankel, J. (2009) *YouTube in music education.* Milwaukee, MI: Hal Leonard.

Chapter 4

Classroom cacophony or chamber choir concert?

Where should singing take place? The aspiration of the National Music Plan is that every student sings regularly and that choirs and other vocal ensembles are available in the area covered by the hub. For 'every student to sing regularly', it is likely that the curriculum music lesson will be the place. 'Choirs and other vocal ensembles' may be extracurricular or may happen within the community. Research reported in this chapter suggests that the most successful schools build their choirs and ensembles upon classroom singing characterized by a 'this is what we all do here' attitude.

Introduction

In this chapter we are going to have to develop the 'why are we doing it?' discussion begun in Chapter 1. We are going to have to explore in greater depth what is meant by vocal work and how this differs from choral singing. Our discussion will need to provide answers to the critique of the advocacy approach developed in Chapter 2, and it will need to respect the points of difference considered in Chapter 3. My most fundamental point is that an unexamined belief that singing is a 'good thing' is insufficient as a secure foundation for the best practice.

The title of the chapter implies something of a continuum from what a listener interested only in the performance of music might perceive as the worst to the best. This is not what is intended, though it might be what is sometimes heard in practice. While there are of course, the three core contexts for singing—the music class, the extracurricular work or curriculum choral programme, and the individual/small group work—the reality is that the three interact in complex ways. We will need to consider how this process is managed. Before tackling that, I need to report and consider a phenomenon that I have observed quite often. I have visited schools where 'little kids' have not been welcome in a chamber choir that is seen more as the preserve of a sixth-form elite. Such a practice is by no means confined to the classical choral tradition. I have observed the development of a boys' rock choir. Again, 'little kids' from the lower school were not welcome. Not only were they vocally unsuitable, their juvenile status was seen by the older boys as intrusive and distracting.

Valuing lower-school voices

Pictures such as these provide a startling contrast with the use of lower secondary school voices in what has been described as 'some of the finest choral singing in the world'. These are the words of Irvin Cooper, founder of the Cambiata Vocal Institute of America, on a study tour to the UK in 1962. He was describing the singing of lower secondary age boys he heard in the English cathedrals and the chapels of public schools (i.e. fee-paying schools). It is as well to face up also to Cooper's impressions of singing in English state-maintained secondary schools: 'widespread ignorance of boys' voices, either no singing at all or a range of inappropriate vocal practices and a complete lack of any systematic training to address the problem' (Cooper 1964). That was written in 1964 and makes an interesting comparison with OFSTED's current observations.

At the root of the problem is the question of value. The voices of lower secondary age boys have long been accorded very high value in what is often called the 'English cathedral tradition'. In recent decades, the voices of similar-aged girls have come to be accorded similar value. Whether boys or girls, children of this age are indeed capable of some of the 'finest choral singing in the world'. Many of them would have better sight-reading ability and reper-toire knowledge than the sixth-form students who do not want 'little kids' in their chamber choir.

It might well be argued that singing of this nature is the preserve of a very small and highly privileged minority and irrelevant to most secondary schools. What is harder to dismiss is the influence of music teachers who have had sufficient contact with this tradition to perceive significant value in the voices of 11–13-year-olds. The evaluation of Sing Up undertaken by Graham Welch and his colleagues demonstrated a clear effect of contact with the cathedral choral tradition on the quality of primary school singing. My own research for this book has revealed that what I suspected might be the case is indeed true. Every school approached on the grounds that the singing was known to be good had on the staff at least one teacher with direct knowledge of choral singing in an ecclesiastical context.

It is hard to know what to say or do about this. On the one hand, I would not really be happy for my words to be used to advance the cause of church schools, still less to recruit children to religion. On the other hand it would be disingenuous not to acknowledge the immeasurable contribution that the Christian church has made, and apparently still does make, to high-quality singing by children. I have worried for many years that if the Church and its music continues to decline, perhaps to a point of near extinction, choral work and high-quality singing by children may suffer a similar fate. For that reason some degree of secularization of choral singing, and of the choral repertoire, seems to me a good strategy, but I find little evidence that this is happening at grass-roots level. What I have observed to be more commonly the case is music teachers who may have, or have had, some involvement with church music quietly working away in schools to promote good singing by the children. They do so to all intents in a secular manner and secular context, but their knowledge of and confidence to deal with the singing of 11–14-year-olds comes from elsewhere.

It is a good deal easier to identify the common ground that secular and sacred might share. This is undoubtedly a belief that the voices of its Y7 and Y8 children can and should be one of the most prized assets of any secondary school music department.

Cacophony?

Would we want to treat one of our most prized musical assets in such a way that the result is cacophony? Not all children will be able to sing equally beautifully and the extracurricular singing groups will in most cases presumably sound better than music classes attended by all. The difference, however, need not be that great. I have certainly witnessed total cacophony in music classes where there is attempted singing. Equally I have witnessed a Y7 class taken for their first singing lesson by a highly skilled and experienced teacher. The class sounded tuneful and pleasant with less than 10 minutes of this teacher's skilful touch. Cacophony is not inevitable and serves no good purpose.

The root of the difference, as said earlier, lies in the value that is placed upon the children and their singing. Are they one of the most prized musical assets in the school or are they an irritating chore and distraction from the 'real' work of GCSE music classes and upper-school productions? Of equal importance to this fundamental question of value is the question of expectations. If it is known and fully appreciated how well children *can* sing, the expectation of the conscientious teacher ought surely to be that they *should* sing that well. If the music department has a clear pedagogic strategy in which singing plays a key role in audiation (the internalization of sound and development of memory and musical thinking), it will surely be the belief of the teachers that children *need* to sing well. How can pitches be heard or intervals internalized accurately if they are not sung accurately?

Some objectivity needs to be brought to bear and there needs to be some recognized indication of singing ability in children. Given all that has been said about progression and continuity, with two out of three key stages taking place in the primary school, there needs to be some objective measure of whether the singing actually has reached its apotheosis in the lower secondary school. It is often assumed that it has, but some children may have advanced little or even gone backwards in the lower secondary relative to the primary school. Much depends on the quality of the experience in both phases. Some children may come underdeveloped from primary schools where the singing is poor or non-existent. The secondary teacher may then need to start almost from scratch in a remedial role. It is equally conceivable that other children may come from musically excellent primary schools. They will have well-developed singing behaviours, only to be let down by a secondary music department where the singing is poor or non-existent.

Measuring singing

Progression is not measured purely in the complexity of the music, or whether the singing has moved from unison to two or three parts. It can also be measured in technical mastery of the singing process itself. If singing is to be useful to children as a key aid to their musical learning, each individual child needs to have developed their singing ability to an adequate level. If they have not, their learning in other areas of music may well be held back. Children are unlikely to develop a secure internal schema of music if their external vocalization is inaccurate or even non-existent. There are recognized measures of children's singing development that have been tried, improved and tested over many years. One is the scale devised in the US by Joanne Rutkowski of Pennsylvania State University. It recognizes five stages of singing development (Box 4.1).

Later versions of this scale have finer subdivisions, but in the form in Box 4.1 it is quite sufficient to provide a clear tool for use with a new cohort of Y7s. In order to benefit from a secondary music curriculum that uses singing as a pedagogical strategy, all students need to have reached at least level 4. Students

Box 4.1 The Rutkowski (1997) scale (abbreviated)

Level 1. 'Pre-singer'. Chants rather than sings the song text.

Level 2. 'Speaking range singer'. Some sustained tones and pitch sensitivity, but only within the normal speaking pitch range (approximately A3–C4).

Level 3. 'Uncertain singer'. Sustains tones but wavers between speaking and singing voice. Unable to lift singing voice beyond about F♯ 4.

Level 4. 'Initial range singer'. Able to use the singing voice consistently as far as the register lift, but not beyond.

Level 5. 'Singer'. Able to manage the register lift and sing consistently across the whole voice.

who will join and enjoy extracurricular choral activities will need to be at level 5. A good many such students will already be at that level on entry to secondary school, quite possibly having developed their voices in choirs outside school. Use of such a scale of course relies on the fact that teachers know enough about singing to recognize vocal characteristics such as the register lift. More is said about this in Chapter 5, but if the concept is entirely alien, the teacher really does need to take some personal singing lessons or perhaps complete an in-service module on understanding of voice.

A majority of the practitioner group expressed the view that the ability range in singing development on entry to Y7 is so great as to present real problems with knowing where to start. This is understandable given the range in quality of primary music provision. Similarly, Sing Up had a mixed evaluation by the practitioner group. There is, of course, huge variation from the Sing Up Platinum school at one end to the non-participating school at the other. Some members of the practitioner group cited a conglomeration of bad habits resulting from Sing Up that had to be unlearned. Others felt that any singing at all was better than no singing. However, to use the contention that the children know nothing as an excuse for avoiding issues of cross-phase pro-gression been found wanting in other subjects.

All should be aware of the comprehensive evaluation of Sing Up carried out by Graham Welch and his colleagues at the Institute of Education (Welch *et al.* 2009b). Using the Rutkowski scale this demonstrated that, in general, Sing Up *did* result in improved capability. Overall, the results were that children in Sing Up schools were on average 2 years ahead in singing development compared to children in non-participating schools. In my view, these results justify pressure

Box 4.2 The Welch (1998) Revised model of vocal pitch matching development (abbreviated)

Phase 1. Chant-like. Words rather than melody the centre of interest. Restricted pitch range dominated by descending patterns.

Phase 2. Melodic outline begins to follow contours of target melody. Vocal pitch range expands.

Phase 3. Melodic shape and intervals mostly accurate. Possible changes in tonality due to inability to manage register shift.

Phase 4. No significant melodic or pitch errors in relation to simple songs from singer's culture.

from secondary music departments to encourage feeder primary schools to use Sing Up or an equivalent strategy.

In addition to the Rutkowski scale, Welch *et al.* (2009b) employed the Welch (1998) scale of pitch-matching development (Box 4.2). This is an extremely useful supplement to the Rutkowski scale. The two go hand in hand.

These two scales complement each other well. The expectation, ideally, ought to be that nearly all children have achieved Welch's phase 4 on entry to secondary school, but this can by no means be relied upon, particularly for boys. Children are unlikely to learn much of what might be intended through vocal work if they have not reached phase 3. If they have reached phase 4, they are likely to benefit from or enjoy being stretched through extracurricular choral work. The evidence would appear to indicate that, where Sing Up has been regularly and competently used in primary schools, most children will have reached these levels by age 11. Where singing has been neglected by primary schools, many boys in particular may not have reached these levels.

Registration and singing competency

The Rutkowski and Welch scales are very useful indicators, but they are probably not sufficient to provide a full picture. First it may be culturally specific to assume that children will progress by level 5 to become 'singers'. Singers are defined as 'using the extended singing range beyond the B♭4 lift point'. There is now a strong tendency to use only the lower part of the voice in class music lessons because it has become highly unfashionable to 'sound choiry' or even 'squeak and shriek' in some children's world view. Nevertheless, children will not develop the whole voice unless they sing regularly a repertoire that takes them well beyond the B♭4 lift point and vocalize *downwards* into the lower voice. The importance of downward vocalization is stressed in almost every text on the development of the child singing voice, and teachers need fully to understand why. It is quite likely that a good many children will never achieve downward vocalization from the upper register, given a widespread tendency of music publishers to pitch school music too low to engage the upper part of the voice.

Whether this is a drawback of the Rutkowski scale or a collective failure in school music publishing is a moot point. It is, however, one of the reasons I would give for seeing progression beyond level 4 as perhaps having to be a matter of choice. For reasons I develop later, it may be more a matter of choosing elective singing opportunities than the normal prescriptions of differentiation and match, though these are still important. Children wishing to extend their singing beyond the classroom will very soon reach level 5 and phase 4 in suitable extracurricular work, provided that extracurricular work of sufficient challenge *is available for the lower school.* Many of those likely to opt for this will quite probably already have reached the highest Rutkowski levels before reaching secondary school.

Testing

Another potential and quite big shortcoming of the scales is that they do not measure such essential other factors as anxiety levels or attitudes. For this reason, useful as they are, the scales cannot be used in isolation from other measures of such qualities. We cannot know for certain whether a child's apparent underperformance is explained better by a high level of singing anxiety or a negative attitude to singing than it is by lack of development or even innate ability. Embarrassment is very likely to result in underperformance in a test, particularly with boys whose voices are beginning to change. Underperformance through embarrassment may be quite widespread, and not just amongst children. Many otherwise competent and confident music teachers may themselves harbour singing anxiety, often communicating this to the students (see Chapter 6). There are validated scales that measure maths anxiety but no direct equivalent for singing. Performance anxiety is recognized and measured amongst musicians, but this is not the same as specific anxiety about the exposure of the voice. Anxiety is also often confused with attitude or even self-efficacy, but the concepts are not the same, as research in mathematics education demonstrates.

Tests have to be administered carefully, sensitively, and patiently. Children may not pitch a note sounded on a piano but they may pitch it from a voice. Whether the voice is at the same pitch as theirs or an octave different may affect their pitch matching. There are permutations such as an adult male an octave below a girl or unchanged boy voice, or an adult female an octave above a changed boy voice. If children are asked to sing any note they like and the listener then pitch matches the keyboard to the child's voice, the child may then be able to sing quite accurately or pitch match to other notes on the keyboard once he or she has started. Sometimes a child might pitch match fairly accurately when given a whole melodic fragment to copy, but not a single note. The permutations are quite considerable and it is highly unlikely that a busy music teacher will have the time or inclination to give the necessary attention to each of a hundred or more new Y7 children.

This is one reason why the Rutkowski and Welch scales are perhaps more useful as tools for the researcher than as tools for the classroom teacher. There is another profoundly important reason, however, that is not often fully appreciated. This is the chorus effect itself. When a number of voices blend together in chorus, the listener perceives that the melody is being sung fairly accurately. Errors in individual voices may be quite considerable, but in the listener's ear these are cancelled out by the chorus blend as well as what the listener actually expects to hear. This is an area in which I have conducted recent research with competent child singers in choirs, and the results are quite surprising. The whole choir sounds accurate, but when an individual voice is targeted through a radio microphone, there may be considerable deviation from accurate pitch or even melodic contour. More is said about this in Chapter 8 where there is discussion about the degree of accuracy needed to ensure that children really are developing musically through participation in the class chorus.

The difficulty of the chorus effect has two main implications for our perception of individuals. First, we cannot gain reliable and valid information about a child's ability and progress in singing unless we carry out some form of individual test. Second, there is arguably a need for a rating scale for voices in chorus as well as individual voices. It should be possible to rate a whole class on a similar scale to the Rutkowski one for individual voices incorporating such categories as 'pre-singing class', 'uncertain singing class', and 'singing class'. Such a scale might have as a minimum standard for Y7 'initial range class' meaning that when the song is pitched below the B♭4 lift point, there is a sufficient number of children accurately in tune to create a chorus effect that is tuneful, even if some individuals cannot sing consistently and accurately in tune at the pitch chosen for performance. If the music teaching is good, such children should be few enough in number not to downgrade their class. The phenomenon is well illustrated when children are asked to clap back a rhythm in chorus rather than sing it. It is extremely rare to witness complete unanimity of clapping. This is certainly not achieved in OFSTED's good practice video of Churchfields Junior School. So inaccuracy within the chorus is to be expected. The question that is not well answered and requires further research is 'how much?'

Another way of approaching the problem is to use tests designed for whole-class administration. The Arnold Bentley tests of musical ability in children (Bentley 1966) have been around for a long time and are still used by some schools. They are what they claim to be—tests of musical ability rather than assessments of learning or musical progress. They were conceived at a time when the idea of innate 'abilities' or fixed 'intelligences' was received more enthusiastically and less critically than it would be now. Though comprehensive and carefully tested for reliability, the Bentley tests have been critiqued on the grounds that the approach is a deficit one that gives a fixed view of what a child might do. The Rutkowski and Welch scales are conceived differently, as indicative of how far a child has progressed developmentally. For whole-class testing the measures of music audiation devised by Edwin Gordon (Gordon 1986) better support a developmental approach. The intermediate version for grades 1–6 is ideal for assessing a new Y7 class (given that G6 is equivalent to the UK Y7).

There are, of course, many forms of 'aural test', not least those designed and published in graded form by the Associated Board of the Royal Schools of Music (ABRSM) or equivalent bodies. The point of any 'aural test' is that it requires the internalization of what is heard. Singing might be used as an intermediate strategy between playing and reproducing. A teacher might play a melody and a student might reproduce it, either in written form or on a keyboard or Orff instrument. Alternatively, the teacher might sing or play a melody, the students then sing it, and after that reproduce or even extend it through other means. If singing is effective as a strategy for the internalization of music, the latter process should yield better results than the former. This strategy is best put to effect in a well-structured lesson where the singing of a song constitutes the first main part of the lesson and work on aspects of the song the second part. Assessment for learning is readily developed through activities such as playing the melody on a keyboard or writing it down to extend it, harmonize it, or analyse its structure. It is possible not only to evaluate how useful the singing has been to the subsequent activities but also to identify what the student is having difficulty hearing. This may well be related to the level of singing development the student has reached.

This brings us to the crux of the matter and Kodály's chief purpose in singing. *All music learning and performance will improve through audiation and the development of the inner ear and this is achieved most effectively through voice.*

Basic singing

Integration with learning objectives

I have seen lessons where little such learning occurs precisely because there is no clear link between what is sung and other activities in the lesson. Singing is seen as an end in itself. Several songs may be sung and the lesson might then proceed in an entirely unconnected way. Alternatively, the whole lesson might be 'just singing' with no direct use made of the power of singing to teach other aspects of music. If a significant portion of the class is below the expected Rutkowski/ Welch levels as a result of poor or no singing at primary school, there may well be some benefit in a crash Y7 course of Sing Up. In such circumstances, 'just singing' probably does have justification, but the class needs to progress toward activities geared to accuracy in the vocal chorus as soon as possible. OFSTED, in their 2013 *Promoting Good Practice* guide suggest the evaluator of any music lesson ask this question:

How robustly is singing taught—with good attention to diction, singing in tune, phrasing and posture? How effectively is the voice and physical movement used to help students internalize and understand music?

This statement goes some way to answering questions about the extent to which any whole class singing activity takes on aspects of a choir rehearsal. If one is working with children, even in the best professional choirs, the work has to include three dimensions:

♦ Preparation of a high standard performance that an audience will be pleased to hear;

♦ Teaching choral technique—matters such as how to watch and follow a conductor's gesture, how to listen and blend with other singers, how to phrase as part of an ensemble;

♦ Teaching singing technique—matters such as how to stand and breathe correctly, how to eliminate tension, how to produce vowels or manage registration breaks.

It is only a matter of emphasis toward one end or the other of a performance–pedagogic continuum that differentiates a music class for all from an extra-curricular rehearsal for elective members of a choral ensemble. To some degree, the class-singing lesson will be a 'mini choir practice'. Depending on the age and experience of the children, one might say and do similar things in a class singing lesson and a choir rehearsal. Music teachers with any form of choral background have the advantage here. Much of what might need to be said and done will be instinctive. Others whose experience is orchestral will soon pick up what is required if they are used to directing ensembles of any kind, willing to spend time observing choral specialists at work, and perhaps take some personal singing lessons.

When I was at school, there was a time each year when class music lessons were given over to rehearsals for a whole-school choral work in which almost every student participated. Usually this would be one of the big works of the Western canon, for example the Poulenc *Gloria* or the Haydn *Nelson Mass*. One year, however, we learned *Joseph and the Amazing Technicolour Dream-coat*. This was not long after the work was first released. Tim Rice and Andrew Lloyd Webber both visited the school and took lead roles in our performance. I have observed practice currently in some of the practitioner group schools where a unit of work is given over to rehearsing a performance. For example, at one school, the final Y7 unit of work is given to putting on a performance of *Roald Dahl's Goldilocks and the Three Bears* (MacGregor and Chadwick 2005).

Although it is good practice to identify some specific learning objectives (to be communicated musically, not through students spending half the lesson copying them down), much that is learned will be part of an unpredictable and ongoing process allied to the preparation of a good performance. The children will learn much of value from a teacher who knows what he or she wants from a good performance. For learning to take place, the caveat that the performance must be good needs to be added. Overpraising children will never achieve a good performance. OFSTED make this quite clear in their guidance for lesson observation, using singing in tune as their example:

Less effective assessment over-praises work which is of poor quality—for example, telling pupils that their singing is 'excellent' when it is out of tune.

Of course, if the singing is out of tune, the teacher will need to know why. The choral specialist might worry about '*a cappella* pitch drift' and whether this is caused by breath control, room temperature, or collective misjudgment of the size of a semitone or minor sixth. In managing the class singing of 11–13-year-olds the causes are likely to be more basic. If a significant proportion of the class is below Rutkowski level 4 in their singing development, there is a real problem that is only going to be addressed by the provision of experiences that were missed in primary school. Without this the singing will remain tuneless, characterized by compressed intervals and lacking unanimity. There is some role in such circumstances for 'just singing' a regular repertoire of songs the children enjoy. The vocal range will need to be such that children progressing toward level 4 will not be confronted by intervals and pitches they simply cannot sing.

Progression

Progression can take the form of introducing songs with a gradually larger range and the teacher modelling accurately the key intervals. The Kodály system is highly developmental in this way. Though most children brought up from infancy on Kodály would be accomplished singers by age 11, it is still possible to start at age 11 with the same developmental sequence of intervals, albeit at lower pitch and with suitable words. Hand gestures pointing up or down (usually up) may also help. The full Curwen system of hand signs used in Kodály can profitably be taught to 11-year-olds. For the technologically minded there are programmes such as *Sing and See* that display pitch on the whiteboard. I have yet to be convinced that these are as effective as good modelling by a teacher, but they can gain some otherwise reluctant children's interest and add an extra dimension to the lesson. Points of technique such as posture, breath control, and articulation can gradually be introduced and the class will begin to progress beyond the 'just singing' stage. The point always to bear in mind is the extent to which children learn singing by imitation, but what they are asked to imitate must be within reach of their current capability. No amount of posture correction or breathing exercise will correct out-of-tune singing that results from inappropriate repertoire selection. If in doubt, choose songs with the smallest viable range in the early stages.

Choice of repertoire becomes important for other reasons in the lower secondary class. Progression through developmental scales such as Rutkowski's becomes non-linear because of the effects of puberty. The singing may go out of tune because children who were previously able to sing wide intervals or fairly high up the scale are confronted by physical changes to their voices. This is such an important topic that it is dealt with fully in Chapter 5, and addressed again in Chapter 7 on repertoire, Chapter 9 on gender, and Chapter 10 on cambiata singing. How to manage the adolescent changing voice is one of the key areas of specialism for the lower secondary music department.

More advanced singing

Knowledge of students

The first point to make in this final section is that there will be few lower secondary classes where there is not a considerable ability range with regard to singing capability. The usual causes, explanations, and arguments about ability variation in any subject may be deployed up to a point. Singing, however, is undoubtedly influenced in quite a major way by children's experience outside school. Children who take part in community music-making, whether it be a church choir, a musical show, or a folk band are likely to be far in advance of peers who do not sing outside school. On the one hand, such children may, perhaps oddly, be amongst the first to volunteer for a school choir. I say 'oddly' because children who enjoy singing well often can't seem to get enough of it. On the other hand the same children may become bored or resigned to suffering in what counts for them as 'silence' during the class music lesson. By 'silence' I mean not using the singing voices they have developed elsewhere. OFSTED have the following to say in their guidance for the evaluation of music lessons:

Third, the teacher should be able to tell you which pupils are benefiting from additional instrumental and/or vocal tuition, and those who participate in regular extra-curricular musical activities—in and out of school. Good teaching would have already identified these pupils through differentiated planning in the lesson observed. (*Music in Schools: promoting good practice.*)

I interpret 'should be able to tell you' as 'off the top of their head', not looking the answer up in a file. The teacher will know these children, not always the easiest of feats in a large department where classes may be seen only once or twice a week. Almost every school I visited while preparing this book was able to show me something like a Y7 workbook where children were invited to record their musical interests and activities outside school. Knowing the musical students is one thing, differentiating for their singing in a class music lesson is a challenge of another order. This is where further understanding of both Rutkowski's developmental scale and the voice change stages of Cooksey and Gackle (see Chapter 5) is called for. If the student is at Rutkowski level 5 and used to singing with the whole voice, he or she may feel a considerable degree of inhibition about doing this in front of peers. This is particularly true for boys, but increasingly a relevant consideration for girls too. Use of the whole voice will take a 12-year-old soaring into the C5–C6 octave and produce a 'choiry' sound even in the octave below. Children who are capable of doing that are very well justified in being wary of how this will be received by peers.

Integration of students

This is an area that I have researched in considerable depth. There is almost no doubt at all that the large majority of lower secondary students regard the use of the whole singing voice, particularly that of a boy, as inappropriate (or to use their jargon, 'weird'). This was not always so, but it has become the dominant musical culture in which we now live. Boy singers have been quite articulate about this when I have interviewed them. They enjoy using their 'head voice' in choir, but in school singing, they will often pretend that they do not have one. This may require their discovering for themselves two distinct modes of voice production. The only reliable means of overcoming this difficulty are through extracurricular work when inhibitions can be left aside under conditions of solidarity.

The problem is dealing with differentiation between Rutkowski levels effectively in the class music lesson that is not a showcase for the choir or exceptional individuals. It may be possible to differentiate by part. The more able singers might be given a lower (or higher) part, or a more complex line that calls on their aural acuity and musicianship to read and hold. Less able singers might have a simple ostinato or even a one- or two-note drone. They might support this by playing a simple instrument as they sing. A simple part needs still to be an integral and valuable part of the piece, and this is by no means always easy to achieve. It is less likely, though possible, that differentiation will be through challenging songs of varying degrees of challenge to rehearse away from other groups in a breakout room or space, particularly with Y9.

Operating against such possible ways of differentiation is always a level of corporate performance that is absent from, for example, the mathematics class. This, indeed, ought to be a celebrated aspect of music-making through singing in chorus. It is about teamwork, corporate identity, and mutual support— elements that can be missing from a culture of unmitigated individualism and competition for exam grades. That being so, the more able singers might be dispersed among the class to boost the singing of the less able. This is a strategy that might work. Equally it might not, because the more able singers may actually be inhibited or embarrassed through being placed in the midst of groups of children for whom singing holds little interest. It depends largely on the relative numbers and the attitude and skill of the teacher.

Extracurricular work

When it finally comes to extracurricular singing for the lower school, I would always ask three key questions.

1. Is there a school choir that eagerly recruits lower-school students because of the value that is placed on their treble voices?
2. Are there singing groups specifically designed to cater for the needs of voices changing during the earlier stages of puberty?
3. Are there separate single-sex singing opportunities for boys and girls in the lower school?

To these three key questions, I would add several other considerations:

♦ Are there regular activities, or is the scene characterized by frenetic bursts of activity for a forthcoming 'production' interspersed by periods when little is available? If there is a tradition of a big annual musical production, this can inevitably take a lot of time and resource, leaving little energy to spare elsewhere.
♦ Are there links into the community and wider musical world? Are children, for example, notified of and helped to prepare for auditions to county or even national youth choirs?
♦ Finally, to what extent is lower-school singing a showcase for the school? Do children from the school go out into the community to sing at local events? Are children who sing in extracurricular groups given equal credit, status, and celebration to sports teams in school assemblies?

All this is very time consuming. Concerning points 1 and 3, the lower-school treble voices will almost certainly need to be divided by gender and rehearse separately, as is done in the professional choirs. Failure to recognize this need almost invariably results in a choir that is mostly girls. The choir will therefore consume at least twice as much of the teachers' limited time. Figure 4.1 shows the priorities of the practitioner group with regard to extracurricular singing. Recognition of the need for single-sex activity clearly ranks highly in those schools where singing was relatively strong.

There are very real questions to be answered about how many extracurricular singing activities can be sustained and what the priorities are. An all-age choir in which lower-school students provide the treble voices and upper-school students the ATB can work well in a boys' school, but is considerably more difficult in a co-educational setting where older girls might provide the soprano line in an SATB choir.

A somewhat different approach, as in point 2, is to run a changing voice choir, perhaps based on the cambiata principles described in Chapter 10. This is a particularly good way of ensuring that boys sing. Strong traditions can be built up through starting with the youngest classes (Y7 in the majority of UK secondary schools) and retaining the loyalty of a good many of the boys as they

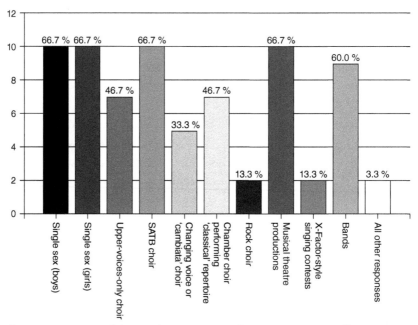

Figure 4.1 Response of the practitioner group to the question 'Do you offer extracurricular singing opportunities to pupils in KS3?'

grow through voice change. Careful thought then needs to be given to what is the most appropriate complementary activity for girls, and whether this is just a 'girls' choir' or one in which an understanding of voice change in girls results in any difference of approach. Such girls' choirs are relatively rare in the UK.

There is then a problem to be faced that if all the efforts and resources go into a changing voice choir, there may be insufficient time for any treble choirs. Although the youngest children can sing with a changing voice choir, it is not ideal. Changing voice choirs are often better without trebles, and treble voices are seldom developed or shown to their best advantage when the time has to be shared with slightly older students who may be learning a rather different approach to singing. To provide for all the possible forms of extracurricular singing is often beyond what is possible for a one-teacher department to do. Other members of staff, whether members of the music department or not, might well be involved in helping to provide a greater diversity of opportunity and more specialized provision for particular needs.

Older students, of course, may well be able to direct and manage their own activities, requiring little more than supervised access to the facilities. This is particularly so for smaller bands and singing clubs. It is often in managing large numbers of younger children that the real skill of an experienced, qualified music teacher is most needed. One thing has characterized many of the most successful teachers of school singing I have observed and interviewed—their absence from the staff room at morning and lunch break. They are absent, of course, because they are grabbing the 20 minutes to work with a particular group of children that makes all the difference to the quality, quantity, and diversity of extracurricular music making in the school.

Part of the answer to the time problem is to be found in an idea that is currently being pushed very hard by OFSTED. Music lessons should consist of music-making, not paperwork and teacher talk, and certainly not lengthy written tasks by students. The following from the guidance to managers observing music lessons ought to be fairly unambiguous:

Good music lessons engage pupils musically straight away—that is, by getting them to listen to and think about musical sound, or by involving them in a music-making task. Learning intentions are shared musically—for example, by the teacher modelling a song performance in tune with good diction, articulation and phrasing to show the pupils the intended musical outcome.

Assessment in music is often overcomplicated. There are only eight National Curriculum levels for music (plus the exceptional performance level). These levels are **not** divided into sub-levels, or separated into individual performing, composing and listening criteria. Teachers that do so often spend too much time explaining criteria to pupils, rather than actually engaging them musically. (*Music in schools: promoting good practice.*)

Teacher time is a very, very precious resource, but it should be concentrated either directly on music-making with young people or indirectly in musical preparation. The latter might even include the teacher taking singing or choral conducting lessons—a preferable use of time to pointless splitting up of assessment into criteria that exist only in the teacher's paperwork-bound imagination. This should be entirely liberating. The music teacher ought to be spending most of his or her time enjoying music-making with young people, not spending hours on paperwork. I cannot think of a better reason to choose music as the subject to teach.

Summary and conclusions

+ There are recognized measures of singing development. These are useful and might be used more.
+ Such measures reveal a progression point that is often a barrier to a large number of students. The highest levels of singing development require the

use of the whole voice and the ability to manage the lift point between upper and lower registers. The upper register is often not used for cultural reasons.

♦ Consideration needs to be given to how far singing in the curriculum music class will progress in the direction of a choral rehearsal in which singing technique and the skills of blending together in chorus are taught.

♦ A significant proportion of many lower secondary music classes may need to learn, for the first time, aspects of singing that could have been learned relatively early in the primary school. Principles, such as those of the Kodály system, may need to be adapted for use with students of lower secondary age. This might involve the provision of more age-appropriate lyrics to accompany vocal exercises that could have been attempted several years previously.

♦ Differentiation in the lower secondary class needs to take account of the effects of puberty on the voice as well as those of prior learning.

♦ The more able singers will only be fully stretched through extracurricular work. However, a range of different extracurricular singing activities is needed to differentiate for all the possible needs. Single-sex groups are important and there is a need to plan for how treble and changing voices might be catered for, and for how the lower-school singers might best be integrated into the overall school singing strategy.

Further reading

Ashley, M. (2009a) *How high should boys sing? Gender, authenticity and credibility in the young male voice.* Aldershot: Ashgate.

Barrett, M. (2010) On being and becoming a cathedral chorister: a cultural psychology account of the acquisition of early musical experience. In *A cultural psychology of music education*, ed. M. Barrett, 259–87. Oxford: Oxford University Press.

Phillips, K. (2013) *Teaching kids to sing.* New York: Schirmer Books.

Welch, G. (2006) Singing and vocal development. In *The child as musician: a handbook of musical development.*, ed. G. McPherson, 311–29. Oxford: Oxford University Press.

Chapter 5

Adolescent voices

This chapter is central to the whole book and explains in some depth what is known about voice change and development during adolescence. All the main theories are reviewed, but particular attention is given to the work of John Cooksey (boys' voices) and Lynne Gackle (girls' voices). Although such work is well known in voice teaching, the research on which this book is based reveals that few practising school teachers are aware of it. The chapter therefore explains it in 'what-secondary-music-teachers-need-to-know' style.

Introduction

Some important principles were established in Chapter 1:

- A child's compulsory music education, in England at least, is between the ages of 5 and 14.
- When transfer to secondary education is at age 11, two-thirds of this education takes place in primary schools, usually with generalist teachers lacking subject knowledge and pedagogical training.
- The final third of compulsory education should build on the foundations of singing established in the primary school in order to capitalize significantly on the singing voice as a means of musical learning in classes taught by music specialists.

The above three bullet points are very much about continuity and progression, the latter in particular. In practice, these things are hard to achieve. We have already seen that inequality of primary provision as well as a huge variation in experience and opportunity outside school can lead to quite challenging situations in Y7. The teacher can be faced with a range of ability from the confirmed non-singer to the advanced choral singer. Faced with this kind of difficulty, many secondary teachers see Y7 as a new start and do the best they can. Starting from nothing does not bode well for progression.

General singing competency

In Chapter 4, we looked at two important measures of singing development, the Rutkowski rating scale for singing development and the Welch revised model of vocal pitch matching development. It is tempting to use these scales as normative measures of what 'ought' to be. Welch reports that 'the latter years of childhood are characterized by a general singing competency for the majority'. He continues to say that a 'wide range of studies' demonstrate that while 30% of 7-year-olds are inaccurate at vocally matching a melody, this proportion drops to about 4% by age 11. Taken at face value, then, the Y7 teacher should begin with classes characterized by a 'general singing competency'. In only 4% of cases should she or he have to differentiate in such a way that learning can still take place without a 'general singing competency'. Perhaps, then, this might be the normative 'ought'?

What, exactly, is this 'general singing competency'? In Chapter 4, I suggested that in order to benefit from a secondary music curriculum that uses singing as a pedagogical strategy, all pupils will need to have reached at least level 4 of the Rutkowski scale. This is not the highest level of the scale. I also suggested that pupils who join and enjoy challenging extracurricular choral work would progress to level 5. By this line of reasoning, the 'general singing competency' might be equated with Rutkowski level 4. That is to say, an 'initial range singer' who is 'able to use the singing voice consistently as far as the register lift, but not beyond'.

Progression does not work quite like this. First, the children who will reach level 5 will very likely have reached it a year or more before coming to secondary school, while many children who attain only a 'general singing competency' will probably never reach level 5. Second, even amongst those children who have reached level 5, a good many may appear to progress backwards during their lower secondary years. They may apparently revert to the capability of a level 4 singer by virtue of the fact that they are no longer able 'to manage the register lift and sing consistently across the whole voice'. Progression in singing development is not straightforwardly linear. In this chapter, we deal with why. Understanding this and how to deal with it is perhaps the very core of the pedagogical knowledge that needs to be possessed by the teacher working with lower secondary singing.

The singing voice

What is the singing voice?

There is sometimes talk of children finding their 'singing voice'. What exactly does this mean? To answer this question, some understanding of vocal anatomy is required. I am going to keep the description here brief and to the necessary point of understanding what the 'singing voice' is. There are plenty of texts that deal in greater depth with the finer points of anatomy and I do not want to obscure the really important points by going into too much detail.

The voice is produced in the *larynx*, which is an assemblage of hinged cartilages located in the neck. Most 11-year-olds have at least some awareness of the larynx and quite commonly refer to it as the 'voice box'. They may also call it their 'Adam's apple', which is to mistake the entire larynx for the protruding bump caused by the laryngeal prominence. We come to that in the section 'Anatomy of singing', because it is important. The principal cartilages are the thyroid and the cricoid, and what needs to be understood is that these are hinged and can move relative to each other in a tilting action. The thyroid is the shield-shaped cartilage that children will feel if you ask them to place two fingers around their 'Adam's apple' and the cricoid is the smaller ring-shaped cartilage below it. Below the larynx is the trachea or windpipe and above it is the pharynx, the tube that leads from the larynx to the oral cavity (or mouth!). The term 'vocal tract' is commonly used to describe the entire system of tubes and cavities that are involved in transforming the crude buzzing sound produced by the larynx into recognizable speech or singing. The pharynx and oral cavity are the most important parts of the tract, but the nasal cavities are also significant. The velum or soft palate can be raised or lowered to engage the nasal part of the tract.

Positioned by the larynx at the top of the trachea are the all-important *vocal folds*, still commonly referred to by the older term of 'cords' and sometimes even the misconception 'chords'. The term 'folds' should be used because it correctly describes the threefold laminate structure, and the development of this at puberty is a critical part of what needs to be understood. The sound produced by the larynx is, as we have said, little more than a buzz, so it is probably misleading to employ the term 'voice box'. The vocal tract is at least as much a vital part of the voice as the larynx itself and the two systems are quite inseparable in understanding the voice and what the singing voice is.

The *lungs*, of course, are also a very important part of singing and probably the source of the greatest difficulty with children's singing. Put simply, children, even when they are quite experienced singers, commonly forget to breathe properly. Breath control has constantly to be taught—as much to the experienced professional chorister as to the raw beginner. Teaching about breath control is often conceived as teaching about singing as a muscular activity. The principal 'breathing muscle', the diaphragm, is often described to children (not uncommonly incorrectly) but less often explained is the fact that highly complex muscular actions are also part of the operation of the larynx and the vocal tract. Singing is, above all, a muscular activity demanding extremely fine coordination.

Anatomy of singing

Two key muscle groups are involved with the vocal folds and essential to understanding what the 'singing voice' is. The first are known as the thyro-arytenoids, sometimes referred to collectively as 'vocalis'. These are actually part of the vocal folds. When they contract, they thicken and tension the vocal folds, which causes a rise in pitch. The second are the crycothyroids. When they contract they bring the two main cartilages closer together through their hinged movement in a process commonly referred to as laryngeal tilt. This also has the effect of tensioning the vocal folds and causing a rise in pitch.

Many 11-years-olds and most 12-year-olds are able to state that the pitch of a stringed instrument is determined by the length, mass (or thickness), and tension of the string. When it comes to the voice, however, it is a little harder to understand. There are these two distinctly different methods of introducing tension to the vocal folds. The first method, the thyroarytenoid action, intro-duces tension and thickness and shortens the vocal folds. Muscles can only contract, and since the vocal folds are a muscle, these things are bound to happen. However, when the crycothyroids contract, the result is different. Tension is certainly increased in the vocal folds, but this is through stretching them by the tilting action. Consequently, they actually increase in length and tension, but decrease in thickness.

The 'rules' for a stringed instrument do not therefore apply in a simple way to the voice. Pitch rises as a result of increased tension, but in the case of thyroarytenoid action although length decreases, thickness actually *increases*. This results in a denser tone that can be rich and interesting but, if uncon-trolled, can also be ugly. In the case of crycothyroid action, pitch again rises as a result of increased tension. However, this time it is *thickness* which as we would expect decreases. Length, contrary to the behaviour of a stringed instrument, actually increases. The result is what the young people may call a more 'choiry' tone. It is perhaps important at this stage to state that any sound produced at all by the vibration of the vocal folds is incidental. The primary function of the larynx is that of a valve to shut off the airway when the body needs to lift a heavy weight or it is necessary to prevent any food or drink reaching the lungs. Talking and singing is an evolutionary by-way!

In normal speech, crycothyroid action has little use. The voice modulates up and down almost entirely through thyroarytenoid action. For this reason, the thyroarytenoid action is commonly referred to as the 'modal voice' or the 'speech voice'. Another term that is sometimes encountered is 'thick voice'— referring to the fact that the vocal folds have thickened and are contacting each other across most of their depth. When, in evolutionary terms, it became desirable to extend the pitch range of the voice, crycothyroid action came increasingly into use. The crycothyroids can add at least one further octave to the range of notes that can be sung. In a child's voice, they do so with great power. Anyone who has attempted to record good child singers will know that as they approach their upper octave of range (from C5 to C6) the power increases exponentially. This is the 'thin voice', the one that is used most of the time by boys and girls who sing the top part in choral music.

Restricted range singing

Children who have no 'singing voice' do not employ this kind of production. They sing only in the limited range of the low or speech part of the modal voice. Children who have well-trained, developed singing voices use both methods of production, though predominantly the crycothyroids. It is the crycothyroids that generate the beautiful or 'angelic' tone of the young choir singer. In simple terms, this is the 'singing voice'. In the parlance of singing teachers and choir conductors, the term 'head voice' is often used to describe this voice, with the term 'chest voice' being used to describe the lower thyroarytenoid production. These are not good terms to use, especially when talking about resonance, because they wrongly imply that resonance shifts from 'chest' to 'head'. Nevertheless, in spite of the efforts of more scientifically minded vocal practitioners, they remain the most commonly employed terms.

It is better, nevertheless, to think of a child with a good singing voice as a child who has learned to employ both types of vocal production, thyroarytenoid in the lowest part of the register, crycothyroid in the higher register, and a skilful blend of the two in the middle. This is the true 'singing voice' and the voice that is never developed by children who do not progress beyond Rutkowski's level 4 (see Chapter 4). When Rutkowski refers to the ability to manage the register lift and sing consistently across the whole voice she is referring to the singer's ability to employ both types of production and manage the transition from the one to the other. This is commonly referred to in singing as 'registration'. Various authorities describe different numbers of 'registers' in the singing voice (between two and four is common), but almost all agree that the objective in good singing is to produce a voice that can shift from one to another register with little or no perceptible difference in tone. It is a highly complex skill that involves not only the control of the intrinsic and extrinsic laryngeal muscles, but also the muscles of the vocal tract since there are subtle and complex relationships between the two in the production of resonance.

With less skilful singers, there is often quite a pronounced change in tone associated with register shift. It is easy to detect once one knows it is there and what to look for. Child and adolescent singing differs from adult singing in two very important ways (other, of course, than the pitch range of the voice). First, register breaks, though they exist in a child's singing voice, are seldom problematic and sometimes not heard at all. Second, as the child becomes an adolescent and begins puberty, register breaks become more obvious and harder to control. For many boys, they become so pronounced and so hard to control that the voice literally breaks into two disconnected halves, with a 'phonational gap' between the two where no notes can be sounded at all. This is one meaning of 'voice break'. Commonly, this is around middle C to E, exactly where a lot of lower secondary singing is wrongly pitched.

We are, however, getting ahead of ourselves and will return to the vexed question of 'voice break' in the section entitled 'The young adolescent'. For the present there is, of course, another reason why registration shifts are not heard in the singing of lower secondary school pupils. This is that they use only one register—the speech part of the modal. There are at least three potential drawbacks to this.

+ The modal voice is not the singing voice. Children are thus not 'learning to sing'.
+ The range of the lower modal voice is small. It becomes even smaller during puberty and is smaller than many of the songs that a teacher might want to use or children might want to sing.
+ When the modal voice is forced too high the tone becomes increasingly strained and tuning becomes less accurate. The resultant sound is not pleasant—hardly surprising since the children have not learned to produce good singing tone.

Nevertheless, a considerable amount of lower secondary school singing as well as most primary school singing is undertaken in the modal voice. There are two cultural reasons for this, both very hard to counteract.

+ Popular singers often use only the modal voice. Most females go beyond the modal range by a technique known as 'belt' and males by going into falsetto. These are the vocal models now familiar to the large majority of young

Table 5.1 Distribution of Key Stage Three boys' singing across sectors

Singing range	Independent schools (6)	State-maintained schools (19)
No singing at all	0%	46%
Singing in modal register	100%	32.5%
Singing in extended range	100%	21.5%

people. Use of the singing voice actually sounds alien to them, whether it be a choral or operatic sound.

♦ We have got into the rather strange situation where most music composed, arranged, and published for use in schools is pitched too low to develop the child's singing voice.

This is first and foremost a cultural issue. It is a very serious and worrying one for any who care about quality singing by children and young people. It is why children in the large majority of schools will only learn to 'sing' if they join an extracurricular choir or take individual singing lessons. It is part of the great divide between those schools that have any kind of choral tradition and those that do not. This topic has been covered in Chapter 3, but the data are worth reiterating in the light of what has been said about singing in the modal voice only and teaching children to sing with the use of their whole voice. Clearly it is the independent schools that do this in the main, but if 21% of state-maintained schools in the sample (Table 5.1) can also achieve singing in the extended range, there is no reason other than low expectations or lack of subject knowledge why more schools cannot raise more children to the full level of singing development.

Developing the singing voice

Unfortunately, schools are not on the whole helped by the publishing industry with its constant output of music pitched too low to develop the upper register. In those schools where children did sing well with their whole voice, the teachers were sufficiently knowledgeable about the subject to critique the work of publishers who might reasonably be assumed by others to know better. Publishers, however, are in business to make money and will print what there is a demand for. It is a cyclic phenomenon that is difficult to escape. Teachers who were successful in developing children's singing voices often created their own arrangements or chose published work selectively.

There are various ways of developing children's whole singing voice. Swoops, whoops, glides, sirens, dogs that woof and yap, birds that tweet, grizzly bears that grunt, rockets that take off, skydivers who jump out of planes, cars that won't start—many such ideas can be found in a good text on children's singing. These, however, are all relatively peripheral to the actual repertoire that is regularly sung and the quality of vocal modelling children experience. The most important single factor in developing children's full singing voices is the regular rehearsal of music that can *only* be sung comfortably when crycothyroid action is employed. In simple terms this means a pitch centre nearer to C5 (treble C) than to C4 (middle C).

A teacher who can model this is likely to achieve much better results than a teacher who can only play backing tracks. Here, though, we simply have to be realistic. There are nowhere near enough such teachers to go round, neither are there any realistic prospects of the situation changing in the foreseeable future. This is an issue that really needs to be addressed at primary school. If children have no experience of using their whole voice by age 11, it is in most cases too late to start. Another problem in any case soon takes over.

The young adolescent

Puberty and change

The lower secondary age span, as defined in this book (11–13 or 14 years), is a particularly difficult one for singing. It is between the ages of 11 and 14 that voice change as a result of puberty occurs for most pupils. To make matters complicated there is a very considerable range in the timing of puberty for individuals and, on average, the process occurs for girls a year or more earlier than for boys. The issue is as much psychosocial as it is biological. It can be very difficult for young people to cope with transitional vocal identities (see Chapter 6). Many people still talk of boys' voices 'breaking' and see the issue as a boys' one. This is seriously mistaken on two counts:

• Boys' voices do not 'break'—they change.
• Girls' voices change as well as boys'.

Voice change occurs because of rapid maturation and growth of the larynx and vocal tract triggered by the same endocrinal changes that stimulate sexual maturation and the other secondary sex characteristics. The voice is now considered to be the most important secondary sex characteristic in boys, but this should never be a reason to neglect what is happening to girls' voices. The most important change for boys is the elongation of the thyroid cartilage from a rounded to a more elliptical shape. Related to this is a significant growth in length of the vocal folds. In simple terms, as with a vibrating string, greater length equates with lower pitch. With boys it can be a virtual doubling of length and halving of pitch from one end of puberty to the other. The key to understanding why the word 'break' is so inappropriate is the realization that no part of the body doubles in size overnight. If a voice 'breaks', you are doing something wrong. The vocal folds also increase in mass and alter in tissue composition, leading to changes in tone and stability as well as pitch. Growth of vocal tract volume is considerable and continues for some time after puberty. This is why newly changed voices, though at the pitch of the adult voice, commonly sound weedy and immature. The process of voice change does not complete until late adolescence, around 20 years of age.

The principal characteristics of voice change are:

+ A deepening of the speaking voice and lowering of the singing tessitura;
+ A contraction in the singing range;
+ A loss of vocal agility;
+ Difficulty in registration and management of lift points or passagio (assuming these had previously been successfully managed);
+ Hoarseness, missing notes and a tendency to 'crack' in boys;
+ Unusual breathiness and missing notes in girls.

As a result of this boys can suffer a serious fear of failure with regard to singing as puberty begins to take hold. They are very easily embarrassed by their voices, particularly if they 'crack' in front of girls. The teacher who understands how to deal with voice change can help boys through with considerable success. Fear of failure ceases to be an issue in the hands of a capable teacher. Where the teacher knows little or nothing of voice change, catastrophe can ensue with boys and it is hardly surprising that the myth that 'boys don't sing' has become so prevalent. Girls do not generally suffer the same level of ignominy, but if they enjoy their singing and want to develop their vocal capability (which they are probably more likely to do than many boys) they can become quite distressed when their voice will no longer do what it used to. The teacher who understands what is happening is able to reassure them and guide them through the difficult times.

How to deal with change

Earlier we considered that if children have not been taught to use their whole voice, their range would in any case be somewhat smaller than that of other children who have been taught more about singing. With puberty this becomes more, not less, of an issue, and it affects children who were previously proficient singers also. The tessitura of the modal voice will contract to as little as a fifth or less, though it is usually safe to work with a sixth. Management of this requires a return to many of the principles established by Kodály for early singing development. There is a huge range of Kodály style material for young voices that does not exceed the range of a sixth. The task is to discover another range of material that will appeal to young adolescents, obviously pitched somewhat lower, but still within the range of a sixth.

Here, there can be an advantage with pop songs. Many traditional folk songs have a range that is far too great for adolescent voices, whereas 'popular' songs often do not exceed a sixth in any case. I once witnessed some considerable success with Y8 boys who sang 'Now I'm a believer' (originally by the Monkees, but popularized by the film *Shrek*). The main reason the boys enjoyed it and sang it with such gusto was simply that they *could* sing it. The range was a sixth and the teacher had selected a key that pitched the song right in the middle of the tessitura of boys midway through puberty. Careful selection of key is vital. The solution to almost everything is knowing where to pitch the tessitura. If the tessitura is correctly pitched and the range is confined to a sixth, problems of agility are unlikely. Agility is partly to do with rapid articulation, but more to do with the ability to negotiate a rapid transition from one region of the voice to another. This happens when the intervals are wide as in, for example, a leap of a fifth. Fifths can usually be managed if they are comfortably within the tessitura. However, given that the tessitura is likely to be less than an octave, leaps of an octave are a 'no' for many boys midway through voice change. Fourths and fifths will also be difficult, of course, if the first note is towards the outside of the tessitura. The vocal folds just cannot change their shape and vibratory pattern quickly enough to pitch the interval and the singing will be an unsatisfactory experience for all concerned.

Relevant research

A substantial amount of research into this topic has been carried out, mostly in the United States. Familiarity with the main findings, principles, and recommendations should be obligatory pedagogical knowledge for secondary music teachers. For boys, what is currently regarded as the definitive research was carried out by John Cooksey and for girls by Lynne Gackle. We will look at Cooksey's work first since the problem arguably is greater for boys. It is certainly more obvious.

Cooksey grouped boys' progress through voice change into six stages. To some degree the stages are arbitrary, but they do correspond to commonly used

Table 5.2 Summary of Cooksey's vocal stages for male adolescents

Stage	Approx. % by year group	Mean speaking note	Tessitura	Full range	Quality of singing voice
0	Y7 50% Y8 10% Y9 <5%	259	D4–C5 (7th)	A3–>F5+	Full, rich soprano. The 'pinnacle of development'
1	Y7 40% Y8 15% Y9 5%	226 (–33)	B3–G4 (6th)	A3–D5	Breathy, strained upper range; little resonance or 'body' in lower range
2	Y7 10% Y8 45% Y9 10%	210 (–16)	A3–F4 (6th)	E3–C5	Loss of agility, falsetto emerges, uniquely beautiful and rich if in range
3	Y7 <5% Y8 15% Y9 20%	186 (–24)	F3–D4 (6th)	D3–A4	Evolution of modal register into baritone range, retention of stage 2 quality
4	Y7 <1% Y8 10% Y9 35%	151 (–35)	D3–A3 (5th)	A#2–D#4	Light and husky, approximating mid-baritone, difficulties with 4ths and 5ths
5	Y7 <1% Y8 <5% Y9 30%	120 (–31)	C3–B3 (7th)	<A2–D4	Body, resonance and power increase, agility recovered, adult qualities emerge

stages of puberty in medical work. One of the most important primary indicators of progression is the deepening of the speaking voice. This is shown in column 3 of Table 5.2 and demonstrated on the supporting website (<http://www.martin-ashley.com/teacher-pages>). The values are given as frequency in hertz and the nearest musical note. When a boy talks his voice will modulate up and down to the extent to which he employs inflexion in his speech pattern (prosody). A deliberately boring task such as counting backwards from 20 will result in the nearest to a monotone at the lowest point of the speaking voice range and this is what should be measured. Measurement may be by ear (pitch matching to keyboard) or, more accurately, by technology such as *Sing and See* or the Speech Test App.[1] The values quoted are means and the range (statistical) is considerable, so caution must be exercised.

---

[1] Created by the author and a colleague as a tool to assess boys' vocal progress through puberty. See <http://www.martin-ashley.com>.

What matters significantly more than an absolute value at any given time is the *rate of change* and subsequent progress through the stages. The sequence is invariant but the rate of progress varies considerably for individuals. This does, of course, make differentiation a considerable challenge. The first significant change is from stage 0 to stage 1. It may not be noticed because the voice still sounds like that of a youngish boy, but if a recording is made of the voice before and after this stage is reached, the difference can be clearly heard. This change is going to happen towards the end of Y7 for about half the boys in the class. It is during Y8 and Y9 that the major changes take place. Less than a quarter of the boys will get through Y8 still unchanged. The majority will experience a fall to stage 2, which is a stage of singing unique to boys of this age. It is sometimes termed 'cambiata' and is of considerable importance. We devote Chapter 10 of the book to cambiata singing. The biggest change of all is likely to occur during Y9. This is when the speaking voice ceases altogether to sound like that of a boy and assumes those characteristics of an immature young man.

Management of Y9 boys' voices is possible, but presents considerable challenge. There is much to be said for an increased use of small-group work in Y9, with differentiation according to vocal stage. There will still be a proportion of boys in Y9 with higher voices, some even at only stage 0 or 1. Equally, there will be early-maturing boys in Y8 who have already reached the final stages of puberty. *These matters require careful and sensitive handling if boys are not to be put off singing for life.* There is much to be said for devoting an entire lesson to puberty and the voice, ideally in single-sex groups and organized collaboratively with colleagues who teach science and sex and relationships education. The beginning of Y8 is the best time for this.

Locating boys' singing range

The most important determinant of where any individual might be is the actual range from highest to lowest notes that can be sung. The terms highest and lowest terminal pitch (HTP and LTP) are used in research. There is a clear relationship between the speaking voice and the LTP. Most people habitually speak near the bottom of what will be their singing range. It will be commonly found that if the speaking pitch is determined, the lowest singing note that can be clearly pitched and sounded is about four semitones below it. Thus, if a boy speaks around the note G to A♭3, the lowest clear singing note is likely to be about E3. In Table 5.2, Cooksey gives a tessitura of A3 to F4 for such a boy and this may be regarded as the most typical for Y8. The boy will not be able to sing at all below E3 and is most comfortable with a song that does not reach this low.

The more important question concerns how high he can go. The top of Cooksey's tessitura is F4 and this may be regarded as 'safe' for almost all boys at this stage. Higher than this, things start to happen. It is during Y8 that the majority of boys will, for the first time in their lives, be able to sing in falsetto. This happens because of maturation of the vocal ligament. The vocal folds are comprised of three distinct layers of tissue. We talked in the section 'Anatomy of singing' about the fleshy 'vocalis' that performs the actual work of contracting the folds. The ligament, which is comprised of collagen fibre, acts to restrain this action elastically. Unchanged voices are less inhibited by the ligament acting in this way, which is why they can often soar with relative ease across lift points to the stratospheric regions of G5 to C6.

For boys who are beginning to possess a mature ligament however, the voice will suddenly jump into falsetto. This is likely to happen for Y8 boys at stage 2 anywhere between A4 and D5. Cooksey gives C5 as the top of the extended range for stage 2 boys. Some may already have reached falsetto by this point, so I would treat C5 with some circumspection and take the boys that high only for the climax of the song. Going across to falsetto is not necessarily a bad thing in itself. Boys will vary between being highly amused by it to deep disapproval of the 'girly' or 'choirboy' sound, depending on the mood they are in. Many boys who enjoy choral singing make considerable use of their falsetto in order to retain their high or 'treble' voices for as long as possible. This is usually acceptable during Y8, but carried too far into Y9 it can be problematic. It is a specialized topic that is dealt with in my other recent book *Contemporary choral work with boys* (Ashley 2014).

There are, however, two significant dangers of which the secondary music teacher must be aware. The first is that of a song that is so pitched that the boys are constantly at the top of their modal range *without* crossing into falsetto. This results in strain, fatigue, ugly tone, and faulty tuning. The second, which is the worst that can be done, is a song pitched so that a significant number of boys have their lift point right in the middle of it. These boys will be forced constantly between modal and falsetto voice with catastrophic results. The ignorant teacher will just assume that 'boys don't sing' and give up. The knowledgeable teacher will transpose the song down a little or choose a different one. If the reader is a beginner and in some doubt, a really safe bet for Y8 boys is 'Mambo Italiano' in the key of A minor or 'I'm a Believer' in the key of A major. A is a good key for Y8 boys. A3 is the bottom of Cooksey's stage 2 tessitura.

Quick reference guide

It may be helpful to conclude this section with a quick, ready reference guide by year group.

Y7 (grade 6) boys

For the majority of boys, Y7 (age 11–12) is, or should be, the 'golden year'. Most will retain high 'treble' voices throughout the year. A little under half will begin to experience the first signs of change during the year, but this is seldom a problem, particularly if the repertoire is not a 'choral' one. Boys and girls can safely sing together in unison and few boys will have a problem with this if the teacher is enthusiastic and just gets on with the job. In an ideal world, all boys would have learned to sing to a reasonable standard at primary school and the specialist music teacher of Y7 should enjoy bringing what has been learned to a final state of perfection before voice change seriously begins. *Y7 is the golden singing year and the vocal foundation of the best musical learning that is to come.*

Y8 (grade 7) boys

Most boys will begin to experience noticeable change during Y8 (age 12–13). While the majority position in Y7 is unison singing with girls, the majority position in Y8 is 'cambiata'. This term is fully explained and further explored in Chapter 10. For the present, we need to understand it as referring to the time when girls and boys begin to part company vocally and serious thought needs to be given to how this will be dealt with (see also Chapter 9). Cambiata itself can range from differing little from the lower part of treble to a unique singing range that is neither alto nor tenor. In Chapter 10 I explain how a complete vocal system based on cambiata can be used. Where this is not used the most commonly encountered fault is to call lower cambiata boys 'tenors' and allocate a singing range that is too low for them. Y8 is also the year of greatest diversity of pubertal stage. Almost every Y8 class will contain some boys who are still prepubescent and others who have completed puberty. The latter might be invited to sing down an octave, but if you have boys singing in octaves the range will clearly be even more limited. Another possibility is negotiating with individuals and giving them permission to choose which octave they sing in at any given point. This is why a good understanding of puberty and voice change by all is to be recommended as an objective early on in Y8.

Y9 (grade 8) boys

In many ways, the situation in Y8 will be reversed in Y9 (age 13–14). The majority will now be singing down an octave. Provided the range is suitably small and the tessitura carefully located, boys and girls can sing in octaves. Some Y9 boys, however, will still be at the upper octave and this can be difficult. They may pretend to sing down an octave but will not actually be reaching the notes properly. The value of such a procedure is doubtful. Depending on how things are handled, some Y9 boys may be perfectly happy singing at the upper octave. Although 'lower octave' singing is likely in Y9, many of the boys will still be at a cambiata stage and will not yet be tenors, let alone basses. The 'lower octave' for these boys should not go below E3 according to the cambiata system (see Chapter 10). Cooksey specifies D3 as the bottom of the extended range for his stage 3 boys and the bottom of the stage 4 tessitura. If in doubt, think of a Y9 range of a fifth, D3–A3. This will not go too low for the boys who are only just approaching baritone and the later maturing boys and girls can safely sing up an octave D4–A4.

Voice 'break' in boys

Everything that has been described is temporary. The singing range will expand again, vocal agility will return. All is not lost! The final word about boys in this chapter must concern the word 'break'. Boys' voices do not break, it was said, they *change* gradually. The main reason the word 'break' persists is because of the old English practice of keeping boys singing soprano up to the age of 16 or so, which is well beyond the completion of puberty for almost all boys. This, surprisingly, is quite possible because the laryngeal cartilages have not fully hardened, the larynx may not have fully descended to the final adult position, and the vocal tract not matured to its full adult size. It is only possible for a certain period of time, however, before the voice literally does break down traumatically. Growth of the vocal tract is the most likely cause of this 'break' as the possible resonances no longer support the high-frequency vibration of the folds. Allowing voices to 'break' like this is now considered very poor practice by most vocal coaches. The sound is also more like a light adult female than 'boyish', hence the term 'soprano' rather than the more familiar 'treble' used to describe a purer, childlike tone (in girls as well as boys).

'Break' can also refer to the separation of the old boy voice from the newly emerging adult voice. This is likely to occur to former treble singers as they progress through stage 3 to stage 4. They may continue to sing in their upper register while also having a new lower register extending down towards D3. At around B3 to E4, there is a big change from thyroarytenoid to cricothyroid production and the voice may not sound at all across the gap—hence a 'break' of the voice into two halves. Ask any Y8 or Y9 boy whose speaking voice sounds in the baritone range to glide down from highest to lowest and you will almost certainly hear an involuntary jump in tone from falsetto to modal voice. That is where the singing break will occur. It is possible to train a boy to cover this gap by vocalizing downwards across it, but this is generally only done in certain kinds of choral work. For class singing, the modal voice only is best, in spite of all that was said earlier about teaching younger children to use their whole voice. Such teaching can resume once voice change has been passed.

If these principles are observed, boys' voices will be considerably less likely to 'crack' in the middle of a singing lesson than in the middle of a PE lesson when they are cheering and shouting.

The female adolescent voice

Voice change in boys is so much more obvious than in girls that the latter have tended to be neglected. This neglect is exacerbated by the fact that adolescent boys are so often more resistant to singing than girls, so gain the lion's share of researchers' attention. However, a number of issues that apply to boys apply equally to girls. Not the least of these is reluctance by adolescent girls to use their whole singing voice. Girls too are influenced by popular vocal models in which only modal voice singing is used, with frequent excursion into belt zone, particularly in music theatre.

Many young adolescent girls will settle, or attempt to settle, in a husky or 'chesty' modal range. They will regard the higher part of their range as 'screechy' and may, surprisingly, be even more reluctant to go there than boys. I have been in classes where the boys actually sing the high notes more confidently than the girls because the girls do not want to go above the register transition they begin to experience at G3. Other girls can get 'stuck' in the higher register and, being unable to find their lower register easily, may withdraw from singing largely unnoticed. All this is likely to happen because teachers (and too often choir directors) assume that girls' voices do not change. With suitable encouragement, boys may just risk all and just sing out!

Lynne Gackle, author of *Finding Ophelia's Voice* (Gackle 2011), can reasonably be described as the John Cooksey for girls. Unlike other conductors who plough blindly on, Gackle noticed an unusual breathiness of tone when taking on a choir of 8–12-year-old girls after previously having conducted a boys' choir. She contacted Cooksey for advice, only to discover that at the time very little was known by anybody about voice change in girls. The characteristic breathiness identified by Gackle has subsequently been noted by other researchers and is now a well-recognized feature of female voice change. Table 5.3 summarizes the stages of change identified and categorized by Gackle.

Table 5.3 Summary of Gackle's vocal stages for female adolescents

Stage	Approx. % by year group	Tessitura	Full range	Quality of singing voice
0	Y7 50% Y8 25% Y9 25%	D4–D5 (octave)	A#3–>F5+	Light, flute-like quality. Register change usually imperceptible
1	Y7 25% Y8 50% Y9 25%	D4–D5 (octave)	A3–D5	Tone likely to turn breathier due to inadequate vocal fold closure. Lift point occurs between G4 and B4 and some loss of agility. Some girls may not access lower pitches
2	Y7 10% Y8 50% Y9 35%	B3–G4 (6th)	B3–C5	Distinct register break, with huskiness in lower register. Contraction of expanded range with discomfort in higher register. The peak of voice change for girls
3	Y7 >5% Y8 40% Y9 60%	A3–G5	A3–G5	Adult qualities appear, including vibrato. Breathiness disappears, agility regained and registration shifts less noticeable

It is often said that puberty comes earlier for girls than boys. There can be apparent evidence of this in the lower secondary phase, particularly Y8 classes, where a good proportion of the girls will be bigger and quite possibly stronger than the boys. It is reflected also in the social behaviour of the girls, which can appear more mature or sophisticated. Boys can occasionally find these things intimidating because it is not 'how things are supposed to be' in a society conditioned by patriarchal dominance and male strength. If not well handled, this disparity can be another reason boys won't sing. It is discussed fully in Chapter 9. When it comes to actual endocrinal progression, however, the situation is not that clear cut. For girls, the menarche (first menstruation) is a clear marker of a universal fixed point in puberty that is easy to employ in large-scale studies. There is no equivalent for boys since assessment must be made by the highly intrusive method of testicular inspection. The obvious ethical difficulties in performing such an operation mean that surprisingly little is known about boys' progression through puberty in large population samples. Assessment by voice is as good as any method and non-intrusive.

Gackle subtitles her stage 1 as 'pre-menarcheal' and her stage 2 as 'post-menarcheal'. Menarche may therefore be assumed to be the catalyst for the onset of register break, range contraction, and vocal discomfort. There is here some equivalence to boys in spite of other signs that puberty occurs earlier in girls. Gackle suggests that female voice mutation peaks between the ages of

Table 5.4 Pre-dominant boys' and girls' voices across the lower secondary phase

Year/grade	Quality of boys' voices	Quality of girls' voices	Safe working range
Y7 (Gr 6)	Full, rich soprano. The 'pinnacle of development'	Light, flute-like quality. Register change usually imperceptible	A3–F5 or above for both sexes (when voices have been well developed)
Y8 (Gr 7)	Breathy, strained upper range. Loss of agility with falsetto emerging. Uniquely beautiful and rich if in range	Tone likely to turn breathier. Some loss of agility. Lift point appears between G4 and B4 with some girls unable to access part of the range	G3–B4 for boys, falling to F4 in summerA3–D5 for girlsA3–B4 for boys and girls together, reducing to G4 in summer term
Y9 (Gr 8)	Evolution of modal register into baritone range. Light and husky, approximating mid-baritone, difficulties with 4ths and 5ths	Distinct register break, with huskiness in lower register. Contraction of expanded range with discomfort in higher register. Some girls beginning to develop adult voice quality	D3 or lower–D4 for boys. A3–C5 for girls D3–A3 and D4–A4 for boys and girls in octaves

12 and 14, much the same as for boys. In theory at least, this should make things slightly easier for the lower school music teacher. Table 5.4 summarizes where the majority of girls and boys will be relative to each other in Y7, Y8, and Y9 (G6–8).

Summary and conclusions

+ The lower secondary years largely coincide with the period of puberty for most young people. The first effects are heard towards the end of Y7 and reach a climax in Y9.
+ Puberty affects the voices of both boys and girls considerably. Boys' and girls' voices change in several ways during puberty and this process of change has a considerable impact on the repertoire that can be sung well.
+ The change in boys is more obvious than in girls, and can be heard in events such as 'cracking'. Boys are very easily embarrassed by singing during this time, and many give up, perhaps for life, as a result.
+ The lower secondary teacher, if he or she is to attempt singing, *must* be knowledgeable about these processes and events. He or she must understand

and provide for the specific singing tessitura that is identified with the various stages of puberty.

♦ Voice 'break' is not a natural event. It is the consequence of poor vocal management and inappropriate repertoire.

♦ Although it is desirable to develop the whole singing voice where possible in the prepubertal child, it is difficult to manage to the full voice during puberty. This can be done in expert choral singing but the balance of specialist opinion is in favour of the use of the lower register only for curriculum music lessons whilst voices are changing.

Further reading

Ashley, M. (2014) *Contemporary choral work with boys*. Abingdon: Compton.

Baldy, C. (2010) *The student voice: an introduction to developing the singing voice.* Edinburgh: Dunedin.

Cooksey, J. (1999) *Working with adolescent voices*. St Louis, MO: Concordia.

Gackle, L. (2011) *Finding Ophelia's voice, opening Ophelia's heart: nurturing the adolescent female voice: an exploration of the physiological, psychological, and music.* Dayton, OH: Heritage Music Press.

Williams, J. (2012) *Teaching singing to children and young adults*. Abingdon: Compton.

Chapter 6

Vocal identity and vocal agency

Music and fashion are the two most important markers of identity to young people. If singing does not give them identities with which they feel comfortable, they will sing only reluctantly or not at all. The previous chapter has described the biotechnical principles of young adolescent singing, but these are of no avail if out of step with a young person's will to present the vocal self-identity they desire. This chapter presents the evidence for this and the practical advice for dealing with it.

Introduction

In Chapter 5 we looked at what is physically possible with the young adolescent voices of the lower secondary school. In this chapter we are going to look at the psycho-social equivalent. What is psychologically and socially possible and desirable? A theme running through this book is that children will sing almost anything if it is put across with warmth and enthusiasm, and is within the physical capability of their voices. This theme coexists somewhat uneasily with themes of anxiety about what is 'cool' and what will be enjoyed sufficiently by the children to motivate participation without groans—or with a positive score on the 'yissometer' (see Chapter 8).

Identity and agency

Vocal identity and vocal agency are concepts through which we can analyse this uneasy relationship. The study of identity is absolutely fundamental to understanding adolescence and how to deal with it. Vocal identity is simply a subdivision of identity studies that looks at what the voice and how it is used says about the identity of its owner. Vocal agency recognizes that the voice is part of the body. We believe in our society today that children have sovereignty over their bodies and therefore, by extension, over their voices. 'Vocal agency' is about the will to act with regard to the voice. It is about the right of the child to present the identity he or she desires through the voice and the way it is used.

Given all that has been said previously about the humiliation of young people through voice in school, this is a matter of primary importance.

What is identity?

Identity is a complex phenomenon that can somewhat imperfectly be broken down into component subdivisions. The whole, though, will almost certainly be more than the sum of these individual parts. The individual parts might include:

♦ Gender;
♦ Social class and social capital;
♦ Age or generation;
♦ Ethnicity;
♦ Religion;
♦ Geo-region

Fluidity of identity

None of these is fixed or static. Children may be born with the physical bodies of boys or girls, but gender itself and the degree of comfort with the given body are highly fluid social constructions. We like to think that our society affords social mobility, whether or not we still believe there is a 'class system' that limits this. Education is often upheld as a means of achieving social mobility but probably even more often fails to deliver on such a promise. Age, of course, constantly and inexorably shifts in chronological real time, and with this the generational relationship to others. There has also been much interesting work on the outlook of different generations into which an individual is born, such as 'baby boomers', generations X and Y, and 'digital natives'. Recent work on how attitudes become fixed within generations during the years of adolescence is of considerable relevance. The British Social Attitudes survey has revealed fascinating differences in generational attitudes to sexual orientation with a significant shift toward greater tolerance in the young.

The region into which one is born can have a considerable impact upon attitude and approach to life. Much is written these days about a great north/ south divide in the UK. In theory, there is a high degree of geographical mobility but studies have shown how this is linked to social class and capital. Those with greater wealth and higher social capital are more likely to be cosmopolitan in outlook than the least wealthy who will also be the least mobile and most strongly identified with often quite a small geographical region. This cosmopolitan outlook (or lack of it) is reflected in musical tastes. Movement from lower to higher levels of cultural capital and social position has been shown to be associated with movement towards more eclectic musical tastes rather than from 'popular' to 'classical'. Identity is highly complex.

Nowhere is there greater fluidity and uncertainty of identity than amongst the 11–14 age group. Saville Kushner once employed the metaphor of the 'building site' to describe the identity situation of the young adolescent (Walker & Kushner 1998). Young people constantly try out and discard different aspects of identity as they begin their adolescent journey of defining an identity of their own distinct from that of their parents. The 'building site' metaphor is helpful to remind teachers that the identities of their charges are far from fixed. Teachers are amongst those adults who might have an impact upon adolescent identity—for good or for ill. Links need to be drawn here with Chapter 3. How often are low expectations associated with stereotyped judgments about identity?

Schooling and identity

Schooling can have a particular impact upon other aspects of identity such as self-esteem and self-efficacy. The degree to which young people experience success and positive affirmation in a general sense will affect their identity with regard to the whole business of education and cultural capital. At a more specific level, children may form positive identities within some subject areas and negative identities within others. Although there is a relationship between this and self-efficacy, probably the strongest relationship at the level of the lower secondary school pupil is that between subject identity and the extent to which the teacher is perceived as an individual to be liked and respected. It could hardly be better expressed than by this 12-year-old girl:

I don't like music, because the teacher don't like me.

Perhaps one of the hardest things for any teacher struggling to build positive relationships with young people is the challenge of relating to individuals whilst maintaining control of the whole group. A class of 12- and 13-year-olds en masse can be a formidable force to confront, but each individually is only a child full of uncertainty, doubt, or even fear about who they are and who they can become. The successful teacher will never lose sight of this. This adolescent angst is what underpins much of the psychology of tribalism. Musical tribalism is a potentially intimidating force for any teacher who has doubts about the strength and adequacy of their own personality for dealing with the tribal allegiances of the pupils. A member of the practitioner group for whom I have a high degree of respect said this to me: 'You have to think like them, you have to be the person who is going to do the singing'. By this she meant think of an insecure child at least as much as a warrior for a particular musical tribe.

Whether or not this is achieved depends in the most part upon generic teaching skills and understanding of young people. Positive identity accrues from positive relationships. The teacher's own identity is a key ingredient of this process. It may be as well at this point to reiterate what pupils expect of their teachers. Fundamentally, they do not expect them to be 'cool', they expect them to be professional. Pupils have defined for me what this means with remarkable consistency across several research projects over many years. The teacher whose identity they respect, warm to, trust and feel comfortable with:

♦ Has a good balance between strictness and fairness;
♦ Can control them and keep order;
♦ Has good subject knowledge and/or skill in the subject;
♦ Can explain things clearly and patiently;
♦ Has sense of humour and can make things fun;
♦ Can be trusted and will respect their confidences.

There is nothing here about what kind of music they like. Of course, given the chance, pupils will be quite eager to find out all sorts of trivia about their teachers. 'Miss, are you married?' 'Miss, do you like Abba?' 'Sir, can you rap?' Anyone who wants to be successful in the lower secondary school will need to know how to cope with such probing into identity trivia. The pupils' inquisitiveness is not disrespectful. It is part of the building site of their identity formation during adolescence. It can be undertaken in a spirit of genuine affection, but pupils can also be remarkably perceptive judges of character when they evaluate the answers they are given. Some schools are putting such uncanny insight to good use in the selection of new staff.

Music, dress, and social media

Dress codes

Music, dress, and more recently, social media are the three principal means by which adolescent identity is established. The music teacher is quite unlike any of her colleagues in the degree to which her subject is a foundation of adolescent identity. This is sometimes the cause of much angst. The right to freedom of expression is expressed in Article 13 of the United Nations *Convention on the Rights of the Child*. The current formulation of this right guarantees that children should be able to 'seek, receive and impart information and ideas of all kinds...orally, in writing...in the form of art or through any other media of the child's choice'. Other media can include clothing or dress, traditionally equal to music as the means through which young people assert their chosen identity or 'tribal' allegiance. A liberal interpretation of this might regard the enforcement of school dress codes, including the wearing of uniform and the banning of certain logos or, more controversially, religious symbols, as an infringement of this right.

However, any right to such freedom is all but neutered in the convention by the proviso that exceptions can be made 'for the protection of national security or of public order (*ordre public*), or of public health or morals'. Any war against school uniform has been all but lost in the Britain of the twenty-first century. Regardless of whether it is demonstrable as objectively true or not, the popular belief exists that there is a close correlation between the smartness of school uniform, general standards of discipline, and academic achievement. Uniform standards are a daily battleground between staff and students in most English secondary schools.

Teachers can complain about learning time wasted or relationships damaged through arguments about straightened ties or tucked-in shirts. In spite of this, rebellious students are likely to be the losers. In schools where I have carried out research, I have found students who willingly support such policies as smart school blazers. They may agree with adult viewpoints that there is greater equality if everybody wears the same clothing to school and disputes and bullying about 'what's cool to wear' are kept out of school. They can even say that the uniform makes them feel 'proud', which is certainly a change from my own distant memories of school days in the 1960s. Reminders to tuck shirts in or straighten ties are accepted as fair game in the daily round of school life by a majority of pupils. Those who consistently defy teachers over uniform may even be demonized by many of their peers as 'chavs'.

Music codes

Can a parallel be drawn with music? The reasons for adult censorship of dress and music derive from essentially the same source, 'order, health, and morals'. Rock music when it first appeared in the 1950s was greeted with horror by an establishment that saw it as corrupting of morals. There is some justification for this in lyrics such as Jim Morrison's:

Father...Yes son? I want to kill you.
Mother...I want to...
FUUCCCCKKK YOUUUU!

It would be naive to imagine that 11–13-year-olds never come across such lyrics on the internet, but the lower secondary school is clearly not the place to promote them. They are, however, just a more extreme example of a characteristic that runs through much of rock music. By its nature, rock music is founded upon rebellion and the perceived need to shock the establishment and older generation. Sheila Whitely has written extensively about a split that occurred early on in the history of popular music between the 'wild boys' of rock and the 'nice boys' of pop (Whiteley 2005). In my own research I was surprised to discover the rapidity of transformation between enthusiasm for 'cheesy pop' in the primary school to a disdain for mass-produced commercial pop in the lower secondary school. Differences in responses were even apparent between Y6 and Y7. A piece of 'cheesy' mass-produced commercial pop sung by a 13-year-old singer elicited responses such as this in Y6:

It's really me and I love that kind of music. (10-year-old primary school boy, Y6)

In secondary schools, the same item resulted in these responses:

It's a bit babyish or for younger children (12-year-old boy, Y7)

It was a bit like a Barbie girl (13-year-old girl, Y8).

He is weird and gay and it is shit and I would rather listen to an old lady sing (14-year-old boy, Y9).

Nevertheless, although song lyrics may be important to some young people, research tends to suggest that the overall sound impression is more important. For the majority of today's adolescents, music provides a mood-enhancing, style-setting background wallpaper. Engagement is passive and music often provides a backdrop to other activities, including homework. Although social networking and internet surfing have replaced excessive TV watching as the focus of adult angst, young people on average consume more hours of music than any other medium.

Young people are not unaware that there is a difference between their leisure choices in music and what might be appropriate for school and their parents.

Y9: Well, that's what the music industry is. There's R&B but we can't do that. How can I say, we do a lot of instrumental music in this school, but we can't do rap.

Y8b: It's quite hard in the music industry to find rap that's politically correct.

Y9: I do like grime. I do listen to it. But it's not graceful if our parents want to come and watch.

Y10: It's all to do with upbringing, if you get angry . . .

Y8b: Yeah, it's quite explicit in all their song.

The vast literature on popular music, adolescence, identity, and style is interesting and we need to be reasonably familiar with it. It is not the primary literature for singing in the lower secondary school, however. School is not 'cool'. Parents are not 'cool' either, but most children and adolescents still love their parents. This does not mean that young adolescents live in a state of blissful harmony with their parents. Rows and disputes are part and parcel of loving a teenager, but most successful young people come from families where such arguments are part of the boundary testing upon which security, resilience and academic buoyancy all rest. Resilient parents build resilient offspring. School uniform can be seen as part of the boundary process. It is not 'cool' but it is the clear water between teen leisure and teen 'work'.

Making it cool?

Singing can be fun and needs to be accessible. Fundamentally I believe that it is a mistake to attempt to make singing in the lower secondary school 'cool', as did most members of the practitioner group. The ultimate result is likely to be the marginalization of music as a 'frill' subject with few students seeing much point in making a GCSE option out of what they spend their leisure time on. If we substituted words such as 'readily accessible' for 'popular' we might be more successful in setting up a progression from singing that will be fun and non-threatening for Y7 to singing that pupils will identify with as part of a stimulating and valuable musical education distinct from the music they engage with for leisure.

Two of the most successful practitioners currently known to me have interesting identities in this respect. One reports that pupils say 'Sir, you're cool because you're just so uncool'. This indicates to me integrity, both interpersonal and musical. The pupils know that 'Sir' likes classical and associates with church choirs. The pupils know that 'Sir' tries to find popular music they will like to sing in class, but fails abysmally to understand or be part of their musical culture. The pupils willingly sing for 'Sir' and enjoy their music lessons because they feel confident, valued, and supported, and because music is explained to them clearly and with humour. The pupils know that they are learning during lessons they enjoy. Their music lessons are so uncool that they are cool.

Another equally successful practitioner confessed to me that she gets by through ignorance of the pupils' music. She knows, of course, that it exists and what it means in the lives of her pupils, but nevertheless claims a constructive naivety. Classically trained at the Royal Academy of Music in piano/conducting repetiteuring and vocal coaching, it never occurred to her on becoming a teacher that pupils might not sing. She is secure in her own identity. 'I'm a musician first and a teacher second'. However, behind this statement lies a natural empathy with pupils and a warm respect for them that I observe whenever I visit the school. She summarizes her philosophy thus: 'You've got to think like the person you're working with'. This merits deep reflection because it shows an empathy that has to be part of the best music making with young people. There may be a perhaps feigned naivety but there is also connection and a two-way dialogue: 'We do sing stuff the kids want to sing. The boys choose stuff all the time. When you do choose it for them there's a mutual respect if you get it right and if you get it wrong, they forgive'.

Learner identity in singing

So far we have talked about musical identity and vocal identity as though they were the same thing, but they are not. Musical identity is primarily the product of young people's *listening*. Vocal agency is an entirely different matter. Vocal agency is primarily a product of young people's *performing*. It is limited to a significant degree by what children can do with their voices. This in turn is determined by the available technologies, singing proficiency and above all the state of the young person's physical development.

Choral programmes

In Chapter 1, I commented on the absence of US style choral programmes from UK schools. Though I am a great enthusiast of choral singing, the view I have been expressing in this book is that 'choral' is not the right term for general use in the lower secondary school. Even amongst children who regularly sing in choirs, *listening* to similar choirs as a leisure activity is relatively rare. Although some children do sing with adult choirs, the idea of a choral programme is in tension with much that goes on in the development of musical identity during adolescence. Paul Freer's recent meta-analysis (Freer, 2012) is something of a challenge to the American 'choral programme' approach, with its findings that boys want to learn useful musical skills rather than concentrate on continuous choral rehearsal and do not like undue pressure not to withdraw from school choral conductors.

Young people who might elect for a choral programme as part of their 16+ examinations portfolio (were such an opportunity available to them) would need to do so in the confident knowledge that choral singer, with all that entails, is part of the identity they wish to develop. This is an identity that needs to be worked on over several years, often requiring an early start in primary school and, in the UK, extracurricular participation in secondary school. Even those children who have established identity as choristers can be more focused on performing than listening when it comes to choral music. Enthusiastic listening to choral music is usually a fruit that ripens some years later. In any case, the average singing class is not going to develop the full vocal range of the proficient choral singer. The time is not available for the necessary vocal training and for a good many children, the high or 'screechy' choral voice will in any case be a step too far and too fast into an alien culture that is 'all ooo woo'.

Authenticity difficulties

There are, however, an at least equal number of pitfalls with some of the alternatives. There are quite often considerable difficulties in reconciling the identities children take on through what they listen to with the identities that are possible for them as performers. For example, a boy of 12 or 13 simply does not possess the physical ability to perform like the rock singer he might listen to. He might try, but the result will lack authenticity and credibility. Agency is not in step with physically possible identities. Here are some of the comments made by pupils who listened to an indie-punk song recorded by a 14-year-old boy whose voice had not changed:

It [voice] was too young for this song, which made it bad overall.

Give up or wait until you're older.

I think he should wait until he's older so that the voice matches the music more.

His voice doesn't suit the song. He should wait to get a bit older before becoming a singer or maybe try a different style.

He should develop his voice a bit more and wait until it's broken [sic].

Authenticity is a desirable element of vocal identity. There is little doubt as to what the pupils think in this case. A boy just turned 14 whose voice has barely reached let alone passed the climax of change is clearly not authentic as a rock singer. This is another good illustration of the mismatch between listening and performing. When they sing in class, pupils sing as children learning music. The class chorus is a particular kind of vocal identity and obviously a very important one in music pedagogy. There is no real equivalent to it outside school. It is the only truly authentic identity for 11–13-year-olds at school, learning music together. We need to explore it further.

Few 11–13-year-olds are going to sound like an older adolescent or adult vocalist. Some may enjoy experimenting at home, but a good many will hate the exposure to peer judgment that will result from being made to try at school.

Much of this difficulty arises from the tendency of popular TV talent shows to judge, not the music or quality of singing, but the personality of the performer. This is just not appropriate for the school music class. Children do not have the voices but neither do they have the personalities of adult performers. Those who are successful in popular TV talent shows are usually successful because they are precocious or cute. Comments directed at children should be in the form of well-informed feedback about musical learning and never directed at the person as in TV talent shows.

Class chorus as identity

There is a much safer alternative to forcing children to take on the identity of an adult vocalist, which they are not. This is to sing in chorus. As I explained earlier, voices in chorus are not the same as choral singing and can constitute an important part of vocal work in schools. Though a good sound can be produced by voices that have not reached the highest level of the Rutkowski scale when in chorus, the defining feature of voices in chorus is that a sufficiently large number of people sing together to anonymize individual voices and render them inconspicuous. The crowd singing at an international rugby match is a very good example of this, and 20 or more children singing together in a music class is another example. None will be adult vocalists, only a few will be choral singers, but all can participate in the class chorus. The class chorus is a particularly suitable vocal identity for all lower secondary pupils because individual voices are anonymized and individual singers are not publicly judged. The chorus is a safe place for children to absorb, at the level that is appropriate to them, what the group is doing. Some singers may be inaccurate. Some singers may be hoarse or rough sounding. Some voices may even not sing at all. These differences are part of individual identities and agencies and children learn at their own pace within the group. The approach is not perfect but those practitioners in the schools observed where singing was strongest across the board were all agreed that it is the best available for lower school class work.

I discussed the matter with one school's pupil music council. I asked them how they would feel if their music teachers introduced something like the *The X Factor* to lower school lessons in order to promote vocal performance by individual pupils. Here are some of their replies:

BOY 1: That'd be throwing them at the deep end if they're expected to come back and do a complete solo performance.

GIRL 1: As a Y7 I'd have cried!

TEACHER: I'd get lot of e-mails from parents!

BOY 2: It's a big step to take if you're doing it on your own on. If you're doing it with everyone else, everyone's feeling the same thing.

GIRL 2: Their comments are so personalized on *The X Factor*, they're going to be judged.

TEACHER: You want them to start singing without realizing they're singing.

SIXTH-FORM BOY: You looked forwards to the last ten minutes of the lesson. Everyone knew that's what they enjoyed more, it was fun.

Whole-class vocal work needs to be a safe place for doubtful singers and this is what is offered by voices in chorus. Some extremely interesting questions of course arise about what individuals are doing during chorus singing, particularly those few who appear reluctant to join in. Those practitioners who used the chorus approach agreed that there would always be a few pupils who would not join in, and that such pupils should not be singled out or forced into confrontation. Questions might be asked about how this compares with learning in other classes such as mathematics. The point about singing together is that level of engagement of each individual is public. Pupils in the mathematics class may look as though they are engaged, but there is no comparable way of telling that they are. Perhaps increased use of active response technologies will change this. It is a very interesting area for research, as is the question of where the boundaries are with regard to forcing children against their agency. I return to the topic in Chapter 7 to look at the important issue of anxiety associated with being required to expose oneself to potential ridicule by peers, imagined or real.

If the class chorus truly is the best identity for the lower secondary pupil learning music, we need to understand why its use is nowhere near as universal as it might be. One reason might be that the distinction between 'choir' and 'chorus' is not sufficiently appreciated. Choirs exist to rehearse and perform choral repertoire. The chorus exists to sing together almost anything that can be sung. A Beatles song could be quite legitimately vamped by a class chorus with none of the niceties that attach to creating a choral arrangement, though choral arrangements of Beatles music do of course exist. This does not mean that one sets out with an anything will do attitude when working with voices in chorus. As discussed in Chapter 4, there will still be a need to teach children some of the basics of singing such as posture and breathing. There is still a need to correct obvious faults. The purpose of doing this, however, is not to rehearse and put on a choral performance. It is to make music lessons enjoyable and motivating, teach children something about singing, develop their facility to internalize musical concepts, and perhaps develop their ability to read and write staff notation. There does not, at the end of the day, ever have to be a performance. I say more about this in Chapter 8.

Teacher identity and the class chorus

If we are going to identify clear blue water between choir/choral work and class chorus/vocal work we need similarly to articulate a difference between choir director and teacher/leader of the class chorus. Few people have only one public identity and many teachers, of course, readily shift between these two particular identities with little conscious thought. The number of schools where there is little or no singing in the lower school means, however, that there must be a good number of teachers who seldom or never take on the identity of class chorus leader. Why this should be is a matter of obvious importance. Perhaps some teachers who are also competent choir directors find it difficult to be motivated by chorus singing that falls some way short of what they may achieve with choirs.

Another possible reason some teachers may shy away from chorus work with their classes is that they do not feel confident in all the necessary skills. For the present, we might conclude this section with a statement about teacher identity made by a member of the practitioner group:

The basic faculty of a musician is to be able to hold a tune with the voice and basic keyboard skills. Keyboard busking can be better than keyboard performance.

In other words, if the teacher has the identity at least of an all-round jobbing musician, she or he should be a person in possession of the basic professional attributes needed to lead a class chorus. Given that nearly every secondary music teacher is a subject specialist, trained in music before teaching, it is difficult to understand why there is so much apparent reluctance to lead the class chorus. Are there now subject degrees that allow the admission to a music PGCE of candidates who cannot hold a tune with voice and do not possess basic keyboard skills? Another member of the practitioner group who has no difficulty working in any of the diverse vocal situations in her school, and regards all vocal contexts as important in their own ways, had this to say:

TEACHER: It's [the class chorus] solidarity, being made to feel equal not different. You have to be able to demonstrate it as the adult. You cannot expect somebody to do any performance if you don't do it yourself.

MA: The teacher I'm describing didn't sing to them.

TEACHER: Well there you go! Take a risk with them. They're just little versions of us. Some days they might do it better. I don't understand this barrier.

We do need to understand the barrier, however. 'Little versions of us' is a profoundly important statement of identity that merits much reflection. In Chapter 8, I explore this issue when I look in more depth at the anxiety and fear that pupils might harbour about singing, and the anxiety and fear that some teachers might have about leading singing. Not being a risk-taker with your own voice is a form of identity, but perhaps we do all have to be risk-takers with our voices if we want to work in secondary music.

Other identities and agencies

Vocal work may also be undertaken by peripatetic teachers of singing. Here the pupil assumes yet another vocal identity—that of the singing pupil. This can be understood as a voluntarily assumed identity in which the pupil expects personal critique of voice and technique. As part of this identity, the pupil will enter into dialogue with the teacher about vocal aspirations and achievements, with the expectation of positive, constructive feedback. A good singing teacher will know how to address both singing technique and musical interpretation. He will not resort to the facile, personalized judgements that are the stock-in-trade of the talent show genre. Most pupils will welcome the opportunity to gain genuine knowledge of singing without the distraction of being 'judged'. Some of course, may seek singing lessons because they dream of stardom. It is all part of the rich panoply of identity and agency.

Small vocal groups can also coalesce around the work of peripatetic teachers in much the way that instrumental groups sometimes do. Some members of the practitioner group enjoy singing with small to medium-sized vocal groups to the extent that they find time to do this during a busy school day. It may be only 20 minutes grabbed during a lunch break, but I have seen first-hand on many occasions how much both teachers and pupils gain from this. It is a first-class way of building relationships with pupils and perhaps what young graduates dreamed of when they decided to become music teachers. The dream needs to remain alive. Some of my school visits are to establishments where there would never be time for such idealism. Others are to schools where it is a priority.

Identity and self-efficacy

Self-efficacy is the term given to a range of psychological concepts and theories that are concerned with an individual's belief about their ability to accomplish a task or succeed in reaching a goal. It therefore has a strong relationship with identity. To cut to the chase, there are individuals who believe that they will be able to succeed in singing and other individuals who do not hold such a belief. By the age of 11 many children will have self-categorized themselves as 'singer' or 'non-singer'. There is a substantial body of evidence that suggests boys are more likely to possess lower self-efficacy in singing than girls. Self-efficacy, though it is an issue for all pupils, is a particular issue for boys. In Chapter 9, we look at the various strategies used by successful practitioners to manage gender issues in singing. In the next section we look at the underlying causes of non-singer identity, particularly in boys.

Self-efficacy and anxiety

Low self-efficacy has a strong and direct relationship with anxiety (see Chapter 8). Low self-efficacy renders an individual particularly vulnerable to the threat of negative evaluation from others. This results in high levels of anxiety and behaviour will be directed towards anxiety reduction. The identity of 'non-singer' needs to be seen as an anxiety-reducing strategy linked to self-efficacy. If the person has decided that he is a non-singer, anxiety and stress levels are reduced because there is no point in attempting to accomplish a task since, by definition of the individual's identity, it cannot be accomplished anyway. The teacher faced with a class, many of whose members have taken on the non-singer identity, will be faced with passive non-participation, mono-tone growling, or active resistance in the form of disruptive behaviour.

Closely related to theories of self-efficacy are theories of self-worth protection. Fear of failure can be a reason for not trying with schoolwork, and research again shows that boys can be more vulnerable to this than girls. It is dangerous to make broad generalizations and the notion of essentialism (that there are biologically deterministic 'boy' qualities) is even less safe. Nevertheless the streak of competitive individualism that characterizes many boys and the hierarchical ordering of boy society compares unfavourably with more socially nuanced behavioural styles of girls. When boys fail, they are more likely than girls to do so on their own. Boys can always blame failure relative to girls on not trying because the subject is 'uncool', or they have 'better things to do' (such as sport), whereas if they do try hard and then fail, the damage to peer standing and self-esteem can be severe. This can matter a lot to a good many boys because of the pressure they are under to maintain 'reputation'.

It is not that boys cannot handle failure at all. Almost every boy experiences losing in sport and most learn to cope. Carolyn Jackson's work has demon-strated that what boys fear more is feminine competence (Jackson 2003). To lose in sport against other boys is one thing, to be shown up in front of girls in academic work is quite another. My own research supports Jackson's and demonstrates that singing is one of boys' most vulnerable areas. Of all the activities at school where the genders might be compared, singing is the one where the girls are most likely to succeed while boys fail. Moreover, singing is one of the activities that matters the least to boys. Reluctance, non-participation, or feigned incompetence is almost a 'no-brainer' under such circumstances.

A large number of boys are at risk of failure at singing for two reasons. First, their pitch-matching skills may be poor and they may have come through their entire primary schooling without ever finding their singing voices. Why this should be so remains unclear. There have been suggestions that because of the way the brain is 'hard wired', boys learn both language and pitch-matching skills more slowly than girls. This is not universally accepted, however, and is countered by more readily demonstrable evidence that boys' development is hindered by low expectations and inadequate subject knowledge in primary schools. Extensive tests of musical ability devised during the 1960s (e.g. Bentley 1966) showed no significant difference between boys and girls at primary school. If there are differences now, environmental causes such as declining teacher expectations perhaps fuelled by media stories promoting the 'boys don't sing' belief are the more likely explanation. Second, whatever pitch-matching skills boys may have been able to develop will soon be disrupted by puberty when the task of pitching a note will become more complicated (see Chapter 5).

Y7 really is the 'last chance saloon' before the male non-singer identity is taken on, perhaps for life. Boys, collectively, in a good many primary schools have already acquired the identity of non-singers. The comments by Y6 pupils listed in Table 6.1 are examples of a range of similar ones gathered during my own research in primary schools. Girls tended to construct boys as incompetent at singing, and boys seemed to believe this image of themselves:

The stimulus for these quotes was recordings of good singing by boy trebles. Neither the children in the schools *nor their teachers* could believe that the recordings were of boys. This was less because they 'sounded like girls' than because of the belief that boys were simply incapable of singing of that quality. The non-singer identity is potentially one of both willingness and ability and it can be difficult to disentangle the order in which these come. It is not unreasonable, though, to suggest that if boys feel themselves incapable, self-worth protection strategies may become operative as self-fulfilling prophecies. Failure at singing can be particularly hurtful because of the deeply personal nature of the voice. It is also very easy for boys to dismiss singing failure as

Table 6.1 Comments by Y6 pupils

Boys' comments	Girls' comments
Girls have higher voices	Boys are more lively
Boys can't sing high notes	They don't have a good voice and they are low when they sing
They like shouting instead of singing	Boys cannot sing
Boys are embarrassed to sing	Boys are rubbish at singing
Boys get teased if they don't sing right	They can't
I don't like my voice, it sounds weird	Boys have got crap singing voices. They crack and break
Boys prefer shouting	Boys don't do singing. They have more gruff voices

unimportant, not least because of the example of so many school managements who set the example that singing *is* unimportant.

The music teacher who is determined to succeed with singing in the lower secondary school is in a double-bind position with regard to continuity, progression and development over the years. As well as looking backwards to primary schools where boys' identities as non-singers are often generated, he or she needs to look forwards to the time when boys' vocal identity changes for the better. By the age of 15 or 16, the trauma of voice change has passed for most boys. They no longer have high voices that could be mistaken for girls and they have also passed the intermediate stages of squeaking and cracking. For the first time in their lives, they have an important new identity. They can be something that girls can never be. They can possess something that is positively desired—an emerging baritone voice (tenor or bass is still some way off, see Chapter 5).

Some will develop a new 'cool' vocal identity as the lead in the school musical. Others will develop equally 'cool' identities through rock bands and there is a host of other options from the lower parts in an SATB chamber choir to barber shop. Younger boys in KS3 do not, in comparison, have the vocal security of older boys in Y10 and 11 who show clear signs of the postpubertal rock-producing masculinity that some of the younger ones 'yearn for but cannot have'. (Mac an Ghaill 2002). We saw in the section 'Authenticity difficulties' the reactions of peers to a boy who tries and fails to sound like a punk rocker. Some girls may find boys of their own age 'immature' or perhaps just 'cute'. A boy from Y10 or Y11 who has a handsome body and a handsome voice may be a more desirable prospect than a boy their own age. Equally, boys in Y10 and above may not welcome younger boys spoiling their singing activity, especially if attractive girls are the alternative.

All these features of vocal identity create somewhat more of a barrier to boys' participation in singing in many schools than OFSTED seem prepared to recognize. It is understandable that many schools are simply tempted to omit the difficult KS3 lower secondary years in the knowledge that enough boys to maintain their school productions or chamber choirs will emerge during KS4 (the upper high school years). In all my many years researching this topic I have yet to better this succinct summary by a Y9 boy of why he and his peers offered so much resistance to being made to sing:

We can't sing like men, so the answer is not to sing, or maybe to sing rap.

Rap is not singing. It is performed in time to a beat but without the requirement for accurate pitching of notes. Although it may be a legitimate art form in its own right that undoubtedly develops the faculties of speech and rhythm, it disengages tonality. Rap will not therefore develop the full faculty of music in the learner but it can be seen by boys as a potential escape route from singing that saves masculine face. It has strong associations with hip-hop and reggae, both genres cited by many boys when asked what kinds of music they like. It is a straw to clutch at for boys whose identity is that of 'shouting instead of singing' or 'crap' or 'more gruff' singing voices. Most boys are aware of the 'politically incorrect' or 'graceless' nature of much of rap. For some, this increases its allure, for others it makes it a tainted product.

Summary and conclusion

Does all this matter? There are many perfectly good secondary schools that have little or no singing in Y7 and Y8 classes. Some of these schools may put on high-quality music theatre productions enriched by talented young male leads from the upper school. Some of these schools may field a range of high-quality extracurricular music performances from rock bands to chamber choirs, even though there is little or no class singing in the lower school. When it comes to singing as part of the lower school curriculum, there is almost an argument for saying that no singing at all is better than bad singing. If the final part of the chapter is to be believed, a poor approach to singing in the first three key stages of education can create lifelong 'non-singer' identities. This is a weighty charge that needs most serious consideration.

As we have seen earlier, particularly in Chapter 2, OFSTED appear to believe that it matters. Merely doing things to 'please OFSTED' or a similar external agency is not a good reason. However, OFSTED do put forward a good reason as their second priority for improving music education: *improve pupils' internalization of music through high-quality singing and listening*. Though they seem unaware of the term, OFSTED here are talking up the importance of audiation. Audiation is how pupils think in music. A significant part of the discussion in this chapter has been driven by analysis of the relationship between singing and listening. A focus on the topic of identity has shown that there is a difference between pupils' passive leisure listening and their active listening. For a good many pupils, a music class where a teacher insists on careful listening with an objective in mind may be the only place where music rises above the background wallpaper of a teenage identity soundscape. A really key point is that the voices pupils actually have are not often the same as the voices they listen to in forging their identities as consumers of music and fashion. Perhaps the most important identity question of all is the extent to which pupils identify with music as a 'serious subject', recognizing a difference between music for leisure and music for learning.

- School music, perhaps more out of biological necessity than social construction, is not synonymous youth music. Teachers have to work hard with biologically given voices to create the identity of pupils learning music.
- Pupils have different identities as listeners and performers. The link is not seamless and can often be problematic.
- The class chorus is a desirable part of the identity of school pupil and musical learner.
- Singing plays an important part in audiation, the development of the ability to hear, think about and rehearse music mentally.
- The percentage of pupils who opt for music as a post-14 examination subject is a key success indicator for the creation of the musical learner identity.
- The degree to which these pupils feel they have been well-prepared for this through their lower school years as well as the gender balance of pupils so opting are health checks on the quality of musical learner identity

Further reading

Ashley, M. (2008b) *Teaching singing to boys and teenagers: the young male voice and the problem of masculinity*. Lewiston, NY: Edwin Mellen.

Bennett, A. (2000) *Popular music and youth culture: music, identity and place*. Basingstoke: Macmillan.

Bourdieu, P. (1984) *Distinction: a social critique of the judgment of taste*. London: RKP.

Warin, J. (2010) *Stories of self: tracking children's identity and wellbeing through the school years*. Stoke-on-Trent: Trentham.

Whiteley, S. (2005) *Too much too young: popular music, age and gender*. Abingdon: Routledge.

Chapter 7

Repertoire and arranging

Repertoire is the most frequently requested area for help. This chapter deals with two difficult questions. Should young people just sing what they already know for enjoyment, or should they be introduced to new material that challenges and broadens horizons? What can and should teachers do if music publishers are not engaging adequately with the research on young adolescent voices? The chapter provides clear guidance on how to write and arrange successfully for changing voices.

Introduction and context

There are, as we have said, three main contexts for singing in the lower secondary school: the music class, the extracurricular activities, and the individual or small-group singing lesson. This chapter is mainly about the first of these. Repertoire for the individual or small-group lesson is mainly at the discretion of the peripatetic teacher who may well be working toward a graded examination syllabus or the personal ambition of the pupil. Repertoire for voluntary extracurricular singing depends largely on whether lower-school children simply contribute to the choral activities of the school as a whole or have their own separate treble and changing voice activities. The latter is addressed in Chapter 10.

Anxiety about repertoire

It has been my constant experience that it is the selection of repertoire that is the most anxiety-provoking aspect of most music teachers' work when it comes to singing. Why this should be demands some reflection. There is, of course, a simply vast range of potential material to choose from. The offerings of music publishers can range from the excellent through the indifferent to the downright dreadful. What is excellent and what is dreadful is to some degree a matter of subjective taste, though there are certain principles and criteria that can be observed. I shall do my best to address them in this chapter.

Nevertheless, the chapter comes with quite a big health warning. This is the chapter where there has been perhaps the least agreement amongst the practitioner group. A high degree of taste and subjectivity is inevitable in repertoire choice. It is with considerable reluctance that I mention *any* compositions or arrangements at all. I do so only to illustrate technical points. Even then, what I have to say reflects my own taste and beliefs about what I would feel comfortable using with lower secondary children. The suggestions should not be taken in any absolute or prescriptive sense.

I cannot help but believe that one of the main reasons for repertoire angst is the fear of singing with young adolescents that we shall explore in depth in the next chapter and, behind this, the old chestnut of 'cool' and 'uncool'. There are probably few things worse than a song that falls flat. No teacher wants to feel that they are pushing water uphill as they look round the class at bored or hostile faces that clearly say 'we don't like this song'. This problem will not be solved by chasing a pot of gold at the end of a rainbow that is marked 'repertoire guaranteed to work'. Whether or not a song falls flat will probably have more to do with the attitude of the teacher than anything else. Children might sing a song quite badly but also with enthusiasm. Poor but enthusiastic singing can occur when the song is technically not ideal but the teacher 'owns' it and communicates his or her positivity. Equally, a technically good song may not work if the teacher communicates anything less than 100% positivity.

The extent to which children engage in singing has a lot more to do with relationships than repertoire. If the teacher concentrates on good relationships in the music class, problems of repertoire will fall into line and the occasional song that falls flat can be quietly discarded. Children aged between 11 and 13 will sing most songs provided that they are of good musical quality, have age-appropriate words, are suitable for the compass of the voices, and are put across with enthusiasm and conviction.

This chapter is therefore very much about practicalities. The intention is that the reader should understand enough about the issues of repertoire to choose music for him or herself. What I am not going to do is to provide a list of repertoire that is supposedly 'what works', though some new starter pieces that follow the principles outlined will be available for those new to the process. A personal playlist of class songs does not have to be large. As discussed in Chapter 6, the teacher needs a degree of ownership of the music to be sung, otherwise it will be hard to put it across with the necessary conviction. This is the disadvantage of published songbooks. The person who has the real ownership is the person who compiled the collection and no successful music teacher can be a clone of the author of a collection of school songs. The experienced and successful teachers observed and interviewed for this book all had their own lists of favourite pieces that worked for them and therefore for their pupils. Such lists are built up through experience and the new teacher has to start somewhere. At least one good, eclectic songbook might be helpful for the less experienced and is likely to be in the collection of most music departments. Ownership by the teacher of the songs to be taught though remains the most important factor. It is a prerequisite for the enthusiasm and commitment that will motivate the children.

Good music for class singing

The following remarks need to be read in conjunction with Chapter 4 where the question of what is good class singing is addressed. Two near absolute conditions must be set out at the very start. First, the music teacher is not there to entertain the children. He or she is there to educate them. Although class singing should be enjoyable, it needs to be done with objectives for musical learning in mind. Second, it is not the duty of the music teacher to steal from young people their own music and destroy any joy they might have in it by making it the subject of school study. The repertoire that is used in school needs to be one that allows teacher and pupils to meet on neutral territory for the purpose of teaching and learning. This is 'school music' and we might describe it as a 'mutually acceptable repertoire'. It is not the most currently fashionable music, but is the most effective for teaching and learning and therefore, in its own way, cool in a different sense.

Contemporary?

There is, without doubt, a dominant view in secondary music that repertoire needs to be for the most part in some way 'contemporary'. This member of the practitioner group speaks for all those I have observed to be successful with singing. There is recognition that it is futile to follow current listening trends, but neither can one pick up a dusty old collection of folk songs and lieder.

Current things they're listening to? No. But they do need to access music from their lifetime.

This is an interesting comment, but what is really meant by 'their lifetime'? These are pupils who have only been alive for 12 years or so, and of those 12 or so years, over 10 were spent as babies, infants, and small children with probably quite different outlooks on music to those currently held for that very brief period as lower secondary pupils. So does the comment mean 'the lifetime of their families and friends', perhaps? Families and friends, as we know, come from many different walks of life with many different tastes and cultural outlooks. Atonal avant-garde music conceived as an apparent challenge to Radio 3 listeners can have been written in 'their lifetime', so we have to be careful in thinking through what we mean. Music that has been around for a long time can also be 'from their lifetime' if it has been rediscovered or repopularized through contemporary media. Here is another view from a practitioner highly successful with singing:

> MA: Do you think repertoire should always be pop?

> TEACHER: What does that mean? I'd say all *contemporary*. Spirituals, gospel, musicals, pop, folk, jazz. Pop is current chart hits or pop bands we know of. Folk, well there's a lot of fusion out there, Mumford & Sons.[1] It's whatever kids bring to table. I wouldn't use 'Danny Boy' in the classroom but we have used it here.

Perhaps an important part of this statement is 'whatever kids bring to the table'. It reminds us that many young people spend considerable amounts of time exploring and sharing music through social media. Their tastes can be diverse and quirky. One thing I have learned over the years is that if it is hard to extract lists of 'what works' from teachers, it is even harder to extract such lists from pupils.

As with so much else, there are some basic principles that are simple to observe but can be forgotten. Finding something that will work well with a class chorus for both enjoyment and learning is not the same as simply finding what is currently the most frequently listened to piece. The relationship between listening and performing, as we have said, is far from straightforward. Work with children en masse requires getting simple things right consistently. When assessing any new item of repertoire, it is as well always to come back to the following four technical questions:

- Does it have a good, memorable tune?
- Does it fit the vocal tessitura?
- Does it have sufficient regularity of metre to suit voices in chorus?
- Does it have age-appropriate lyrics?

Two further more subjective questions may also be referred to:

- Is it mutually acceptable and authentic (i.e. the teacher can feel ownership of the process of putting it across enthusiastically and the pupils' identities will not be compromised)?
- Does it contribute to a balanced and culturally inclusive programme?

---

[1] A British folk rock band.

A good, memorable tune?

Above all else, a good memorable tune will be *simple*. Simplicity has to be seen as the greatest virtue and if there is any doubt about this, Benjamin Britten's masterly *Friday Afternoons* collection might be referred to. Closely allied to simplicity is repetition. Repetition may result from the structure or form of the entire melody or verse, as in the classic AABA structure. It may result from the device of sequence (a motif repeated perhaps several times at rising or falling pitches to construct a phrase). Simplicity is necessary for two reasons. First, to create what Green refers to as the necessity for a high level of familiarity with the musical syntax in order to create inherent meaning. Second, the contour of the melody must be readily negotiable by the relatively unskilled singers who will be the majority in the lower secondary class. The syntax needs to follow conventional rules such as leading notes that rise and fourths that resolve down to thirds if pupils are to grasp any inherent meaning. Try pausing an unknown tune on the leading note and asking the children to sing where it goes next. Few children of lower secondary age are unable to recognize that a tune paused on the leading note urgently cries out to rise to the tonic. This is indicative of the absorption of musical syntax and inherent meaning.

A good memorable tune will also have a clear sense of tonality, clear implied modulations and obvious progression away from and back towards the tonic. There will usually be a sense of location between the tonic and dominant and the tune will be driven forwards by the implied underlying harmony. Children and the musically inexperienced often confuse the 'modern' and the 'classical'. Most songs that are perceived by young people as 'not classical' probably have a clear sense of tonality with a very conventional and conservative implied harmonic underlay, often little more than IV, V, I. It is the truly 'modern' or contemporary 'classical' music that is the least likely to have a sense of tonality and finality of progression through leading note to tonic. Such music is more likely to appeal to those who are so thoroughly grounded in conventional syntax that they are questing for something different. A good, memorable tune also has clear melodic contours. This means a balance of strong intervals such as the perfect fourth, fifth, or major sixth with ascending or descending scales or arpeggios inside the interval. One particular interval may be a dominant feature of the tune, as in the perfect fourth at the start of 'Amazing Grace'. If the tune is well known, it can become an aide-memoire to recognition of the characteristic interval.

If too little heed is paid to these considerations, the result is likely to be excessive support from the piano or whatever other backing is used, and only a vague impression of an approximation of the melodic contour. Individual voices may be singing intervals quite wide of the mark, the tune being only recognizable as the 'average' of each individual's pitching errors. Much of the pedagogic object is then defeated since few individual children are internalizing the tune and its intervallic structure accurately. A good test of this is whether the pupils are able to reproduce what they have just sung by ear on the ubiquitous digital keyboards.

Educators who place considerable significance on the principles of Zoltán Kodály stress the importance of the falling minor third from dominant to median (or so–mi) and the closely associated jump of a fourth to the sixth note of the major scale (as in the near-universal childhood figure of so so mi la so mi). These are steps towards the pentatonic scale and, if they are followed as a pedagogical principle, children are much more likely to sing in tune (provided the tessitura is correct for their pubertal vocal stage). The pentatonic scale avoids semitone intervals, in Kodály's pedagogy for reasons of accuracy and progression. It is clearly seen in the tune 'I'd Like to Teach the World to Sing', played only on the black notes of the keyboard. A strong tonal centre around the tonic is thus not the way children's apparently inherent sense of pitch relationships is harnessed in the early stages of this system. Once the 'black notes only' (or prepared Orff instrument) principle is understood, the potential range of repertoire is in fact vast and certainly culturally eclectic. It includes 'Amazing Grace', 'Swing Low Sweet Chariot', 'How Can I Keep from Singing?' and literally thousands of others from Chinese folk to Indonesian gamelan. Kodály's ideas at this level of development were conceived with quite young primary or even nursery children in mind, but they are ignored at the peril of secondary teachers whose children sing out of tune or pitch intervals inaccurately.

Does it fit the vocal tessitura?

The vocal tessitura should by now be well understood if Chapter 5 has been studied and a few practical tests carried out on actual pupils. In order to illustrate the point, I am going to give an example of unison singing that will and will not work for Y8 boys. If it is assumed that the majority of boys are at the in-puberty phase, their safe tessitura will be from about G3 to E4 and will extend to A4 if they have done a reasonable amount of singing. Below G3, a fair number of the boys will begin to lose tone and cease to be able to phonate at all by about E3. Above A4, boys at this stage will rapidly start to break into falsetto and the majority will have done so by around C5. If they do not cross into falsetto, their modal or lower register will be increasingly strained and uncomfortable once A4 is reached. The tuning will certainly be faulty.

The song 'Mambo Italiano' by Bob Merrill is probably not one that many pupils will have in their iPod playlist but it is quite upbeat, powerfully and straightforwardly rhythmical, and has amusing and 'harmless lyrics' (see section 'Age-appropriate lyrics'). It is in the key of A minor with a tessitura of A3–E4 and has repeatedly iterated notes on A3, an ideal region of the voice for in-puberty boys with doubtful pitching skills. The range extends to a prominent A4 that might be 'growled' down an octave by the odd few without too much disaster. The actual pitch centre of the song (i.e. the mean pitch of all the notes) is 321 Hz or just between D♯4 and E4. This is as near ideal as it gets for Y8 boys at the in-puberty phase. Provided the teacher presents the song positively and with conviction, most boys will enjoy it and sing it with gusto.

Most girls will also be able to sing it, though it is lower than ideal for some female voices and may encourage jaw tension or larynx depression. During Y8, if it has not already been done in Y7, thought is going to have to be given to the divergent needs of the two sexes. Choice of key is extremely important and the teacher of the class chorus absolutely must be prepared to transpose. Transposition is a core skill for the teacher of lower secondary music. A is certainly a good key for the reasons stated above. Here is an extract from an interview with a practitioner where we discussed this issue:

TEACHER: I choose keys that allow them to sing in their natural range.

MA: What is their natural range?

TEACHER: It's quite wide. In Y7 it's from A below C to a tenth or eleventh above. In accessing the top you've also got to how to teach them to use the bottom. You've got to choose keys carefully.

I certainly agree that children should always be encouraged to use the whole range of their voice. If they are choir singers, they may well need to be taught to 'use the bottom' but for non-choir singers, this is usually the part of the range most likely to be used. A below middle C is still a good bottom note for Y8 (grade 7), though a good many boys can by that age get two or three tones below it. Y8, in general, will have problems reaching a tenth or eleventh above where Y7 (grade 6) can go and the range needs to be smaller.

Transposition considerably widens the possible choice of repertoire and is also a key strategy for differentiation. Boys and girls can sing at different times in the lesson in different keys, though this creates at least as many problems as it solves. Another way of dealing with differentiation and range accommodation is to split a unison song into sections for higher and lower voices.

For example, the Coldplay song 'The Scientist', if transposed into a key such as
D♭, allows the verse to be sung by the lower voices and the chorus, where the
Coldplay singer transitions to falsetto, by the upper voices. It cannot be
assumed, however, that 'high voices' means girls and 'low voices' means
boys. Plenty of Y8 boys will still have a tessitura within the treble range.
Some Y8 boys for whom puberty has come sooner will easily drop an octave
on the chorus, while others for whom puberty is later may try to drop the
octave but not reach 'it would be this hard' in the lower octave. Whether octave
switching constitutes best practice is debatable. If such a device is used purely
in the whole-class music lesson and boys are counselled to do what seems right
for their voices at the time, it may well be preferable to the alternative of an
indifferent songwriter writing something specifically for children. I personally
would not have voices dropping in and out of octave transposition as part of a
concert performance. It sounds ugly.

The discussion in Chapter 5 of voice change in girls is often forgotten or
simply not known about. Most Y8 girls will have a lower tessitura than they did
as primary school children and many will be at least as reluctant as boys, quite
possibly more so, to cross a passagio into the upper register. At least boys can
make humour out of falsetto. Girls will just not want to sound 'choiry' or
'screechy' and the majority who do not sing in choirs conceive singing as
something done only in the lower, speech register. I have sat through lessons
where many girls drop out of singing because the teacher does not realize that
the song has gone too high for comfortable rendition by girls in their lower
register.

An example that is problematic for boys and girls equally is 'You Raise Me
Up' by Rolf Løvland and Brendan Graham. This is in many ways a beautiful
song that satisfies admirably the criteria for a good, memorable tune. It is also
one that is likely to be relatively well known by pupils, particularly since its
popularization by the band Westlife. It is not, though, at all a good choice for
general unison singing by young adolescents, primarily because it has a range
of a twelfth. The lowest key it might be pitched in for a Y8 class is C major, to
give a bottom note of G3. The refrain will then go up to D5, taking the large
majority of in-puberty boys into their falsetto region and some girls into their
belt zone. Again, the choice for boys is to drop an octave, or force the lower
register too high with resultant strain, unpleasant tone, and faulty intonation.
Where you have trained young singers, of course, the situation is different as
they will be able to use their whole voice and manage register transition, but
this does not apply to the majority in the curriculum music lesson. This
reminds us that songs for all, as in class singing, should be chosen because

they will comfortably fit the voices, not because the teacher or anybody else has them in their playlist of favourites. Problems such as these are not going to go away. They will generally become more acute as Y8 progresses. They are dealt with in greater detail in Chapters 9 and 10.

Regularity of metre

This is a potentially difficult and certainly controversial issue. It is related to the divide between aural and written traditions of singing and therefore strongly linked to the question of learning to read and write music through singing. Many popular songs have grown out of a predominantly aural tradition and are conceived for solo or small group singing. The rhythm follows both the words and idiosyncratic interpretation of the vocalist, anchored by an incessant drumbeat. Notation can often be superfluous to such a process. The songs, of course, *can* be written down and often are for sale as sheet music. The result, however, can sometimes be a complex notation of irregular note values, syncopations, and frequent ties across bar lines in the attempt to convey the live, quasi-improvisatory, speech-driven performance of a vocalist.

If this is compared with more classical compositions conceived specifically for large numbers of singers in chorus, it will be seen that the notation of the latter is usually much simpler. Music designed for large numbers of people to sing in chorus is based on a clear, regular metre designed, among other things, to hold together a thousand or more voices in a large church or cathedral. Almost all traditional hymnody follows this principle as in a block, homophonic tune such as the Old Hundredth. 'Swing Low' sung at a Twickenham rugby final might be a secular equivalent. More adventurous rhythmic writing with syncopation is still based upon the principle that the singers have first mastered regular duple, triple, and compound time and can count accurately. The nub of the matter is found in the 'rhythmic suggestions for middle school boys *who are learning to read music*' (my emphasis) currently provided by the Cambiata Vocal Institute of America:

Metres: 2/4, 4/4, 3/4, and 6/8. Although mixed metre is possible, the complexity of asymmetrical and mixed metre combinations are probably too challenging.

Rhythm should be presented in patterns and in repetition of those patterns.

These guidelines are presented on the assumptions that pupils will actually learn to read music through their singing. That this is a pedagogical objective seems to be taken for granted. Behind the injunction to keep to relatively straightforward rhythms is the suggestion that few pupils are ever going to learn to read music if they are only ever presented with the complex syncopations, bar ties, and asymmetrical metres that characterize a popular song learned by rote.

Learning by rote, as in call and response, is the central issue here. Almost all members of the practitioner group used popular songs, often presenting these to their pupils in written notation. Here is an extract of an interview in which I discuss this issue:

> TEACHER: There are no issues with syncopated bar lines; *so long as you've got it right yourself.*
>
> MA: It's perfectly possible for 50 people to sing a Beatles song then?
>
> TEACHER: Oh gosh yes. It can become choral if it's arranged.

The emphasis is mine, because I think it confirms that the children are likely to be learning the song aurally by rote and not reading it. How useful it is to present them with the notation is perhaps an important research question. It is often said that boys and girls who sing in church choirs are good sight singers. This may be less true than it is assumed to be. The impression may be given that the music is being read, but learning it by ear and imitation has almost certainly preceded the pure process of translating previously unseen notation into previously unheard sound. Once the piece is known, its contours might be followed on paper and an impression of how notation works gradually assimilated.

So I would not argue exclusively for one approach or the other. Both have their place and, as in many things, it is a question of developing a balanced, blended approach. I return to this discussion in the next chapter when the additional complication of learning through the aid of solfège and its associated symbols is raised. Meanwhile, I would issue the usual plea for critical, reflective practice!

Age-appropriate lyrics

There are some song lyrics that are clearly not appropriate for the lower secondary class. Probably no teacher would think it appropriate to use the Sex Pistols' anarchy song:

Right! Now, ha, ha
I am an antichrist
I am an anarchist
Don't know what I want
But I know how to get it.

How many, though, would pass these lyrics written by a Y9 boy, perhaps as an example of songwriting to share with Y7 or Y8?

> This arsehole's giving me a pain
> Manipulated by your hairy scary wife

Some might, others might not. It is, after all, Y9 language. It was once suggested to me that 'Men of Harlech' would appeal to boys because of the way it is featured in the film *Zulu*. Appleby and Fowler's well-known *Sing Together* book includes 'Men of Harlech', but I eventually decided not to pursue the Zulu connection:

> From the rocks re-bounding
> Let the war-cry sounding...
> Raise the loud exalting chorus,
> 'Britain wins the field'.

Perhaps such cowardice on my part might be dismissed by some as 'political correctness'. After all, thousands of people sing outrageously jingoistic words accompanied by much international flagwaving every year at the last night of the Proms. It is so over the top that nobody takes it seriously—do they?

One answer might be to discuss the lyrics of a song with the class, pointing out the historical and political context. Pupils of lower secondary age are quite capable of appreciating that 'we don't actually believe that any more, but it tells us about our history'. How often might a class sing a well-known spiritual such as 'Oh When the Saints' without any attempt to explain the deep meanings associated with slavery? On the other hand, each year as Christmas approaches, the boys in the church choir sing about 'the truth from above':

> The next thing which to you I'll tell
> Woman was made with man to dwell
> Thus we were heirs to endless woes...

Is this to be taken seriously? Does it result in the subconscious subversion of young boys who will grow up to be misogynists? Do children in church choirs reflect on some of the arcane and archaic theology that constitutes their weekly diet of song lyrics? Might they be so keen on their singing if they actually appreciated what they are singing about? I have often discussed the concept of Original Sin with pupils of lower secondary age and St Augustine is seldom popular when it comes to the vote.

The Sarah McLachlan song 'In the Arms of the Angels' was selected by Simon Cowell (or his advisers) for his young teenage band Angelis to sing:

> in the arms of the angel
> fly away from here

from this dark cold hotel room
and the endlessness that you fear
you are pulled from the wreckage
of your silent reverie

The singers may have been hyped up as 'angels' but the song is about depression, the contemplation of suicide and drugs.

I have interviewed several music teachers whom I respect who have all recorded their distaste at the thoughtless use of lyrics in the lower secondary school. Their main concern was with lyrics of interest and appropriateness for much older adolescents being used with younger pupils simply because of the tune. This brief tour of the hazards of song lyrics might alert us to the difficulties of choosing 'clean lyrics' once we probe beneath the surface. Not that long ago, I was involved with a performance by boys of *Adiemus* and I confidently wrote that nonsense words were a way round the fact that there were so many 'good tunes' that had words (usually about pretty flowers or maidens) one wouldn't really, for whatever reason, want to use with young teenage boys. Although they sang it really well, a number of the boys didn't like *Adiemus* 'because the words don't make sense'. One can't really win, but one ought to keep trying and each year brings new classes who may react differently.

Music for children

These difficulties raise the thorny question of whether there should be music specially composed or arranged for children. Kodály argued that only the best is good enough for children. The quotations below are often reproduced:

Only art of intrinsic value is suitable for children! Everything else is harmful...

Let us take our children seriously! Everything else follows from this...only the best is good enough for a child.

It remains the case that wherever the Kodály system is properly employed by teachers who understand it, children's singing is almost invariably of a high standard and sometimes of a very high standard indeed. Not only is the singing of a high standard, but the musicianship and internal ear that guides instrumental music-making is also strong and secure. It is sometimes necessary to issue reminders that Kodály devised his system with precisely that goal in mind. The Kodály approach is not an end in itself. Kodály had definite views concerning music for children and the practice of composing or arranging music specifically for children. He is sometimes accused of a narrow outlook that privileged Hungarian folksong, but only those who do not really understand the principles would do that.

Classical or classic?

What, though, *is* the best? We have already considered the key principles of *simplicity* and repetition allied to a secure grasp of tonality, implied harmony, contour, and metre. We have considered that such conditions may require some degree of restraint resulting from knowledge of how the vocal tessitura changes and develops as children grow, particularly during puberty. Another way of evaluating whether children have been taken seriously and provided with the best material is to look at who the composer or author of lyrics is. One of my most recent interviewees reminded me that children learn 'great music' with much more ease than they do the works of lesser composers. This is where we run into the old problem of defining 'classical' again!

It is undeniable that Kodály, like Holst and Vaughan-Williams in England, was enthusiastic about folk music. He was particularly enthusiastic about Hungarian folk song and the reasons for that were to some degree political. Hungary had suffered German domination and needed, in Kodály's view, to recover and value what was distinctively Hungarian. The enthusiasm for folk song, however, goes beyond nostalgia and nationalism. Certain tunes have become part of collective folk memory simply because they *are* good tunes. Well-known folk tunes come into being out of a process of evolution within a primarily aural tradition. As in all matters, time is the key to evolution. It demands a composer of very high calibre indeed to come anywhere near to achieving what evolution and the 'survival of the fittest' principle can do to a melody.

I remember as a child a poster on the wall of the main music teaching room in the school I attended. It was a timeline of musical history and it had the words 'popular music is commercialized folk music'. That was in the 1960s! The claim fascinated me then and it must have had some impact to be recalled almost half a century later for the writing of this book. Another verse that I have remembered from childhood is 'Let us now praise famous men' [sic]. Perhaps the forgettable bit is 'men' but the fascinating and memorable part was:

such as found out musical tunes and recited verses in writing

'Found out' musical tunes? Exploration of the meaning of this could easily occupy a whole book. In the short space available here, I am going to recall the concept of 'how popular musicians learn' and link it to that of evolution and folk music. Some tunes are 'found out' without the need for lengthy conservatoire training in composition and proved by a process not dissimilar to natural selection. In this way, certain songs that appeared initially with all the support and hype of the CCM industry[2] have survived to become 'classics' in their own right without such support. Songs from *Joseph and the Amazing Technicolour Dreamcoat* have become as perennial as any traditional folk. Louis Armstrong's 'Wonderful World' is certainly an early classic that children can sing in chorus. Eric Clapton's 'Tears in Heaven', Johnny Cash's 'I Can See Clearly Now', Sting's 'Field of Gold' and Rod Stewart's 'Sailing' have all endured and translated successfully to singing in chorus because they meet all the criteria listed above. More recently, Coldplay's 'The Scientist' looks a possible contender.

Music does not have to be 'classical' to be classic. What makes a song classic is simply its ability to endure through its intrinsic merit and stand without the marketing hype of the commercial music industry. Music of *any* genre and from anywhere in the world can qualify in such a way as repertoire that children might know and through which children will learn music and musicianship. If this becomes a key principle, the question arises as to why it might be thought necessary for lesser composers who have failed to make a living composing for adults should try writing for children instead. The reader may guess that my answer to this question, in many cases, is that they shouldn't. I have wasted too much public money in the past on commissioning new works for children by composers and poets who are relatively unheard of in the 'real' musical world. In stating this, I feel myself at one with Zoltan Kodály.

Composing or arranging?

The production of repertoire lists for lower secondary aged children to sing is, nevertheless, not simply a matter of compiling two or three really great tunes from each genre in the syllabus. The tunes may be very fine. They may be part of a multicultural heritage we might want to pass on to children, but they may not be appropriate for the vocal compass of changing voices. They may be classics when performed by the original vocalist, but they may not translate into suitable material for a class chorus to grasp quickly with sufficient accuracy to form a pedagogic resource for key elements of music. The tune may be wonderful and require little more than transposition to an appropriate key, but the words may be hopelessly inappropriate. Sometimes it is justified to modify, arrange or compose specifically for children.

---

[2] Contemporary commercial music (CCM) includes jazz, pop, blues, soul, country, folk, rock, and music theatre.

Lyrics

Let us begin with a little more on words. It is not always necessary to reduce words to what is imagined to be the level of children's literal comprehension, nor should children ever be denied the cadence of great language. There could not be a better example of this than some of the great metaphysical poetry or King James Bible texts that are used in liturgical singing. Perhaps it is justifiable to substitute 'people' for 'brothers', but some of the banal attempts to dumb down great poetry that are sometimes seen are just insulting to the people who might sing them, children included. This has always been the advantage of liturgical texts. Children sing them as a 'job' but their memory remains as a treasure to be revisited in ever-growing depths of appreciation throughout adult life. A full literal comprehension at the time of first acquaintance in my view at least is neither achievable nor necessary. The process of appreciating a great text is lifelong and may begin in childhood with a feel for the rhythm and cadence of the language itself.

So many secular texts, however, are themed around love and lovers, unrequited passion, or the death of maidens. This does not have to mean the sex, drugs, violence, and misogyny of heavy rock. Take, for example, 'My Bonnie Lies Over the Ocean', now almost universally popular since a certain person invented standing up and sitting down on every word that begins with a b. Are 12-year-old boys *really* to take the part of the virgin maiden dreaming of her absent sea-faring lover? Sometimes we can just conveniently ignore such difficult dilemmas, but it becomes quite challenging when there are just too many pretty flowers. Over-reaction to this problem can lead either to a surfeit of social realism, perhaps more with girls in mind, or the limiting of boys' horizons to endless songs about football. Social realism, of course, is not always bad. As with all things, moderation and variety are the watchword. An example of social realism is Howard Goodall's song 'Refuge':

There's always someone standing on their own outside the crowd who looks bewildered and confused

They try to make some sense of all the jostling and the jokes but still they don't look that amused

What place, what did they leave behind?

What sights, what sounds, what thoughts are on their mind?

This is found in a collection boldly titled *Twelve Songs Worth Singing*. All are original compositions for adolescent singers. Why might somebody consider them 'worth singing'? 'Refuge' is an example of serious writing with young people in mind. It could be a good choice for the lower secondary school because the range is a near to the best possible compromise for all voices likely to be found in a mixed gender class of 12- or 13-year-olds. It would be something of a cheek to claim that the composer has adhered to all the guidelines I have set out above, but in effect, he has! The composer is, after all, an established one who has made a good reputation in the world outside schools. This is writing that can be effective through its simplicity. It is easy for voices in chorus to sing accurately and instructive in terms of musical learning and making sense of the syntax of music. No young person who has learned this song should be in any doubt about what a perfect fourth is. However, I am informed that more experienced singers find this song boring and lacking melodic interest—to the extent they change the name from refuge to 'refuse'!

In the same collection is Lyn Marsh's original pop ballad 'Believe'. Marsh is a prolific and respected composer for young people. The range and compass of this song, though, is less suitable for changing voices than 'Refuge'. A good many changing voices will be pushed by the top note in the verses of C5 that will take many Y8 boys just across the boundary into falsetto. At the same time, the mean pitch centre is too low to develop the whole voice, so many children will sing it entirely in thyroarytenoid register (see Chapter 5). The chorus then modulates to B♭ with a range of an eleventh up to E♭5 in the lower part. Domination by female voices will almost certainly be the result, so it does not have quite the gender neutrality of Goodall's 'Refuge'. On the other hand, the melody is more lyrical and memorable than the admittedly prosaic contour of 'Refuge'. Rhythmically there is a good balance between word rhythm and regular metre. The inspirational lyrics are admirably suited to lower secondary pupils and, aside from the issues of gender neutrality and suitability, it is arguably a beautiful composition that I know has worked well in some schools.

Another prolific and popular composer for schools is Alan Simmons. I have seen good use made of his song 'Turn to Drink!' in a Y7 class and there is also a high-quality concert performance of it by the Warwickshire County Boys Choir in the BBC Choir of the Year contest.

> Work like a slave for a cruel master
> Fast as you can but they want it faster
> It's a hard life

This is not contemporary social realism. It is the story of historical working conditions that should be part of the social and historical knowledge of lower secondary aged pupils. It is musically very strong and again illustrates robustly what I have tried to explain in my guidelines for what will work well as material for singing in chorus. The rhythm is very powerful and should teach any class to count, feel a strong pulse, and stay together. The rest at the end of each opening phrase is excellent for teaching breathing. It illustrates the power of a minor key (not always 'sad', as children are often told) and the main melody is strong, simple, and readily grasped. It is pitched at the bottom of the upper head voice range but the lower part can equally well be sung in the lower chest voice by almost all children with unchanged or early changing voices. The part writing allows good and effective differentiation. A teacher who understands singing and the management of young adolescent voices should be able to get a lot out of this song.

Lyrics, tonality and melodic contour

Simmons's 'Roller Ghoster' seems to have found its way into a good number of Y7 classes as an example of the children's 'fun' genre, combining funfairs with 'bumps and ghosties':

> We're not scared, we're terrified!
> Everything is churning up and down inside
> No-one warned us such a ride
> Would be guaranteed to make us feel sick
> Let us just remind you,
> Keep on moving look ahead
> Something's right behind you!
> Maybe we should have stayed in bed

Personally, I would only use this song with a treble choir, and a well-trained one at that. Although it can be great fun to sing and children may enjoy it, it requires a lot of work to achieve a good performance. It is beyond the capability of most Y7 or Y8 general music classes to sing *accurately*. Frequent use is made of chromatic sequences, as in 'we're going down' which may throw the tuning and ignores some of the well-tested principles of Kodály. More worrying than this is the fast tempo combined with pitching of the top of the range just beyond the B♭4 lift point. The song begins with a C major arpeggio that then rises very quickly to D5. This will strain both boys' and girls' voices if there is little experience of using the upper register. A declining vocal agility, as happens at pubertal onset, may also be a problem. If any boys' voices have started changing, it could well be little short of a disaster. It will push them right across the break into falsetto with little chance to adjust production. Strained tone and faulty tuning will be almost inevitable. I have an embarrassingly bad recording of this song by boys who ought to have done better that confirms my contention here.

If 'bumps and ghosties' are to be the theme for a Y7 or Y8 class, I would be more inclined to recommend 'Suppose There Were Ghosts' by Gareth Malone and Hannah Finch:

Ghostly footsteps,
Have you ever heard them?
Stomping in the basement
Who goes there?

The key is B minor which gives a much better range for young voices on the cusp of change. There is good word painting through an onomatopoeic, four-square 'ghostly tread' rhythm that is easy to sing well. There is skilful but simple part writing that allows the class to be split between those that can sing above the lift point and those that cannot. The phrase in bar 16 'where do you find a ghost?' beautifully teaches a perfect fifth and a triplet and the following bar the first three notes of the minor scale. Finally, if I wanted to introduce chromaticism to inexperienced singers, I might well choose this song. The phrase 'there's nothing I am scared of' is built round the leading note with a very secure sense of tonality.

I really do worry about endless songs about football for boys. Some of the ones I have seen really are musically poor with trite lyrics, but perhaps the greater objection is the same as applies whenever authors of material for children resort to crude stereotypes. The matter is well addressed by writers on boys and masculinity such as Wayne Martino. To assume that boys will be motivated only by sport, or by 'war, guns and cool tough things' (Martino & Meyenn 2002) is to have low expectations and ultimately to fail to educate them. It is interesting that the focus for boys seems to have shifted from war and guns to sport, but the reductive essentializing is still the same.

The National Youth Choir of Scotland (NYCoS) commissioned *Going for gold: a sports cantata* by Tom Cunningham and Derek Roberts for the year of the London Olympics (2012). This was a much more eclectic and inclusive approach to sport than those that assume all boys like football and can only be interested in anything if there's a football in it. The range of events covered is broad and could appeal to girls as well as boys who either are or are not obsessed with football. Coming from the NYCoS stable is a recommendation in itself and I have it on good authority that it scored well on the 'yissometer' when copies were given out. On the other hand, the Olympics are now well past and the concept has dated, for the time being at least. The cantata as an entirety might be attempted as the final project of all the classes in their final term in Y7.

What, finally, of traditional folk? Though people have tried, nothing, I'm afraid, will ever convince me that 'Danny Boy' (the *Londonderry Air*) should be chosen. The range is just far too big and there are so many recordings of it by 'cute' child singers that have made it complete hackneyed. 'Waltzing Matilda' similarly has a range that is hard to manage and I have heard some truly awful performances of it by primary school children since it was put in the Sing Up song bank. 'The Ash Grove' is a good song if the dead maiden theme can be borne. The pentatonic 'Camptown Races' has a more suitable range, as does 'Cockles and Mussels'. Both can be sung without having to worry too much about unrequited love, dead maidens, or absent sailors. With so much material to choose from, why pick anything that there might be doubt about when there are alternatives that a more clearly pedagogically sound whilst still being fun and satisfying to perform?

Creating your own arrangements

Several of the most confident and successful teachers in the practitioner group spend quite a lot of time creating their own arrangements. One school, in fact, uses exclusively its own arrangements, and that is a school that sings a huge amount. If you are going to do this, the first thing you need to understand is what the legal position is concerning copyright. The arrangements in the UK are surprisingly generous, thanks to an agreement negotiated with the Music Publishers Association. As well as legal photocopying of music for the class chorus (but not for individual vocal tuition), teachers are permitted to create arrangements that for 'primarily practical reasons such as a change of instrumentation or key ... [to] make the musical work performable by the Licensee's instrumental or vocal resources'. The full document, known as the Schools Printed Music Licence, is available from the Copyright Licensing Agency and knowledge of its contents should be part of the professional knowledge of any secondary music teacher.

Prioritizing the time

There has to be a reason for the time-consuming process of arranging music. Arranging music to suit the particular needs of the performers has often been part of the duties of the music director and his or her staff in many situations. The clear message from OFSTED is that the content of music lessons should be music-making, not teachers talking or pupils copying out writing about music. Similarly, the work of the music teacher should be musical work related to this objective. Creating arrangements for the children to sing is certainly part of this, probably one of the most instructive and creative parts. If the reason for not having time to create arrangements is 'too busy' it might be well to audit how much of this business is justified in the light of the priorities clearly set by OFSTED for musical teaching without inappropriately complex assessment tasks.

Another very good reason for the teacher to create his or her own arrangements is that this gives *ownership*. Children will sing a remarkably wide repertoire provided the teacher is thoroughly familiar with what she is putting across and presents the material with enthusiasm and conviction. Provided the principles of arranging are well understood, the teacher will feel confident and enthusiastic and the pupils will be happy to sing the material. Importantly, if the arrangement is an appropriate one, the pupils will be able to sing it well, and this will increase their motivation too. Closely allied to the concept of ownership is the notion of 'bespoke'. The regular teacher of a class will know the pupils better than anybody. She or he will know far better than any published arranger their likes and dislikes, their capabilities, and their foibles. There is also something intangibly positive about the effect on relationships if the pupils think 'did you really write that for us, miss?'

It is for reasons such as ownership and the creation of bespoke repertoire for particular classes that I feel so uncomfortable about being drawn into specifying repertoire as I have reluctantly done above. I feel less uncomfortable, on the basis of many years of research, in stating that expectations should never be too low. The real skill and art is to have high musical expectations in tandem with a high level of knowledge of the physical properties and capabilities of young adolescent voices. Most teachers will be familiar with Vygotsky's zone of proximal development (ZPD). The teacher who can pitch bespoke arrangements within the differentiated ZPD for pupils in the classes being taught really is in the premier league. The ZPD for a song would be a level of difficulty that stretches the pupil beyond 'just singing' but never to the point of frustration, poor-quality performance, or repeated failure.

Arrangements by pupils

Sometimes the pupils themselves might be involved in composing or arranging. I have seen some remarkably adept attempts at song writing and vocal composition by pupils of lower secondary age. There is no better way to improve one's own knowledge of arranging than to teach the key principles to pupils who may have some musical talent but do not yet understand certain things. There are several really key points to remember in writing for any part for young adolescent voices that are changing. Teacher and student composers/ arrangers equally need to:

- Know what the tessitura is and stay within it most of the time;
- Know also what the extreme range is and how often it can be used (typically at the climax of a song);
- Know where the lift points or passagio regions are and avoid them whenever possible. *Never* write a line that is pitched so that it constantly crosses the known passagio for singers of a particular stage;
- Realize that some young adolescent boys may quite commonly develop a phonational gap where no notes can be sounded. Know where this is likely to occur and avoid too much pitching in that region for boys at that stage of development (the middle C–E area is very dangerous for boys approaching the climax of voice change);
- Understand how vocal agility decreases during puberty. Avoid rapid articulation anywhere near a passagio point and treat leaps of a fifth or more with great caution. Octave leaps are particularly to be avoided during voice change.

If in doubt, this can all be simplified to 'stay within a range of a sixth that is pitched neither too high nor too low'. Time spent with pupils experimenting with what their voices can do and gaining a practical feel for what all the above actually mean is time very well spent.

At the simplest level, arranging can amount to little more than transposition. Shifting the key to suit the voices available can make an enormous difference and is now so much easier to accomplish through digital technologies than in the days when keyboard transposition skills were essential. In doing this, the arranger absolutely *must* understand what the tessitura of the target voice group actually is. If the range of the song is too big, transposition will simply shift the problem from one extremity to the other. Chapter 5 needs to be studied carefully in this respect, but it is equally important to test out the pupils' voices to confirm where they actually are in relation to where they might be in theory. Of course different pupils will be at different stages, so the next step in arranging might be to divide the song up into different sections that might be sung by groups of voices with a tessitura appropriate to the particular section of the song. We have already looked at Coldplay's 'The Scientist' as an example of this.

From unison to part writing

To go beyond simple manipulation of unison passages requires a feel for part writing and, obviously, an at least basic knowledge of harmony and counterpoint. Hopefully, this will have been part of the teacher's musical training, whether from an instrumental or vocal background. The first thing to remember about part writing is that most pupils are used to singing the 'tune'. There is a paradox here. The more musically experienced and capable pupils will be the ones more able to hold a part other than the 'tune', yet this part may be simpler and less interesting than the 'tune'. The extreme version of this would be giving boys who were capable singers as trebles a lower part that is little more than a drone or series of minims on I and V (IV if lucky!) For some classes, this might be exactly what is needed if there are a few newly changed baritone voices who are also inexperienced singers. Other classes might require a more interesting baritone part.

The visual layout is important. If one is confined to G and F clefs only, thought needs to be given to the minimization of additional ledger lines and the point where it might be better to use a treble clef with octave transposition. Incredibly, I still visit lower secondary music classes and find pupils who have not received sufficient explanation of how staffs are grouped in systems. As I did as a small boy 50 years ago, they have got halfway along the tenor line of the first system when everybody else has finished.

Taken to its highest art form, arranging for lower secondary changing voices will include splitting a melody and sharing it across the parts. In this way melodic contour can be preserved and a range that is too great for any individual group of voices can still be sung by the group as a whole. Knowledge of simple counterpoint and descant writing is going to be really helpful here. Such part-sharing is more likely to be between the first and second voices, but can extend to the lowest voices (if there are any). If you are going to share a part between first, second, and third voices, be careful about taking the first voice too high if the melody has gone to the second or third voice. Children's voices increase in power exponentially in the upper octave and the melody can easily be obliterated. Ground bass or ostinato if it can be worked in is a good strategy for inexperienced singers to learn a harmonizing part. Classic FM may have made Pachelbel's Canon the most hackneyed composition of all time, but it will probably still be new to many pupils and lends itself to an almost infinite variety of arrangement possibilities. I am wary, though, of attempting to sell classical music to children by writing 'child words' to an orchestral theme. I have seen some cringingly banal attempts at this. If in doubt, don't do it. A good tune can always be 'Swingled' (sung to oos, ahs, and dooby dahs).

Pachelbel's Canon (at least the theme thereof) is simple. I cannot close this chapter without reiterating the importance of simplicity. I have seen too many arrangements that follow the guidelines above in a technical sense, but are more to do with showing the arranger's technical skill than consideration of what will produce a satisfying, musical result for the singers. In the hands of a masterful composer, 'simple' does not mean low expectations. It means 'genius'.

Summary and Conclusions

♦ It is neither possible nor desirable to specify a definitive repertoire list of 'what works', still less to define a simplistic canon of songs that should be known by all children.

♦ Class repertoire cannot be built around current chart hits. A better approach is to think in terms of mutually acceptable repertoire that is still enjoyable for children to sing but also reliably teaches aspects of singing and music. This is *school music* and it is for children whose identities, *when in school*, are those of learners.

♦ The most successful teachers in the schools visited were greatly more inclined to create their own arrangements than to rely upon published songbooks. Where published songbooks were employed, successful teachers generally used these selectively, compiling their own bespoke class singing books.

♦ Ownership is a very important concept. Children will sing a surprisingly wide range of music, provided it is put across with warmth and enthusiasm and the conviction that comes from ownership. The most successful teachers had researched and developed a relatively small number of songs that they knew really well and which had been proven to work with their particular classes.

♦ It is possible to identify clear guidelines to assess the suitability of a song for class use in the lower secondary school. These include memorability of tune, fit to tessitura, suitability as an aid to learning (including learning to read) and appropriateness of lyrics. The genius of simplicity is probably the greatest of all virtues and not at all the same as low expectations.

♦ The principles of composing and arranging music for young adolescent voices are still not widely understood. Much published material is unsuitable. The most successful teachers understood this and used published material critically and selectively.

Further reading

Barham, T. & Nelson, D. (1991) *The boy's changing voice: new solutions for today's choral teacher*. Van Nuys, CA: Alfred Publishing.

Bobetsky, V. (2009) *The magic of middle school musicals: inspire your students to learn, grow, and succeed*. Lanham, MD: Rowman & Littlefield.

In keeping with the content of the chapter, the best solution to the repertoire question is to network with other teachers, e.g. through Choralnet of the American Choral Directors Association, or in the UK, through the Teaching Music website.

Chapter 8

Leadership and conducting

The book is perhaps a little more sympathetic to teachers lacking confidence than OFSTED have been. Successful singing with young teenagers can only take place when there is a first-class understanding of classroom behaviour management, as described in this chapter. It also depends upon absolute confidence, fearless leadership, and a deeply personal ability to build good relationships around the mutual enjoyment of singing. Can these further necessary qualities be taught or acquired? The book does not underestimate the magnitude of the problem but provides some candid and often soul-searching insights that will provoke and inspire.

Introduction

We have considered the justification for singing in the lower secondary curriculum and the need for high expectations (Chapters 3 and 4). We have looked in some detail at the young adolescent voice (Chapter 5) and we have considered the impact of that voice on young adolescent identity (Chapter 6). We have looked at some principles for the selection and evaluation of repertoire (Chapter 7). It is possible to be well-versed in all this knowledge yet still end up with 'no singing at all' because the most vital ingredient has been overlooked. This is the teacher's ability to be a strong leader. We said a little about the teacher's identity in Chapter 6. We considered in that chapter that the teacher needs to be a professional in the same sense as all the other teachers on the staff. This means that he or she will have specialist knowledge of the subject and its pedagogy. He or she will need to have undergone the same generic training as any other teacher. This of course includes behaviour management and how to implement the various policies necessary for a smooth-running secondary school.

There are plenty of good texts that cover such matters. In this chapter I want to look at two questions that will not be found in such texts: the leadership of singing and the extent to which the teacher in charge of a music class is also a choral conductor. The skill set required for good vocal work within a curriculum music lesson is not the same as that required for the training of a choir made up of singers who enjoy and volunteer for choral work. To be sure, there is a cross-over of skills and the majority of the practitioner group were involved in both sorts of activity. However, there are other issues that confront the music teacher in charge of a class chorus that do not confront the conductor in charge of a proficient choir. The class music teacher must know how to manage significant numbers of children who do not have the necessary aptitude for accurate choral singing, still less the inclination to acquire it.

Teacher or conductor?

The third chapter of Wiseman's *The singing class* is entitled 'The points of good singing—accuracy'. The chapter is written as though the class singing lesson were a choir rehearsal. There are other related chapters in Wiseman's book on conducting technique, rhythm and phrasing, and, importantly, learning to read music through singing. Perhaps conditions were different in Wiseman's day but I am surprised that he does not recognize more the most fundamental difference between a choir rehearsal and vocal work with a class. Unlike the choral conductor, the class music teacher may have to confront classes with a negative view of anything that might be called 'choir'. They may be apathetic or even hostile to any form of singing together. Overcoming this apathy and hostility requires a good professional knowledge of the difference between choral work and class vocal work, but above all it requires strong leadership. Whether or not the music teacher has the personality needed to be a strong leader undaunted by apathy or hostility is a matter that requires more careful consideration than is sometimes given. It is something that needs to be got right at the initial selection stage. We can, however, say a little about what underlies much of the apathy or hostility that the teacher of class vocal work needs to understand.

Leadership

Fear, anxiety, embarrassment, shame, humiliation. These, not repertoire, are the primary source of apathy and hostility. They are therefore the main obstacles to the class chorus and it can take strong leadership to overcome them. The OFSTED triennial reports set out a clear vision of what is wrong with lower secondary school music and what needs to be done to put it right. It is hard, though, to accept that OFSTED fully appreciate the difficulties of a lone music teacher working with little support in a school where no tradition of singing has been inherited and popular TV talent shows define the cultural horizons of singing for many students. It is hard to accept that OFSTED come anywhere close enough to recognizing that the root causes of many of the problems they describe are fear (if not outright terror), anxiety, embarrassment, shame, and humiliation.

Overcoming fear

Leadership, amongst many other things, is about overcoming fear. Fear or anxiety about singing affects many students but it can also affect teachers. If the teacher has not confronted her own fear and anxiety, she will stand little chance of helping the students overcome theirs. I sometimes use the metaphor of choosing the right lifeboat on the *Titanic*. When all is terror and panic, it is the officer who exudes cool, calm, confidence, and fearlessness whose lifeboat will be the one of choice. People who are afraid need a leader who is not.

Students' fear and anxiety is easy to identify. Shortly before writing these words, I found myself 'lining up' with some Y7 students outside the music room, waiting for the teacher to arrive and unlock. Here is the dialogue:

MA: Are you looking forwards to this lesson?

CHORUS OF STUDENTS: No! No way!

MA: Oh? Why not?

GIRL: We've got to do *singing*.

MA: I thought girls liked singing?

THREE GIRLS: No! (said with rising inflection as though the answer were obvious)

MA: What about you?

BOY 1. No. I don't like singing.

MA: Why not?

BOY 1: I just don't.

MA: Just don't isn't an answer. There must be a reason.

BOY 1: (shrugs)

BOY 2: He's embarrassed. He doesn't want to do it. He's too embarrassed to try and too embarrassed to say.

This kind of embarrassment is natural and can be overcome by a determined approach. Harder to deal with is a deep sense of resistance resulting from past humiliation. Graham Welch begins a chapter describing the 'sense of embarrassment, shame, deep emotional upset, and humiliation, usually accompanied by reports of a lifelong sense of musical inadequacy' (Welch 2006: 312) felt by older adult respondents in one of his studies. Recalling painful moments from their distant past, these adults spoke of how school had destroyed them as singers. It is particularly the case for many men who have never sung again since some thoughtless teacher told them to stop spoiling the singing with their 'breaking' voice.

My own adult daughter is now a professional singer and tours the world with a much-sought-after choir. She sang as a child in a prestigious cathedral choir. It was very nearly not so. I recall the upset when early in her career the primary school headmistress told her that her 'out-of-tune singing was spoiling the school choir'. I prefer to recall the unbridled joy when I received a phone call from the cathedral's music director to tell me she had passed the audition and he'd like to offer her a place. I was, of course, thinking how to break the news if she had failed the audition. One thoughtless remark by a headmistress could have changed a life. How many other cases might there be? Why do some schools seem to get it so spectacularly wrong? Why are some teachers so cruelly judgemental?

It would be good if we could be entirely confident that music teaching has progressed beyond what was experienced by these older adults, or more recently even at my daughter's primary school. The majority of schools have progressed a long way in terms of empathy and respect for students. In our own age, though, humiliation of wannabe vocal stars has become the stock-in-trade of the TV talent show. Thoughtless adaptation of the methods of the TV talent show in some schools suggests to me that perhaps we have not progressed as far as we might in understanding the necessity of dealing with the natural sense of reticence that is felt by most young adolescents asked to expose their voices. 'A breath of air travels through your body, taking on the colours of your thoughts and emotions, and when it re-emerges, it's filled with your essence' (Love 1999). Humiliate the voice and you humiliate the soul deep inside the person.

I have always had mixed feelings about eisteddfods and musical contests. To be sure, children are used to taking part in all sorts of competition. Many boys in particular inhabit a world of intense sporting contest and accept winning or losing as part of life. Resilience is an essential disposition, though how it is best developed is another matter. I have never thought anti-competitive sports days where everybody 'wins' a satisfactory answer. Losing at singing, though, is a more intimate and deeply personal failure than losing at sport, and the large majority of boys are less motivated to win than in sport. Perhaps part of the reason is that it is *unnecessary*. Singing does not *require* winners and losers in quite the way that sporting contest does. In my view there can sometimes be something 'precious' about some eisteddfods and singing competitions that is just not there in sport. Perhaps it is something to do with the relative numbers taking part or the self-importance of some of the judges. It is difficult to put one's finger exactly on it, but I am not convinced that all those who judge singing competitions really understand the world of adolescent boys. At the very least, to avoid the humiliation of children through singing, teachers should:

+ Promote the value of chorus singing where everyone's voice is valued no matter what its solo quality;
+ Know how and when to differentiate and include children who may not readily sing at the same pitch as the majority;
+ Know their own limitations and *never* blame children for their own failure to get a chorus singing together and in tune;
+ In the self-reflective knowledge of their limitations, undertake the necessary training and development.

Appreciation of a solo talent that emerges from that chorus is likely to be far warmer if the soloist with the unusually pleasing voice is 'one of ours'. If children wish to *volunteer* for a competitive singing festival, there is no reason not to enter.

Singing anxiety

Having disposed of the extremes of fear and humiliation, we may now turn our attention to the very real problems of anxiety and embarrassment that are an inevitable part of singing in the lower secondary school. Much is written and researched about something known as 'mathematics anxiety'. Anxiety about one's mathematical ability is often traceable to teachers who pressurize students in inappropriate ways. Mathematics is usually thought of as an 'essential' or 'basic' subject, but such is the prevalence of maths anxiety that our society has made an inverted virtue out of not being able to perform mathematical tasks whereas an inability to read or write basic English would more probably be hidden in shame.

Singing anxiety is in a number of ways comparable to maths anxiety. Large numbers of people are affected by it and included in the population of the singing anxious are many teachers (including some secondary music specialists) and a large proportion of adolescents, particularly young males. Singing anxiety is not the same as performance anxiety or nerves. Many of the greatest performers suffer from severe nerves and there are recognized psychological measurement scales for performance anxiety. Mathematics anxiety has been defined as an 'important non-intellective factor that contributes to mathematics avoidance behaviors and to disruption of mathematics performance' (Suin & Edwards 1982) or the 'presence of a syndrome of emotional reactions to arithmetic and mathematics' (Dreger & Aiken 1957). In comparing singing anxiety to mathematics anxiety we can draw on a number of concepts from the latter:

+ There is a difference between a general psychological tendency to anxiety (trait anxiety) and specific anxiety-provoking situations or activities (state anxiety). Trait anxiety is the potential, or tendency to experience state anxiety;
+ People suffering from a state anxiety tend to avoid the anxiety-provoking activity (in boys, this is most commonly manifest in challenging or disruptive behaviour, and/or denigration of the activity);
+ There is an affective dimension of state anxiety manifest through self-esteem and emotional disposition to the activity, and a cognitive dimension manifest through self-efficacy and perceived competency in the activity.

Factors identified by researchers of mathematics anxiety that could equally well contribute to singing anxiety include:

+ A generally stressful learning environment created by teachers who are insensitive or have difficulties with class management;
+ Demands that are shaming or promote intimidation (e.g. demonstrate a maths solution on the board or sing in front of the class before the student feels ready);
+ Insufficient opportunity to practise or develop the activity;
+ Unpleasant memories from previous experience;
+ Pressure from teachers, parents, friends, or siblings.

Many people do not like to hear the sound of their own voice recorded (though some children may not be able to get enough of this). Recognition of and empathy with this simple fact should alert the sensitive teacher to the deeply personal nature of the voice and the ambivalence felt by many toward the rarely heard public and the familiar private vocal self. There are some fairly clear anxiety triggers in singing and the teacher needs to be aware of these and plan the course of the lesson to avoid them as much as possible.

+ *Judgement by others leading to loss of credibility/reputation/public image.* It is critical that the music teacher establishes that it is the musical learning that is being judged, not the individual (as in talent shows).

◆ *Self-comparison with others*. Individuals need to come to terms with a realistic self-assessment of their singing. This does not mean overpraising; it means feedback that is both honest and sensitive. A focus on musical accuracy that it is within an individual's power to change rather than vocal quality or 'voice print' that is more personal and nebulous will go some way to allaying fear and uncertainty.

◆ *Exposure of vulnerability and the public gaze on privacy*. For a good many individuals, enforced exposure of the voice amounts to an invasion of personal privacy.

◆ *Inability to control events*. Young adolescents undergoing voice change may not be able to control aspects of their voice such as 'cracking'.

◆ *Self-reproach*. Paradoxically, in spite of the above, a good many people would like to be heard singing and can mentally punish themselves for not overcoming their inhibitions.

The practitioner group was asked to rate students' 'yissometer' response when a singing activity was announced. The results are shown in Figure 8.1

The 'yissometer' is an essential item in the toolkit of the sensitive, reflective teacher. For most of the time, students in the classes of experienced practitioners 'just got on with it' when singing was announced. It may be an indicator

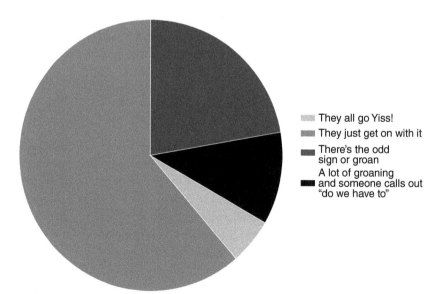

Figure 8.1 Response of the practitioner group to the question 'Please rate your pupils' "Yissometer" response when you announce a singing activity.'

that your repertoire choice is badly wrong, but it would have to be so for a sustained period in order to build up the expectation in the students' minds that they will never like the songs you make them sing. *It is more likely that you have failed sufficiently to take account of anxiety triggers.* When older children groan about singing, it is likely to be a learned behaviour and the result of failing to mitigate some or all of the anxiety triggers referred to above. There is, in my data archives, no shortage of evidence that boys, even more than girls, enjoy singing provided they think they can't be heard by anybody who might judge them. Here is a good example:

DAN: I don't like singing in front of people, but I sing to myself in my room.

MA: Why don't you like singing in front of people?

DAN: You might be embarrassed by your voice. But when I'm singing in my room, my Dad says I've got a good voice.

MA: What stuff do you sing in your room?

DAN: I just ... *just sing* along to my CDs [my emphasis]

MA: You like to sing to your CDs?

DAN: Yes. But not if someone can hear. . . .

Who has taught them that they don't want someone to hear? This is an example of a more recent conversation with a Y7 boy who registered a groan on the 'yissometer' at another school:

MA: Don't you like music?

BOY: Yes I do. I do like music, but not singing!

MA: Why don't you like singing?

BOY: I'm no good at it.

MA: Who says?

BOY: My sister.

To the extent that singing anxiety is a learned behaviour, it can be unlearned. It is always a pleasure to visit a school where students sing without the inhibitions that show up on the yissometer. These are all schools where, if the teacher does harbour any personal singing anxiety, he has learned to deal with it sufficiently to create a secure environment for the students.

Fear and anxiety in teachers

The more subtle disguise of teachers' fear is stripped away in a dialogue between students and teacher such as this (taken from an actual lesson observation).

> Miss? Are we doing singing in this lesson?
>
> I'll answer that later.

Why the prevarication? Why not just give the student an honest answer: yes. Better still, why keep the students in suspense? Why not begin the lesson with a singing warm-up that they will all enjoy, putting them in a positive and relaxed frame of mind for the learning that is to come? I have seen subtle prevarication time and time again. In another Y7 class I observed recently, the students moved through several different tasks during the lesson. At each transition, the teacher simply gave an instruction that the students followed with little fuss. However, each time this happened, the teacher also said 'we're going to do some singing later in the lesson'. The advice I gave was not to keep telling them that singing was coming but just to say, in a similar way to her other transition points, 'Right, on your feet, deep breath, I'll sing a line, you sing it back to me...' Would the *Titanic*'s officer of choice keep saying every fifteen minutes 'Later on, we're going to board the lifeboat' to disguise his fear?

Singing anxiety in teachers is likely to have three main causes:

- Doubts about the quality of one's own voice or how it will be received by students and compared with singing voices they rate highly;
- Insufficient study, practice or preparation with regard to the ability to demonstrate or model the singing behaviours that are required;
- The belief that the students do not think singing is 'cool' and will not like or identify with the chosen repertoire.

Concerning the first of these, it undeniably helps if the teacher has a good singing voice. Such a teacher is likely to have positive vocal identity and a relatively high degree of vocal self-esteem and self-efficacy. The students may even enjoy listening to his or her singing. However, lack of a good singing voice does not have to be an impediment and can even be an advantage. It is possible to boost the students through comments such as 'this will sound better with your voices than mine!' This has always been the strategy I have employed throughout a long career of working with young people who can produce a more pleasing sound than I can myself. I know many successful choir directors whose voices possess none of the beauty or eloquence that is hoped for from members of their choir.

It is not beauty of tone but accuracy of demonstration that counts here. The latter can be acquired through practice and preparation in a way that the former may not. If the students are mis-pitching an interval, the teacher has to be able to sing the interval accurately to them. If the students' singing is insipid or breathy and the teacher requires a firmer, bolder tone with glottal attack, the teacher has to be able to demonstrate that. *Good demonstration almost invariably works whereas talking about what is wanted almost invariably fails.* The ability to demonstrate can be acquired by almost anybody who is prepared to work on his or her voice. There was quite a strong feeling amongst the practitioner group that there is no excuse for not doing this. The group felt that the ability to perform basic vocal demonstrations was a *sine qua non* of the secondary music teacher. Do not contemplate a career in secondary music teaching if you are not prepared to take this on board, in other words.

This attitude was reflected by the PGCE cohort who were asked at the beginning of their course 'Please indicate how you would feel about singing in front of a class of 13-year old-students next week'. Their responses are shown in Table 8.1

There is complete agreement here that singing to and with the children is indeed 'part of the job'. It is what the trainees expect to do, but with varying degrees of enthusiasm. Just fewer than half the sample was really looking forwards to this, and just over half might be harbouring in varying degree some form of anxiety. Whether this anxiety goes up or down will of course be largely determined by their experiences in the first years of teaching. The same may be said of enthusiasm. Much will depend here on the newly qualified teacher working in a school where there is enthusiasm for singing. A newly qualified teacher whose attitude was 'brace myself and have a go' would not be likely to develop singing in a school where there was none at the time of appointment.

The fear that the students won't find the music 'cool' really is entirely genuine. It is perhaps almost inevitable, given all that has been said elsewhere in the book about the role of music in young people's lives and the fundamental

Table 8.1 Feelings about singing in front of a class

You must be joking! Hell!!	0%
I would feel really uncomfortable, but I'll brace myself and have a go	21%
I'll just get on with it. It's something I'm expecting to have to do	36%
I'll positively enjoy it	43%

part music plays in young adolescent identity. It is a fear that I experienced myself as a young teacher. The word usage 'cool' was unknown in those days, but I felt distinctly uncomfortable about consciously liking a different kind of music from what I suspected the students would like. What bothered me most was that differences in musical taste might drive a wedge that would compromise my ability to form the positive relationships I wanted with the students. So strong was this worry that I opted for a number of years to teach other subjects, returning to music only when I felt I had got over it. One has, I have learned over many years, simply to 'get on with it'. Never doubt and never apologize. Never ever say to a class anything as crass as 'you might not like this song but the curriculum says we have to sing it!'

Anxiety about repertoire

The frequency with which questions about repertoire are asked on training days is, nevertheless, another indicator of anxiety. Teachers who are in any way anxious about singing with lower secondary children clutch desperately at the straw that someone will tell them 'what works' in repertoire, thus relieving them of making a decision they do not feel confident to make. Another way of dealing with the problem is to ask the children to choose the music themselves. I have seen approaches where the children are asked to find a song on YouTube and adapt it to their own performance, karaoke style. This can hardly be described as strong leadership of singing and may yet again conceal an underlying anxiety.

If it is desired that the children make significant progress in learning about music through singing across a diversity of musical genres, approaches born out of anxiety really are not the best. The teacher must be in charge and must 'own' the music that the children are to sing. 'Owning' the music means neither choosing what the teacher likes personally nor choosing something purely because somebody else thinks it's 'what works'. It means choosing what the teacher believes he or she and the students will enjoy together through knowledge of self and class and painstaking research of what is available. Knowing this is inevitably a product of experience, so it is admittedly difficult for the new teacher. The concepts of neutral territory and mutually acceptable repertoire have already been discussed in Chapter 7 where some starter suggestions were given. The point I wish to reiterate here is that cool is not the central issue. The children really will sing almost anything provided it is not too far beyond their capability and the teacher puts it across with warmth, confidence and enthusiasm. Do not wear 'not cool' like a millstone round your neck!

There is one secure piece of anxiety-alleviating advice that *can* be given, particularly with regard to choosing repertoire that teacher and children will enjoy together. I know of very few expert practitioners who would start children new to singing with a song that none of them knew. The first song, therefore, does have to be popular, or preferably, accessible, in the sense of 'likely to be familiar to most students'. Thereafter, anything at all unfamiliar needs to be heard and sung many times—and within a positive context in which there is some fun or enjoyment. The key piece of advice here is not to choose too much repertoire and not to underestimate the necessity of repetition. There are many subtle ways of repeating. For example, sing it five times in different keys and have the students discuss which one was most comfortable for their voices. If your approach is an aimless Cook's tour, flitting from one song to another, students will never know any song well enough to sing it accurately, get to like it, and learn from it. They may therefore groan and say they don't like it when a little bit of judicious persistence might persuade them otherwise. Most people get to like the music they know.

To do this, the teacher has to know the song more intimately often than even the original performer. The teacher has to be able to perform the song himself or herself. This means a command of the vocal lines so that they may be demonstrated. The ability to clap or beat the rhythm is as important as the ability to sing the notes, some would say more so. The teacher must always be ready to demonstrate any aspect of any given fragment of the song at any given instance. She or he has to be absolutely clear about what the students will learn from doing this. What are the learning objectives that underpin the song and how do these relate to other work the students will do in the lesson? Does the chosen song really support the desired learning objectives? Reflecting on this need not be a complicated process, but it does need to be done.

It also means a command of an accompaniment. If preparation has been thorough enough, this will include the ability to transpose instantly to fit the song better to the tessitura of the group. There was a time when this demanded fairly advanced keyboard skills, but in an age of digital technology, there is usually a handy transposer function for the pianist with limited numbers of fingers. Practise using it if there is a need! If you are not a pianist, practice singing the song yourself in several different keys. The guitar is a good alternative instrument for leading children's singing because it allows good eye contact. The same advice about tessitura and transposition nevertheless has to apply. Thorough preparation and ownership of the song in this way is an extremely good antidote to anxiety, but it is often overlooked. My advice would be to take OFSTED at their word. Cut down on pointless bureaucracy and spend the time instead actually rehearsing the song you are to teach. If need be, convince the senior leadership of the importance of this.

To conclude this section, the old rule 'little and often' is a strong lifeline for anxiety. Ideally, children should sing for a part of every lesson. This in itself reduces anxiety because it regularizes and normalizes the activity. The ideal to aim for is the children *wanting* to sing because it is one of their favourite parts of the lesson. This is perfectly possible if you make singing an expectation of every lesson and a fun, enjoyable part of every lesson. The aim is a judicious blend of scarcity and regularity. Allow the children to enjoy and have some fun with their singing and *move on to another activity when you are winning*. In planning this, it is perhaps helpful to bear in mind a formula such as:

♦ A new piece that is being introduced;
♦ A piece which is known but being worked on both to improve singing knowledge and performance and to underpin other musical learning objectives in the lesson;

And *sometimes*:

♦ A favourite piece chosen by the children from their repertoire as a treat to end the lesson.

Many of the most successful teachers I have observed have a surprisingly small repertoire that they use regularly, making occasional changes to keep it fresh. They have found out what works for them and their classes. This is the best antidote to anxiety I know. Careful preparation pays enormous dividends. Careful preparation of a limited repertoire is part of the process of gaining ownership.

The pedagogy of the class chorus

It has been one of my constant arguments that the use of singing in the music class is not just light relief from the rigours of teaching and learning elsewhere in the school. It is part of a pedagogical strategy for learning music.

Choir or chorus?

I once observed the following exchange in a Y8 music class in a boys' grammar school. At the time of my visit, the only singing in the school was extracurricular and of a fairly traditional 'chamber choir' nature. The recently appointed teacher wanted to introduce singing to the curriculum, and a greater diversity of styles in extracurricular work:

TEACHER: If I asked you how many of you enjoy singing when on your own, how many of you would put your hands up?

(almost every boy raises his hand)

How many of those of you with your hands up would join a new choir in school?

(all but one of the boys lower their hands)

Part of the problem here may be with the use of the word 'choir'. It is not that boys do not want to sing, per se, it is that they are anxious about the identity membership of a choir will give them. Perhaps they may also worry about the level of commitment demanded. The frequency with which the large majority of young people, girls and boys, consistently use the two words 'posh' and 'elderly' when talking to me about choir membership is unrelenting. A young person perceived as a lackey of the posh and the elderly undoubtedly will be seen as uncool in all but a few cases.

Similar worries have been reported about other aspects of music making. The lower secondary student who carries a violin case across the schoolyard is advertising his status as a string player. He might then be a lackey of the posh and elderly who like 'slow music with violins'. It is reported anecdotally that children who have begun learning certain instruments in primary school give up at secondary school for reasons such as this. There is a need for further research on the topic. The extent to which it is an issue is heavily dependent upon the status of music within the school. As we discussed in Chapter 2, it is largely missing the point to address this as an issue of popular versus classical. It is more a question of 'frills' versus academic rigour. If music is respected as a serious academic subject and it is a perfectly normal thing to walk across the schoolyard with a violin case, there is less likely to be a problem. If the school has a string orchestra, its young people will still engage in a wide variety of music-making, including the creation of rock bands. Opportunities for music making will simply be wider, tastes more eclectic, and choices better informed.

Musical literacy and singing

It is my belief, admittedly in need of refinement by future research, that the question of musical literacy, of which the ability to read music is a key element, might be seen as a divisive marker here. Reading music is not hard, and well within the capability of any primary school child capable of learning one or more modern foreign languages—which is most of any primary school's population. Yet a mystique has been allowed to develop in which primary school teachers repress, conceal, or deny any potential inadequacy that attaches to musical illiteracy. The collective paralysis in many primary schools with regard to teaching children the basics of how to read and write musical notation has made the musically literate child the exception rather than the rule. A parallel can once again be drawn with mathematics anxiety. Our society has convinced itself that being poor at or anxious about mathematics is somehow socially acceptable. Anxiety about musical literacy can go one stage further. It can pathologize the musically literate as 'posh', or as the music teacher's little band of favourites.

Crucially, musical literacy is not just a question of cognitive knowledge of how to decode abstract symbols. It includes the ability to look at those symbols and hear their meaning inside the head. This ability cannot be divorced from the ability to internalize musical sounds and give outward bodily expression to what is heard inside the head. The musically literate can see two notes on paper, recognize them as a fifth, and reproduce a fifth accurately. The question of whether and how children become musically literate through singing merits examination. It is a long-standing question the importance of which, in my view, has yet to be fully recognized. Kodály recognized the importance of the process I have just described, of course, but I do not believe that the wider musical community has recognized the importance of researching Kodály-style pedagogy or to *examining alternatives aimed at the same end* of universal musical literacy.

We considered in Chapter 4 that there is a difference between vocal work undertaken to teach music to all children and choral work undertaken with the more musical children who elect to join a choir. Contrary to what Wiseman might have hoped to see, I have not observed during any of my visits to the practitioner-group schools an ordinary class rehearsing its repertoire to the same exacting standards that I observe when visiting a good choir. Nor would I expect to, or do so with a class myself. In this section our task is to position vocal work with the class chorus in the right place between 'just singing' and choral work. We need to consider how far it is appropriate to demand 'good singing' and 'accuracy' of the ordinary class, how much time should be spent on this relative to other aspects of the music curriculum, and what contribution is actually made to musical literacy.

Central to the necessary discussion is the question of what degree of accuracy to expect from each individual student. Many readers of this book may be confident in directing some kind of instrumental ensemble. They will have the experience to know what are the parameters of acceptability with regard to the accuracy of individual players within different levels of ensemble playing. They may have less knowledge of pedagogy that develops vocal accuracy. They may also consider it a matter of lesser import if the attitude is it's 'just singing'.

The role of accuracy

Wiseman devotes a whole chapter in *The singing class* to the question of accuracy. He makes no distinction between teaching a song to a class and rehearsing a choir. This, I think, is a great mistake. One cannot expect the same level of accuracy from the singing class as from an elite choir. A critical feature that distinguishes one from the other is that of differentiation. Differentiation in choral singing is largely through curriculum voluntarism. One is either in the choir or one is not. Once in the choir there is a part to be sung and those allocated to the part must all sing it with preferably equal accuracy. Where there is a requirement for choral accuracy and, for example, a mistuned interval is identified, the rehearsal may well need to stop and the source of the problem be found. If the singers are young ones, perhaps something like 'no, that's a fifth as in "Baa Baa Black Sheep"' will be said and the conductor will go through the passage until every singer has got the fifth accurately (assuming she is not corrected by a student saying it should be 'Rainbow Sheep').

It is not necessary to take on the autocratic approach of some choral conductors. A 'command and control' approach based on 'do everything I say and nothing else' can be perceived by youngsters outside the choir as bordering on the despotic. The need is simply to understand how to achieve a degree of accuracy that positions the learning within Vygotsky's well-known Zone of Proximal Development (ZPD). If this can be achieved, the right balance between 'just singing' and choral work will have been found. You will have got as near as is reasonably possible to a pedagogy of appropriate vocal work for your class chorus.

This inevitably raises two critical questions:

♦ Differentiation for individual learning needs;
♦ Where the class chorus is positioned on the continuum from cacophony to chamber choir (see Chapter 4).

The considerable difficulty in answering these questions, particularly the first, without also raising anxiety levels leads many to sidestep the whole problem. This can lead to a form of class singing where accuracy is abandoned altogether. There is no 'conductor'. The teacher leads by a combination of busking from the piano and call and response. Students join in to the extent they are willing and able and to that extent differentiation is by the somewhat dubious 'outcome'. If a class chorus is approached in this same way, the differentiation problem in reality is neatly sidestepped.

Critically, we must then ask what each individual student is gaining from whole-class singing. One of the perhaps surprising results of the practitioner survey was the relatively low importance attached to singing as a means of developing musical literacy. A 'means of teaching notation and reading' was considered the least of the contributions made by singing to students' progress and development. This is not something I can entirely agree with. It may be a personal view, but understanding notation is one part of a holistic package of musical literacy, and listening and singing another part of the same package. If no attempt is ever made to ascertain the degree of accuracy achieved by each student in the singing class, one has little more than 'just singing'. Ascertaining the degree of accuracy emphatically does not mean demanding the student sing on his or her own as in the choir rehearsal, perhaps. That goes against all that has been said about singing anxiety. There are more subtle approaches.

If the singing is a properly integrated part of a well-designed curriculum, there will be other ways in which the student's accuracy and understanding might be assessed. For example, how well do they perform on a computer programme or tablet app that asks them to identify intervals? Does this performance improve after a particular song, the learning of which has stressed a certain interval (see previous chapter for examples)? If we think in terms of progression, this is a necessary activity. In Chapter 4, we looked at the Rutkowski and Welch singing scales. Phase 3 in the Welch scheme is achieved when the melodic shape and intervals are mostly accurate. It was stated that at least this much should be the ideal starting point for Y7 and such an expectation is entirely reasonable, at least from Sing Up schools. Progression to level 4 'no significant melodic or pitch errors in relation to simple songs from singers' culture' ought to be happening during Y7, but how do we know whether it is for each student and where do we go from there for the more able?

A recently completed piece of research I undertook with a cathedral choir was extremely revealing in this respect. The accuracy of the singing as a whole by the choir was assessed. Needless to say, there were 'no significant melodic or pitch errors'. Each member of the choir was then individually assessed and quite a few errors of pitch and even melodic contour were found. Unsurprisingly perhaps, the frequency and extent of individual errors was largely proportional to the age and experience of the individual boys. Perhaps more surprisingly though, was what happened when the choir was synthesized by mixing together all the boys who had been first recorded individually singing with a piano accompaniment. The errors that were clearly audible in the individual recordings miraculously disappeared when all the boys were heard together. Very few listeners could tell apart the actual recording of the whole choir singing together and the synthesized version of the choir created by mixing together all the individual voices with their errors of pitch and contour.

The impression of 'no significant melodic or pitch error' was the result, then, of individual errors averaging out to create an apparently accurate choral blend. Once listeners had been alerted to this, they began to notice subtle differences between the two recordings, particularly with regard to unanimity of consonant placing. But these errors were not detected on the first play-through. What we hear as apparently acceptably accurate chorus singing is an averaging out of individual errors. This might be seen as the musical equivalent of finding that, though some students in the mathematics class were answering enthusiastically and correctly, others not detected by teacher questioning were daydreaming and not understanding the work. What then, other than a busking of the song itself by the whole class, is actually being taught? What are individuals learning? How are we helping those making a greater than average number of errors and is this inaccuracy an impediment to the development of their inner aural acuity and reading ability?

If the answer to such questions is along the lines of 'it doesn't really matter, singing is just for enjoyment' the case for including singing in the class lesson is considerably weakened, particularly given the evidence that so many children apparently do not particularly enjoy class singing. What we are dealing with here is the integration of singing as a useful component of the whole package of all children learning music. It raises another controversy, perhaps the greatest of all. This is that of whether solfège should be used, and within that controversy, the further one of whether do should be movable or fixed. Few English secondary teachers today use solfège, and none of the practitioner group was observed to do so. Yet movable-do solfège is a foundational pillar of the Kodály system, still highly regarded across the world for the astonishingly good results it can produce in accurate sight singing.

Is there a place for solfège?

A key argument for solfège is that singers must learn to create their own pitch and relative pitch. This is an important argument in choral pedagogy because if it is really true that singing combined with listening develops musical memory and aural acuity, it is difficult to see what positive role is played by inaccurate singing and misjudged intervals that are seldom corrected. There are similar arguments to be made about the use of the French rhythm patter names of Aimé Paris. According to Wiseman, 'these should be part of every teacher's armoury against rhythmical faults'. For those unfamiliar with the system, the pulse is always called ta and ta is always used as the first sound of a divided pulse. Thus, two half pulses are ta-té and four quarter pulses ta-fa-te-fe and so on. The system builds up into a complete means of achieving rhythmic accuracy and can be mastered by any musically competent teacher prepared to spend a little time on it.

Arguments for solfège are countered by the claim that the most accurate readers of all are string players and other players of non-fixed-pitch instruments. These musicians have both to use their ear to create the pitch of their instrument and to master the conventional notation that is *de rigeur* in orchestral playing. The argument would be that if orchestral musicians can do this, so should those whose instrument is the voice. Personally I have never met a class that does not take readily to solfège and patter, at least in the initial stages. Children are unencumbered by the various prejudices held by teachers that seem sometimes to be based upon ignorance of the method and its principles. Is it, as one commentator has suggested, simply snobbery based on the idea that students who have learned conventional staff notation through instrumental tuition do not *need* solfège and patter?

I have a video recording of 50 children of upper primary and lower secondary age performing spontaneously in Liverpool Cathedral an improvisation for vocal chorus that was inside my head. They simply followed my Curwen hand signs and it took no more than a morning to teach them how to do this. On the other hand, I have to admit that when I study texts on how to use solfège to teach sight-singing I feel confronted by mumbo jumbo and the feeling of 'Why do we need all this? Why do we need "do re mi" when we can do equally well with "1 2 3"?' The reason for my doubt has become clear after a little reflection. I myself learned to read notation through learning first the piano, then the organ and trombone. My ability to sight-sing (such as it is) is the result of transferring those relevant skills learned as an instrumentalist to my choir singing. Is this as good as a gradual transfer to staff notation through, for example, attaching note stems to solfège symbols placed on a staff? Sometimes, even now, my ear will let me down in a difficult choral passage and I will sneak redress on the fixed pitch of the keyboard when the rest of the choir has gone for tea break. Perhaps this would not be necessary if my music teachers had known about Kodály. Research has not yet told us the answer to this question.

The above reasoning may be anecdotal, but it is a good example of what we mean by 'reflective practice'. Through this reasoning I am inclined to favour a 'blended' approach. The music curriculum these days is a great deal broader than the 'singing class' about which Wiseman wrote. It is possible to teach universal musical literacy through a Kodály approach, but this has never found favour in English secondary schools, nor is it likely to when there is so much to cover in a time-constrained curriculum. A high degree of musical literacy and aural acuity can be achieved when children use both voice and instruments as well as a range of other approaches, certainly including IT. All these approaches, however, must work together within an integrated scheme of work of which aural acuity through voice and ear is a foundational pillar. That is why I am so against 'just singing' and so in favour of further research that investigates the relationship between the singing voice, the digital keyboard and notation software. There is all the difference in the world between 'just singing' or 'just playing with the keyboards', and a well-planned and integrated lower secondary music scheme.

Summary and conclusions

♦ There are many adults who have been put off singing for life by bad experiences at school. No singing at all is probably preferable to bad singing under the direction of an insensitive teacher who knows or cares little about adolescent voices.

♦ Singing anxiety is a real phenomenon and underlies the embarrassment and reticence towards singing shown by many lower secondary students. It can also affect teachers. Teachers need to understand its causes and how to deal with it.

♦ Strong, confident leadership resulting from 'ownership' of the material, careful and thorough preparation, and continuous development of personal skills in keyboard busking and vocal demonstration is a key element in dealing with students' singing anxiety.

♦ Whole-class singing requires a pedagogy that is more than just learning a song through call and response. This pedagogy is not the same as the pedagogy of the choral conductor, but shares certain key aspects of it in terms of working towards accuracy, good vocal technique and reading and writing staff notation.

♦ Anxieties also exist about the ability to read music and these can be quite divisive. They are sometimes wrongly confused with debates about popular and classical music. A good musical education will develop musical literacy, whatever the genre or paradigm.

♦ Musical literacy is more than just reading and writing notation. It includes the ability to absorb music through the ear, hear music inside the head, express what is heard internally through the body, and relate this directly to what is written.

- A blended approach in which singing, music technology, and instrumental tuition all have a role to play is to be favoured as the strategy to achieve this.

Further reading

Beadle, P. & Murphy, J. (2013) *Why are you shouting at us?: the dos and don'ts of behaviour management*. London: Bloomsbury.

Chaplain, R. (2003) *Teaching without disruption in secondary schools: a model for managing behaviour*. London: Routledge Falmer.

Durrant, C. (2003) *Choral conducting: philosophy and practice*. London: Routledge.

Dweck, C. (2006) *Mindset: the new psychology of success*. New York: Ballantine.

Emmons, S. & Chase, C. (2006) *Prescriptions for choral excellence*. New York: Oxford University Press.

Wiseman, H. (1967) *The singing class*. Oxford: Pergamon.

Chapter 9

Boys, girls, or boys and girls: the management of gender

Boys' underachievement has prompted a number of coeducational schools to experiment with single-sex classes. There is strong evidence that temporary, subject- or topic-specific sex segregation of 11–14-year-olds matters a great deal for singing—possibly more even than for sport. This chapter looks at the evidence and at some schools that have overcome the logistical difficulties to achieve a strong singing culture of which selective sex segregation is part.

Introduction

In Chapter 3 I made reference to the 'motherhood and apple pie' notion of equality with the promise of expanding on the issue of gender and singing in Chapter 9. Nearly everybody, it was suggested, presumes the pursuit of equality to be a good thing, yet something akin to a postcode lottery operates with regard to the way music education is delivered. Singing in the lower secondary school is demonstrably subject to a postcode lottery and singing by boys even more so. It is not, according to OFSTED, that schools are unaware that 'many more girls than boys participated in choirs'. It is that 'far fewer [can] provide evidence of concerted action that they had taken to overcome these differences'.

The missing males

In Chapter 6 we considered self-efficacy as a key part of vocal identity. Evidence was presented to suggest that boys, on average, have lower self-efficacy in singing than girls. This, it was argued, is almost certainly related to OFSTED's failure to find concerted action in the face of a clear and genuine problem. A diverse and substantial number of authors over many years have referred to problems described in terms such as the 'missing males' in singing. Even when the postcode lottery is taken out of the equation, the experience of many practitioners and many researchers over many years is that singing with boys presents an unusual level of challenge.

We returned to the issue again in Chapter 8 where we examined singing anxiety and the necessity for music teachers to be strong leaders if this is to be overcome. Once again, this emerged as a particular issue with boys. Reasons were presented as to why singing anxiety and the associated fear of failure should be a particular issue with boys. OFSTED, rather predictably, have stern words to say about this. Their criticism, moreover, is not just of demonstrably poor schools. There is a lack of singing by boys, even in schools that are otherwise good. This comment from *Wider still and wider* is an admirable summary of what my own research has found time after time:

Students were performing songs from notated scores with good attention being paid to improving diction and tone quality. Of the 25 students present, just two were boys and these were from Years 7 and 8. The girls were from all year groups, including the sixth form.

There is nothing too much wrong with the singing here. Good attention is being paid to 'improving diction and tone quality' and there would even seem to reading from staff notation. The problem is that there are hardly any boys. Otherwise effective music departments, it seems, do not have either the knowledge of what to do or the will to do anything about it. In *Making more of music* we read:

Teachers in the music department of an otherwise effective school highlighted the problem seen elsewhere. They did not know how to engage boys in vocal work when their voices changed (*they wrongly referred to them as breaking*). They thought the boys would not be motivated by singing activities and shied away from building more vocal work into the curriculum.

In Chapter 5, we looked at the subject knowledge issue. Hopefully nobody who has read that chapter would 'wrongly refer to [boys' voices] as breaking'. We return to the issue of subject knowledge and how to apply it in the next and final chapter. In that chapter we shall look in an entirely practical way at how to accommodate boys' changing voices. Before doing that, we need to consider that, in spite of OFSTED's fulminations, there may be no smoke without fire. There must be reasons for why so many scholars and teachers over so many years have reported on difficulties with boys and singing. There must be very good reasons to justify an entire chapter on the management of gender in the lower secondary music class.

Gender in music

There is no shortage of research that reports on gender as an issue in music and music education. Much of this research has to do with matters such as choice of instrument. Girls, it is said, prefer demure forms of instrumental music making, choosing gentle instruments such as the flute or the harp. Boys like to make a lot of noise and will be found wherever there are brass instruments or drums. The advent of technology has considerably enhanced this gender divide. If electronic amplification can increase the amount of noise, boys will be found playing with it. Music in the curriculum will be predictably split between a majority of boys attracted to music-technology-based routes and a majority of girls to more traditional instrumental ensembles or, most of all, to singing. Previously, boys had to become organists if they wanted a complex technology that made a lot of noise. Now, the exclusion of girls from male territory has shifted to rock music and the guitar.

The need to manage gender

A strong culture of band contests dominated by boys' rock groups is emphatically not indicative of successful management of gender. One has immediately to ask why girls are under-represented. At least one whole book could be written about this important issue. Our concern here, though, is with the absence of boys from other forms of singing, ranging from the choral to differential levels of participation in the class chorus. If one is enthusiastic about boys' singing, it is good to have an agency such as OFSTED 'banging the drum' (advisedly, so to speak) about the lack of boys' participation. However, I cannot help but think that in this case OFSTED either do not fully understand the relationship between boys and singing or have not fully appreciated the difficulties teachers face. Even the practitioner group, chosen for its above-average level of expertise and success in lower secondary school singing, had failed as a whole to crack the issue as the chart in Figure 9.1 shows.

'More boys than girls' is largely accounted for by the fact that some single-sex schools were included in the sample. Only a very small proportion (11%) of the expert practitioners known to me had really overcome the gender barrier. They received at my behest this gentle endorsement in the National Music Plan:

Annex 4: Case studies

1. Success in boys' singing

It can be particularly difficult to motivate boys to sing when they reach secondary school. However, some schools avoid this problem by recognizing that boys can be embarrassed about singing while their voices are changing, especially in front of girls. These schools understand that boys' voices do not 'break' but change gradually, a process that is sometimes referred to as the cambiata principle.   (DCMS 2011: 44)

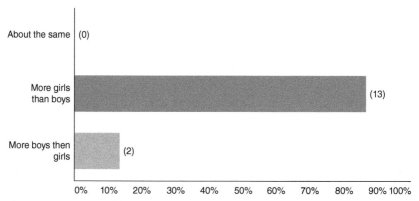

Figure 9.1 Response of the practitioner group to the question 'How would you describe the relative participation rates of boys and girls in extracurricular singing?'

Behind these innocuous words lies a gender management struggle of titanic proportions. Only the strongest and stoutest hearted might embark upon such an epic endeavour.

The voice and bodily display

A place to begin might be Lucy Green's book, *Music, Gender, Education*. In it she proposes that singing is a form of bodily display. Traditional constructions of masculinity have proscribed male bodily display. 'Classical music' according to Green has to some extent circumvented such proscription because such music has 'inherent meaning'. People are not supposed to go to classical concerts or opera in order to gaze upon the body of the singer. Feminist writers complain frequently of the notorious 'male gaze'. There is little doubt that, whether or not classical music truly has risen to such lofty ideals, the commercial music industry has never even attempted to. Much money is made from singing as an activity where males gaze upon female bodies. A particular form of aggressive body display, going sometimes to such extremes as hurling microphones or smashing instruments on stage, is reserved for males. Female exclusion from such activity is far more heavily policed than ever was female exclusion from choral singing.

There has been some breaking down of these barriers in more recent times. Passive male bodily display has become more fashionable with famous footballers posing in their underwear. Calendars of 'hunky firemen' are published and females are occasionally permitted a reverse gaze as in the Chippendales or films such as *Magic Mike*. Recent research into schoolboy masculinities (McCormack & Anderson 2010) has also revealed a softening of attitudes and greater acceptance of boys perceived as or who come out as gay. Nevertheless, society remains fundamentally patriarchal and such changes are generally still brought about only upon male terms, a condition referred to in the literature as the patriarchal dividend. There is a long way to go before significantly more boys either feel confident enough to display their bodies through voice or are permitted to do so unfettered by social attitudes. It is still far safer for boys to 'hide behind' music technology as Green describes.

My own work has shown that there are further complications that affect the lower secondary school. A boy of 12 is not a hunky fireman. He does not have a man's body. He certainly does not have a man's voice. The 'essence' that emanates from his soul through his voice is, to say the least, ambiguous in gender terms. Significant authors on male gendering such as Martian Mac an Ghaill talk of boys' 'yearning for an adult masculinity they cannot have' (Mac an Ghaill 2002). If he is an accomplished singer, a boy of 12 may well be the subject of the female gaze. The gazers, however, will be grandmothers, middle-aged women, and schoolgirls, all of who think him 'cute'. Anybody familiar with Benjamin Britten's relationships with boy singers will also be aware of an underground homoeroticism that is a far more difficult issue than OFSTED appear to recognize. To all this must be added all that was said in previous chapters about singing anxiety and fear of failure. The rational behaviour for most boys is to avoid singing, which they quite understandably do.

The 'problem with boys'

Most teachers and parents will be well aware of the fact that singing is not the only area where there is thought to be a 'problem with boys'. Boys are said to underachieve right across the curriculum, to be at far higher risk than girls of exclusion, and significantly more responsible than girls for the 'constant low-level disruption' that plagues so many secondary school classes. Music and singing are not the only gendered subjects. There is often said to be a problem with boys' literacy. English is to some degree seen as a 'feminine' subject, though most boys reluctantly acknowledge its necessity for 'getting a good job'. Modern foreign languages, perceived as somewhat less necessary, suffer to a similar degree to music as being 'for girls'.

Various strategies have been proposed over the years for dealing with this. Perennially popular is the preoccupation of politicians and the media with the need for male role models. Those of further right-leaning tendencies sometimes go as far as demonizing single mothers. Strategies such as 'boy-friendly curricula', meaning English lessons based on 'war, guns, and cool things' are proposed. There is certainly an equivalent in music with the endless demand for songs about football that will supposedly motivate boys. There are 'boy-friendly' forms of school organization too, such as setting subjects by gender or the more extreme measure of resisting demands for coeducation altogether.

Research has tended to show that these strategies can misfire in all sorts of ways. Giving boys more male teachers has been shown to result in increased 'laddism' among teachers. Weaker male teachers simply play to the boys' gallery, which benefits neither boys nor girls. Setting by gender or coeducation may slightly improve boys' behaviour and results, but girls' results are improved even more and the gender gap widens rather than closes. At the same time, the benefits of coeducation are lost and my own research has demonstrated the possibility for alarming degrees of laddish misogyny during boys' music lessons in single-sex secondary schools (Ashley, 2010b).

Unsurprisingly, there has been a considerable backlash against the 'problem with boys'. Some writers have simply expressed themselves tired of the whole discourse with titles such as 'Do we really need more books telling us there is a problem with boys' underachievement in education?' (Zyngier 2009). In Australia the gender equity movement has developed a strong critique of 'recuperative masculinity politics' (e.g. Mills & Keddie 2007), perceived as necessary in the face of strident right-wing male politicians who push the need for boys to 'catch up'. Some of the more erudite writing in the UK has successfully pointed out the extent to which gender can never be seen in isolation from social class. The concept of the 'renaissance child' (Skelton & Francis 2010) has been invoked in analysis of high achievement by both boys and girls, not without irony drawing on the term renaissance *man*, considered to be everything that is ideally 'boy'—tall, athletic, muscular, confident, and handsome.

I have always found it very difficult to position singing within these dis-courses. As mentioned in Chapter 1, my own upbringing was very much in the Platonic, classical tradition where sport and music were equally important as the next things to be added to the curriculum of a boys' school after the 'three Rs'. I have argued consistently that music and singing are very necessary parts of boys' education in order to develop cultural and emotional literacy, avoiding what I call the 'football monoculture' or what Mac an Ghaill succinctly describes as the 'three Fs'—fightin' fuckin' n' football (Mac an Ghaill & Haywood 2006).

Such arguments are difficult to uphold against a background of patriarchal hegemony in music where most classical composers have been men, and the commercial music industry continues to be dominated by men who have ruthlessly exploited females as fodder for commercial pop. Most difficult of all has been the enforced exclusion of females from the most exalted forms of choral singing for not far short of two thousand years. To argue that boys must be given the opportunity to sing through the maintenance of single-sex choirs often cuts little ice with those seeking redress for this great historical inequity. In the face of the critique of recuperative masculinity politics and its 'boy-friendly' schools and curricula, it can often look singularly lame. Nevertheless, it is to this that we must now look as we analyse the work of those practitioners who have been most successful in 'providing evidence of concerted action that they had taken to overcome these differences [of boys' and girls' participation in singing]'

The diamond model

The practitioner group was asked the question 'Do you ever organize single-sex music teaching or singing groups?' Comfortably over half did for extracurricular work, which is a significantly higher figure than would be found in any other subject with the probable exception of sport.

Justification for sex segregation

The term 'diamond model' is sometimes used to describe the practice of beginning with mixed-gender singing groups in the early stages, splitting to parallel single-sex groups in the middle stages, and resuming with mixed-gender in the later stages. This, with very few exceptions, was the approach favoured by those members of the practitioner group who were most successful in engaging boys with singing (Figure 9.2). The single-sex phase of the diamond quite neatly coincides with the lower secondary years, so the implication is that anyone who is thoughtful about 'providing evidence of concerted action' to engage boys needs to consider it seriously.

   The main disadvantage of the diamond model is that it places considerable extra demands on what are often already hard-pressed music departments. Although there are some single-sex choirs that exist in their own right, any organization charged with the welfare of boys and girls needs to provide equality of opportunity. If there is a boys' choir, there must also be a girls' choir. It has certainly been the case that whenever I have visited a coeducational school to hear or work with the boys' choir, there has been a girls' choir as well. The cost of this is that almost everything needs to be duplicated. Boys' and girls' singing groups might both appear in the same concert programme, but obviously there need to be separate rehearsal times, a separate process of

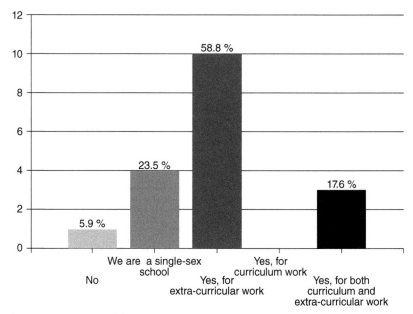

Figure 9.2 Response of the practitioner group to the question 'Do you ever organize single-sex music teaching or singing groups?'

repertoire selection, and so on. If the music department is small, with perhaps only one full-time member of staff, this is a very big ask.

The main justification is that without such an approach, few boys will sing. It has been a near-universal experience for those running previously boy-only choirs to find that they lose almost all their boys once the choir is opened to girls. Where previously there may have been a thriving boys' choir, the admission of girls will almost certainly reduce the choir within less than 2 years to what OFSTED found: 'Of the 25 students present, just two were boys and these were from Years 7 and 8.' This situation is repeated almost *ad infinitum* up and down the country if not across the planet. It is often found also in primary schools, certainly towards the end of KS2 when boys in Y5 and Y6 can desert singing activities unless strong proactive action is taken to prevent this. Often it is not, the loss of boys being accepted as inevitable. Quite when the genders should diverge on their journey through the diamond is therefore a matter for some serious consideration.

It has been a major task for me as a researcher over the last two decades to understand and explain why boys of 10 to 13 or so years of age are so reluctant to sing with girls. The process of understanding is ongoing. I cannot claim to have the whole answer. Nevertheless I can reasonably confidently state that those who simply declare that there must be equality and therefore there will be mixed-gender singing are doomed to almost certain failure (unless 25 girls and 2 boys is considered to be 'mixed gender'). The forces that need to be understood are powerful. Equality is more subtle and complex than crude demands that everything boys and girls do should be identical.

To some degree, there might be a comparison with sport. The normal justification for single-sex sport is that men are usually stronger, faster, and play the game harder. While coeducational sport at amateur level can increase socialization and even 'civilize' men in need of this, the experience at adult level has been that men's enjoyment of the game is restrained by the need to be 'gentle', women can be frustrated by not being taken seriously, and inter-sex injuries can be potentially serious. These considerations do not in theory apply at primary school level where the difference between average height, weight, and strength of the sexes is much less (though the important work of Christine Skelton (2001) on boys, football, and male primary school teachers should be noted). At lower secondary level, the difference can even be reversed, with girls who begin puberty earlier actually being bigger and sometimes stronger than the boys.

There are key similarities and differences between sport and singing. First, the bodily androgyny of the primary school child is very directly replicated in the voice. There is little difference between the voices of boys and girls under the age of 9 or so and the potential singing range is very similar. There is no *physical* need to separate boys and girls in either sport or singing. If they are separated, it is for cultural reasons, or in sport perhaps to prepare them for the way things will be in the future. At upper secondary level, boys have low, changed voices that can often reach adult male singing ranges. This is the vocal equivalent of the athletic, hard-playing sportsman. Indeed, with singing the sex difference is even more the case. Although women who devote their minds and bodies to it can achieve considerable feats of strength and sporting skill superior to many men, very few women can sing tenor and none bass even if they try for a lifetime.

This latter point provides a very strong reason for the sexes coming together again after a period of separation. A four-part singing ensemble with males on the lower voices and females on the upper voices could hardly be a stronger statement of the fact that there are physical differences that make the two sexes complementary. This is perhaps a slightly contentious statement in a culture that favours socially constructed views of gender and is struggling to put sex discrimination and homophobia behind it, but for the director of a singing ensemble it is almost a 'no-brainer'. This much should all be fairly obvious. It is what happens in the crucial 11 to 14 years that is far less obvious to those with no in-depth knowledge of singing and gender.

The first point to be understood is that there are physical changes to be accommodated. Though puberty affects the physical body in ways significant to sporting development, its effect on the singing voice and the way it can be employed is considerably more. These physical changes and sex differences are not socially constructed. They are a biological given, peculiar to the lower secondary age group. They cannot be legislated against by a political agenda regarding how gender equity is achieved. Though a biological given at the fundamental level, the social constructions that are subsequently possible through mismanagement of the biology are considerable. The most obvious of these is that 'boys do not sing'. Almost as frequently encountered is 'boys who do sing are not real boys' (Ashley, 2010a).

We have largely covered much of the necessary ground in previous chapters. The key points can be brought together here and earlier chapters studied again for better understanding as significance dawns. The list is fairly formidable and it is easy to see why so few boys sing!

♦ The vocal ranges for boys and girls begin to differ. Girls can continue with the familiar high voice and the extensive repertoire for it. Boys must find new voices that are temporary and for which only a very limited repertoire exists.

♦ The voices of both boys and girls change in functionality and quality during puberty and these changes disrupt singing ability. The changes are much greater and considerably more disruptive for boys. If teachers do not understand how to manage these changes, boys can wrongly believe that they cannot sing. This belief may endure for the rest of their adult life.

♦ Singing ceases to be an enjoyable activity for boys if they are given repertoire that they can no longer sing well or vocal tasks that they can no longer perform comfortably. Surprisingly few composers, arrangers, or publishers of music have any in-depth understanding of boys' changing voices. Many published arrangements are inappropriate, and inexperienced teachers can understandably be misled. The most successful teachers usually create their own arrangements.

♦ Many boys already harbour high levels of singing anxiety and are extremely vulnerable to fears of failure and feminine competence. The rational defence is to assume a non-singing or anti-singing identity.

♦ There is evidence that girls can exacerbate this problem by taking revenge on boys during this difficult period—perhaps for years of boys' domination of the primary school playground space for football and sometimes harassment through 'kiss-chase' type games.

♦ Boys go through a vocal identity crisis that can last two or three years any time between the ages of about 11 and 15. During this time they can be a vocal nobody—neither the child they once were and sometimes wish they still were, nor the adult they wish they could be but sometimes fear becoming. Vocal nihilism is an obvious corollary of a more general adolescent nihilism that can affect boys at this time.

♦ A powerful system of diminishing returns operates. When boys feel in a minority, they begin to doubt the appropriateness of the activity for their gender. The more that boys leave the more that it appears that only 'weird' or 'wimpish' boys remain. 'Weird' and 'wimpish' boys then discourage other boys who would not want to be seen having that identity.

♦ Many senior leaders of schools have little understanding of the singing voice at puberty. In consequence, they readily believe social constructed misconceptions such as 'boys don't sing' and do not understand the necessity of strategies such as the diamond model.

The remarkable thing about the diamond model is its ability to overcome all the above difficulties. With the exception of the last, which is where a diamond model might itself become stillborn through the occasional blind opposition of an intransigent management, the diamond model provides an answer to almost every one of the above difficulties. This is why it is so important for senior leaders in schools to have a much better understanding of the issues but above all a much higher expectation of the boys and what the music department might or should achieve with them.

'Boys' stuff'

The singing will often be less refined than the sensitive musician might desire. A singing activity deliberately designed to encourage young adolescent boys may be tackled with boyish enthusiasm but little choral delicacy. What is remarkable about this is that audiences often love it. For all sorts of reasons, people like to hear boys sing. Again, a formal research project might furnish a better understanding of this phenomenon, but my impressions have grown over many years that boys singing reassures people at a deep level where the psyche might fear laddism, underachievement, unemployment, yobbishness, and a growing cultural worthlessness of a large section of the male population.

I have on many occasions experienced reactions from pleasant surprise to incredulity by school managers when it is shown to them that boys in their lower school can and will sing. Not that long ago I was invited to a school to run a boys' singing workshop. The hall was filled with a large number of Y8 boys who initially glared at me with defiant looks of 'try and make me sing, then...our last supply teacher's funeral was a week ago'. Three hours later, these same boys were performing in three parts to parents who had come to hear them at the end of the afternoon. My most abiding memory of that event though is of having nearly to pick the deputy head up off the floor because of the shock to his 'boys don't sing' belief. School managements need many more such experiences.

The key to all this is making singing 'boys' stuff'. For Y8 boys I work with, this has always included an element of education about puberty and the impact it is having on their voices. Most find this fascinating and listen with rapt attention while many old myths and fears are disposed of. Once boys can be persuaded to join a singing activity, the diminishing returns problem then goes into reverse. One of the schools I visit fairly regularly has 160 11–16-year-olds in its boys' choir, but the teacher started from nothing with just a handful of boys and worked at it. A member of the choir put it succinctly:

> Once other boys see there's nothing wrong with it, more boys come.

Equally remarkable is the way boys' embarrassment evaporates once they are in an all-boys group. I have many times seen the delicate subject of 'cracking' turned into uproarious fun as boys are encouraged to experiment with falsetto and explore their voices. There is so much that boys need to learn about singing and voices that is irrelevant to or of only passing interest to girls. Time is needed to discover and explore new vocal ranges. Many boys relish attention to their voices once girls who might threaten their 'reputation' through criticizing them are removed, and I don't think I've ever had a problem with boys whose voices are at different stages of change. There will always be some boys who will sit quietly and hope they are not called upon, but for every one of these, there are usually at least two who will volunteer for anything before they even know what is being asked. They might have high squeaky voices or low growly voices—they will just delight in being the centre of attention for a moment.

Perhaps most important of all is that boys can work at their own pace. In a mixed-gender group, girls often have to wait while boys struggle to master new parts. Girls do not have this problem. They continue with what has always been familiar. They can understandably become impatient and bored, though this emerges in more subtle ways perhaps than with many boys when impatient and bored. Boys nevertheless pick up the signals. Boys can feel that girls either think they are a nuisance or are secretly laughing at them. So many times have I seen teachers add to the problem through their own lack of patience with boys. Boys are usually told off for their behaviour while girls are usually called on to demonstrate. At the end of the day, the girls carry the singing and save the lesson or rehearsal from disaster.

In concluding this section though, there is just one final and important caveat. There is very little recognition in our culture for the boys' changing voice. There is no real place for boys' changing voices *en masse* in most recognized genres, where the conventional ranges of SATB are all but universal. Activities that can appeal to boys such as rock choir, glee club, or barber shop need adaptation if they are to accommodate the changing voice. There is very little published music for changing voices and the sound of boys' changing voices is unfamiliar or even alien to most listeners. What is expected is either 'treble' voices or 'broken' voices. (This is reflected in the graph in Figure 4.1 on p. 84 that shows what extracurricular singing opportunities were offered to lower secondary pupils.)

The most frequently encountered activities are SATB choirs or music theatre productions. Boys' changing voices probably are loosely accommodated in musicals such as *Oliver*, and wherever there is a solo lead part for a boy it can sometimes be adapted to whatever voice the boy has. Often, though, this does not happen and the boy is forced to sing intensively outside his range with potentially harmful results (see Baldy, 2010). The voices of girls and older boys are likely to dominate in SATB choirs for all the reasons we have discussed. One-third of the sample reported that they offered a changing voice or 'cambiata' chorus/choir. Unless there is a strong tradition of treble singing, this is really the only place where lower secondary boys can thrive.

In one sense, one-third of the schools offering a changing voice chorus or choir is encouraging, but it has to be remembered that the sample is skewed towards practitioners who are successful with singing. This very important matter is addressed again in Chapter 10. First, though, we have to consider the management of gender in the lower-school music class that is compulsory for all pupils.

Catering within the music class

There was a broad consensus across the practitioner group that the diamond model for extracurricular singing is a strong one and the most likely to result in good participation levels by 11–14-year-old boys. It is a model I endorse personally after a lifetime of choral work with boys and many years' serious research into the topic.

Lack of consensus

There was no such consensus with regard to how the problem of boys and girls should be tackled in curriculum music classes. For example:

+ *Practitioner A* insists on having all the boys on one side of the room and all the girls on the other side of the room for his lessons.
+ *Practitioner B* stood by the door and made the children enter boy/girl/boy/girl, insisting that they sat in that order.
+ *Practitioner C* remains completely and deliberately blind to where the children seat themselves and regards it as wholly irrelevant to her passionate value of total gender equality.

Here we have three complete extremes. Each produced equally good singing by both boys and girls in lessons where gender appeared not to be an issue. What is even more interesting were the justifications given by these experienced practitioners for their approaches.

Practitioner A believes that if boys and girls are not separated, the boys become embarrassed through being near to girls. He insists that he was once made by a senior manager who did not understand this to mix the boys and girls up. The singing was then not as good. He successfully argued with the senior manager and reverted to the old arrangement. The senior manager then had to admit that the singing was much better, particularly the boys' singing.

Practitioner B believes that if boys and girls *are* separated, boys will sing less well because groups of boys may form where one or two cynical, sporty boys ('jocks') intimidate other boys. When boys are next to girls, nobody worries, it's not a big deal, and everybody just gets on with it. The singing in this lesson was also observed to be very good, with plenty of enthusiastic participation by boys.

Practitioner C becomes 'incensed' with people who believe that boys won't sing because this is an affront to her all-important aim of gender equality. She 'just gets on with it', expects the boys to sing wherever they are seated, and they do. Interestingly she adds a telling little caveat, saying that 'boys need to let their hair down safely, and be emotional. OK, it's not normally cool for boys to show emotion but here we do it in a controlled environment'. There is no doubt that boys sing in these lessons. Singing is usually towards the end of the lesson, looked forward to, and the children leave 'happy, calm, or hyped up' according to what they have just sung.

My own personal inclination is perhaps towards Practitioner A, but it is my job as a researcher to report on, document, and analyse what I see, not to push my own personal preferences. Perhaps what matters here is that whatever an individual teacher feels most comfortable with will work for that particular teacher. We are back in the familiar territory of the personality, style, and confidence of the teacher, which seems inescapably the most significant variable in whether or not the singing is of a good standard and boys participate at all.

However, it is also worth recounting observations made in a Y8 class taken by Practitioner D. On the surface, Practitioner D was similar to Practitioner C. She did not have strong views on dictating where the children sat. She began her lesson by having all the children randomly stand in a circle in order to undertake some 'warm-ups' she had learned about through observing the *Voces8* method at a conference. The gender distribution in this circle was largely random and little difference in participation level between boys and girls could be observed. However, when the children were asked to return to normal seating, they themselves sat largely boys in one area of the room and girls in the other. In this particular lesson, the boys then out-sang the girls in volume and commitment of participation.

Children of lower secondary age do tend, when given the freedom to do so, to cluster by gender. This was not by any means the first lesson I had observed where boys actually out-sang girls—with no particular encouragement to do so. I once observed a singing lesson in a primary school where the children were standing in a circle. Again, the boys out-sang the girls. The lesson was based on a Kodály-style singing game where the child who was 'it' sang their part of the song and could then choose the next singer from the circle. A good many boys clamoured eagerly to be chosen, whilst several girls avoided eye contact and hoped they would not be. One girl who was picked was too shy to sing at all.

Gender and expectations

Finally, two more practitioners; E and F. Unlike Practitioners A–D, these were both teachers in schools which, though good, were not at the time known for the quality and extent of their singing. No particular seating directions were given with the Y7 class of Practitioner E, but boys of themselves gravitated to one area of the room and girls to another. In this lesson, girls clearly dominated the singing, though most boys were at least giving it a go. Interestingly this practitioner chose a group of girls to lead some call and response singing in the style of 'Singing Playgrounds' (as promoted by the group Ex Cathedra). Most of the boys joined in, some enthusiastically. However, boys were given no similar opportunity to lead the singing.

In the Y7 class of Practitioner F, boys and girls again self-selected gender-segregated seating. The children were given the opportunity to practise in groups of two or three a section of a warm-up the whole class had sung. Almost all children engaged enthusiastically, leading to a high but purposeful noise level. Several groups of boys appeared to be enjoying themselves and, unlike any of the girls, were making up actions to the song. Towards the end of the lesson, the teacher called the class to order and asked for volunteers to demonstrate what they had been practising. Four groups of girls were chosen. One group of boys was finally chosen at the very end of the lesson but had their available time curtailed by the bell and did not have the opportunity to show off what I had observed, as children were becoming restless and preparing to leave for the next lesson. When asked after the lesson why four groups of girls had been chosen but only one group of boys at the very end of the lesson, the teacher seemed surprised and said that the choice was random and coincidental.

What lessons can be learned from these practitioners? It is difficult to conclude other than that, though the last two teachers may have been well-intentioned, lower expectations were held of boys than of girls. These may well have been subconscious, but the message given to the children was clear. Boys cannot be trusted to lead singing or are incapable of doing so. When a demonstration of what has been learned is required, girls must be asked as boys probably won't have learned very much or are incapable of a performance from which the rest of the class might learn.

Practitioners A–D were all from schools where the singing is strong and gender differences were far less marked. In some cases, boys out-sang girls and in others girls out-sang boys, but the differences were relatively marginal and it is in any case not (or should not be) a competition. In all four of these schools, the singing by both boys and girls was good. The real point is that, in the hands of highly skilled and experienced practitioners, there is no real difference between the singing participation levels of boys and girls. Although it is tempting to attribute this to a particular strategy to manage gender, such as seating arrangements, the evidence does not support this. It made little difference whether the children were deliberately segregated by sex or deliberately mixed by sex. Perhaps this makes a difference to the way the teachers feel about their work and the confidence with which they undertake it, but this is part of the subjective rather than objective domain.

A possibly more supportable explanation is found by contrasting the first four schools above with the last two. The first four were visited because they were ones that stated in the survey that they offered a cambiata or changing voice extracurricular singing activity for boys. They were also schools known for the strength of their singing and the level of involvement of the lower school in activities such as boys' choir. The desire was to observe, not the extracurricular work, but the classroom practice that went on in these schools. The other two schools had been randomly chosen from a list of schools that claimed or demonstrated no particular achievement in lower-school singing.

The factor common to the four schools where participation of boys and girls was largely equal in Y7 and Y8 lessons was a positive attitude to gender equality marked by a deliberate intention to involve boys wherever possible in extracurricular singing activity. Closely linked to this were high expectations of boys. It was simply not on the agenda to consider that boys would not sing, nor was there much tolerance of the wide diversity of primary school experience as a justification for not attempting singing in Y7. The interview responses of these teachers were strongly and consistently characterized by attitudes such as 'what's the problem? or 'we just get on with it!'. The first statement below sums up the kinds of attitude found in schools where there were no significant gender issues and boys' participation was at least equal to girls':

> It's all about what teachers introduce as normal, it's all about their attitude to the subject.

There is recognition in the next extract that this is not easy. The teacher in this school has been in post less long and has had less time than the previous interviewee to make singing for all boys and girls in lower school music lessons 'normal'.

I'm experimenting because I'm working to remedy a non-singing culture. It was 'just play the keyboards' when I came... If it's not really entrenched in the school culture they find it hard to accept. In the Swedish tradition they just do it.

In this next example, from a school where a teacher new in post achieved significant changes in less than a year, there is a clear statement about identity. The pupils are ascribed the identity of children learning music, their singing voices being part of the pedagogical strategy:

They don't have an option, no choice. Do they walk into a maths lesson and say 'I'm not a mathematician'? For the first bit we want everybody taking part and enjoying it. Tuning and not shouting is important. 'Shouting is cheating'.

Though this practitioner was highly knowledgeable about adolescent voice change, he was not too concerned about providing repertoire that would exactly fit the known tessitura of each individual pupil in the class. In a Y8 lesson observed in this school, boys were simply told to drop an octave if they needed to. Not infrequently, references were made to how far boys had developed their new voices. The boys seemed to accept what was said quite happily, showing autonomous knowledge of which part of their voice to use. In the next extract from another school, a positive attitude and high expectation again seems to trump all matters, including the inevitably wide range of pubertal status of the pupils:

> TEACHER: We just sing! We don't make a big deal of the changing voice. We don't draw attention to it. That makes them feel unsafe. We just get on with it.

> MA: What happens for Y7 boys who reach puberty early? Can they drop an octave? Is that difficult?

> TEACHER: They just get on with it! And it does NOT make it harder to do singing with Y9 than Y7!

Nevertheless, this teacher operated the diamond model for her exceptionally successful extracurricular work, as did all the teachers featured in this section who had achieved gender equality in their class teaching.

> In the classroom I'd always go for what all of them can do. In choirs I'd differentiate for boys and girls.

OFSTED call for 'evidence of concerted action…to overcome these differences'. What seems to have characterized the most successful all-round practice in the schools visited was a combination of high expectations unmediated by specific gender provision in the curriculum work, but an equally strong focus on gender separation for key aspects of extracurricular work where the specific and differing vocal needs of boys and girls were given serious consideration. This is a strange paradox that demands further detailed research.

Summary and conclusion

In my own consultancy work, I commonly request to speak to the boys alone when I work in schools. My reason is that the content of what I have to say to them has a strong orientation toward the aspects of puberty that are specific for boys. The lessons I give are unashamedly about 'boys' stuff' and the way boys sing is very much part of this. Most schools have been quite willing to accommodate this and have arranged for classes to be redistributed for the music period. It is clearly possible to do this, but none of the experienced and successful practitioners was sufficiently motivated by the possibility to confront the difficulties in making a more permanent arrangement of it. For extracurricular work, however, all were prepared to make the sacrifices required by the diamond model. Twice the amount of time and effort was taken up in getting boys to sing outside music lessons, but this was considered worthwhile in view of the almost inevitable alternative of '24 girls from across the school and 2 boys from Y7 or 8'.

In Chapter 6, I put the case that there is some justification in the claim that singing in the lower school music class, particularly with boys, is difficult. I have suggested that OFSTED perhaps underestimate the total sum of difficulties faced by lone music teachers. So many factors combine together, not least a cynical media that promotes the 'boys don't sing' belief and works actively in so many ways against many teachers' efforts to reduce gender stereotyping. Nevertheless, while many boys will quite happily both play sport *and* sing, far fewer will miss sport in favour of singing. It is difficult to argue that this is merely a stereotype in the face of overwhelming empirical evidence. Those teachers who not only give up extra time to run extracurricular vocal work for boys and girls separately, but go the additional mile of negotiating a time with the sports teachers when boys will not be compromised, truly are exceptional. Somewhere in the middle of this perplexing maelstrom is the postcode lottery, or what the UK's current chief inspector has recently more simply called 'luck'.

♦ The necessity for higher expectations of boys, a consistent theme of this book, is once again shown to be critical.

♦ The attitude and values of the teacher seem to play a more pivotal role in achieving gender equity and boys' participation than do more tangible 'fixes' such as the management of classroom layout or the application of specific subject knowledge about adolescent voices.

♦ Given the importance and significance of attitudes and values, a very high level of attention should be focused on the process of initial selection of which graduates should become music teachers. Attitudes and values are formed from childhood upwards and seem to trump the effect of training.

♦ The most successful schools visited differentiated between extracurricular work and classroom work with regards to setting by gender. In the most successful schools boys and girls sang quite happily together during curriculum lessons, yet were split by gender for many extracurricular vocal activities.

The last point is explored more fully in Chapter 10. Although there is clearly a need for a pragmatic response to the difficulties of setting by gender, there are also significant issues of vocal identity, vocal management, and the teaching of singing and choral work.

Further reading

Green, L. (1997) *Music, gender, education.* Cambridge: Cambridge University Press.

Jackson, C. (2006) *Lads and ladettes in school: gender and a fear of failure.* Maidenhead: Open University Press.

Jarman-Ivens, F. (ed) (2007) *Oh boy! Masculinities and popular music.* London: Routledge.

Lingard, B., Martino, W. & Mills, M. (2009) *Boys and schooling: beyond structural reform.* Basingstoke: Palgrave Macmillan.

Chapter 10

The cambiata movement

Cambiata, which means changing, is a movement to provide for young adolescent voices which began in the United States. A key cambiata principle is that the song should fit the voice, not the voice the song. This is illustrated by musical examples linked to clear explanations of the vocal ranges. The UK has been very slow to embrace cambiata principles, but that is now changing following leads set by the National Youth Choir of Scotland and the National Youth Choirs of Great Britain. This final chapter shows how schools can create their own cambiata singing groups which come together for regional gatherings such as Cambiata North West or Cambiata Cornwall.

Introduction

In Chapter 5 we looked in some detail at the young adolescent voice and how it differs from the voices of either children or older adolescents. We may be enthusiastic about a song or choral arrangement we would like to share with young people, but no amount of enthusiasm in the world will make up for what is either impossible altogether or simply inappropriate for young voices that are changing as a result of puberty. We might, on the other hand, be distinctly lacking in enthusiasm for such challenging tasks as getting all the 13-year-old boys in a class to sing. The factor common to both conditions is a lack of knowledge about how to present young adolescents with material that they are *able* to sing, and will *enjoy* singing on account of its particular suitability for the physiological and acoustic properties of their voices.

In Chapter 6, we examined in some depth the ideas of vocal identity and vocal agency. Not only do we have to understand the physical properties and capabilities of young adolescent singers, we also have to understand the social and cultural factors governing what they will tackle with enthusiasm as opposed to what they will tackle reluctantly or even refuse to tackle at all. All the knowledge in the world of acoustics, physiology, and singing technique is of no avail if there is no corresponding understanding of how young people relate to music, popular culture, and their own singing voices. In Chapter 7, with both Chapter 5 and Chapter 6 in mind we looked at the particular issues of repertoire, composing, and arranging. In Chapter 8 we looked at the key role of the teacher in motivating children's engagement. Children of lower secondary age, it was said, are far more tolerant and open with regard to repertoire and singing than is often imagined—provided that the teacher puts the material across with enthusiasm, conviction, and warmth.

Finally, we reserved Chapter 9 for a special consideration of the management of gender, acknowledging that it is true that singing with boys can be particularly difficult and has been so for a long time—over many decades, not years. Once again, the attitude of the teacher emerged as the single most important factor, very closely linked to the levels of expectation held. We saw quite clearly in that chapter that where the attitude is positive and the expectations are high, boys sing. It could be argued that there is not really a 'problem with boys'. The problem, when it exists, is with music teachers, composers, and arrangers. It is also with much of the musical canon and establishment within which those individuals operate. Finally, and by no means least, it is with a popular media that promotes gender stereotypes and low expectations, including the 'boys don't sing' one. This is to be my theme for the final chapter. The problem is not with boys. It is with what we ask them to do and the way we ask them to do it. This final chapter is about cambiata, which is a different way of going about things, premised upon exactly this argument.

What is cambiata?

I am by no means the first to suggest that the reason boys may not be singing is because there is something wrong with the music teaching, not the boys. The word 'cambiata' is derived from the Italian *cambiare* which means 'to change'. It is sometimes encountered in place of 'mutare' as a change directive as in, for example, change to a new key. Students of strict counterpoint will be familiar with the term 'cambiata note', used in Palestrina's lexicon to denote a dissonant passing note on the beat. Over half a century ago, a young music supervisor who was later to become a major figure in adolescent voice research gave much thought to the question of why boys in American junior high schools were not singing during music classes. That young supervisor was Irvin Cooper and he found a new use for *cambiare*. He 'changed' *cambiare* to 'cambiata' creating a neat word play to describe the changing adolescent voice.

Voices do not 'break'!

Cooper's ideas were radical for a variety of reasons. They were so radical that they have yet to become widely appreciated in the UK. As we have seen, a widespread problem in the UK is that people continue to talk and act as though boys' voices 'break'. One wonders whether it is with feigned shock or tongue in cheek when OFSTED report that:

teachers in an otherwise successful school... did not know how to engage boys in vocal work when their voices changed (they wrongly referred to them as breaking).

This is perhaps a little unfair. Cooper himself on a study visit to the UK remarked on how in English cathedrals and public schools, some of 'the finest choral singing in the world' might be heard. To this day, most music directors in these establishments continue to refer to boys' voices as 'breaking'. It is a little disingenuous of OFSTED, perhaps, to criticize state school teachers for using the term 'break' when that is the term used by conductors of world-class boys' choirs as well as presenters on BBC Radio 3 who, presumably, ought to know better.

Voice change in both boys and girls has already been explained in Chapter 5. In that chapter we referred to the work of John Cooksey, still recognized as probably the world's leading authority on the adolescent voice. Cooksey was adamantly against the term 'break'. Here are his actual words:

The destructive concept of an adolescent broken voice is completely indefensible. It bears no resemblance whatever to the dynamics of vocal growth during adolescence (Cooksey 2000).

The reason for the persistence of the term 'break' in England is explained by the American author Kenneth Phillips in his book *Teaching kids to sing*. It is related to what we have said in earlier chapters about the Rutkowski singing scale. Phillips states that what he calls 'English choirboys' employ only the crycothyroid muscles, which is more popularly understood as singing only in the so-called 'head voice' (another dubious term!). It is perfectly possible, when taught to sing in this manner, for boys to maintain a high singing voice throughout puberty and even for some years beyond the completion of puberty. There comes a time, however, when they simply cannot do this any longer. The voice will no longer transition between its upper and lower registers and people call this 'broken'.

If you play recordings of 12- and 13-year-old boys singing with only the crycothyroid muscles to classes of 12- and 13-year-olds in the average English state school (as I did extensively in my research project, inviting the children to express freely their real thoughts) you will field remarks such as:

Girl, girl, girl! (laughter)

OMG it sounds like *she* is screaming! (The boy's voice was genuinely mistaken for a girl's.)

You are being an idiot. Sing in a lower voice.

Stop sounding like a girl. Become a man with a lower voice and become a proper singer.

The conductors of world-class boys' choirs in the UK usually ignore this because they need the emotional and musical maturity of adolescent boys who sing in a high voice during puberty to lead their choirs and interpret the music. The vast majority of teachers and conductors working outside the world of elite boys' choirs cannot afford such a luxury, nor would most want to, given all that was said in Chapter 6 about vocal identity. We can therefore dismiss the term 'break' as an anachronism and concentrate and what is best for the large majority of boys whose voices begin to change at around 11 years of age.

Fitting the song to the voice

This chapter, then, is all about 'knowing how to engage boys in vocal work when their voices change'. We will never again talk of voices 'breaking'.

Origins of cambiata

To understand where Irvin Cooper was coming from, we have to imagine Canadian Boy Scouts seated around their campfire in the late 1950s. It is said that Cooper derived his inspiration from such an encounter. Cooper had, after emigrating from the UK and teaching for 15 years in Montreal high schools, been promoted to the position of music supervisor for the entire Montreal system. He became increasingly perplexed on visiting the schools for which he had responsibility to find middle-school boys 'not singing'. Indeed, in some schools, he found that so formalized were the teachers' expectations of that young adolescent boys would not sing, that the boys were excused music classes for extra study in other subjects.

This did not square with his experience of the same adolescent boys on scout camp, where they sang lustily into the late evening around the fire. It dawned on him that what was different from school was that these boys chose their own pitch for their singing. At school, teachers would force boys to sing in unison with the girls. At scout camp the boys sang spontaneously without the constraint of a formal keyboard pitch. This spontaneous pitching was lower than that of the girls at school, but higher than that of adult men. Cooper undertook extensive research on this phenomenon during the next phase of his life at

Florida State University. It is said that over his lifetime he analysed the voices of over 114,000 adolescents, which puts my own 'over 1000' into perspective! Through this work he devised his key tenet of the Cambiata concept:

No attempt should be made to make the voice fit already existing music. The music should be made to fit the voice.[1]

Like all great discoveries, this idea on the surface is blindingly obvious and completely simple. Yet it still has to find widespread acceptance, in the UK at least. The problem is with the 'already existing music'. There is an awful lot of it and composers, arrangers, and publishers keep producing more of it, largely oblivious of Cooper's key tenet. In choral singing, there is of course in the 'Western canon' a vast heritage of great composition from Dufay, Byrd, and Palestrina through Bach and Mendelsohn to the late and much lamented John Taverner. This is what 'English choirboys' (and girls) sing. Nobody is seriously going to suggest that a major music publisher declare SATB voicing to be inappropriate and produce a version of Bach's B Minor Mass rearranged for the parts unique to adolescent boys.

When it comes to school singing, however, the situation is very different. Here, there is perhaps less excuse for composers, arrangers, and publishers to continue churning out material that shows no recognition of what is known about adolescent voices, and is at best of mediocre suitability in consequence. Ignorance of adolescent voices and how to write for them is not excusable in my view when there is so much research evidence supported by clear guidelines and exemplification of those guidelines available. On the other hand, following these guidelines without straying too far into the 'uncool' really is extremely challenging for any composer or arranger. Shortly we will look analytically at examples of how it should and should not be done. First, though, it is necessary to reflect a little more on the ideas underlying cambiata.

Less often recounted but presumably part of Cooper's gestalt moment was the fact that the Canadian Scout movement did not then admit girls. Perhaps the boys were singing lustily at least as much because they were engaged in homosocial bonding in a safe all-male environment where no girls were going to judge their singing. We have already discussed such matters fairly extensively in Chapter 9, so there is no need to repeat what was said here. Second, we have also had extensive discussion spread across several earlier chapters about what is cool (see Chapter 7 in particular). I have said several times that teachers

---

[1] See Cambiata Vocal Institute of America web pages: <http://www.cambiatapress.com/CVMIA/TheCambiataConcept2.html>.

worry too much about this and that boys will sing quite a wide range of repertoire if it is put across with conviction, warmth and enthusiasm. I wonder, though, whether a 1950s Boy Scout campfire is just a bridge too far.

Not only were Cooper's Boy Scouts singing at their own pitch, they were also singing their own music. By this, I mean in the main *not the music they were given in school*. Many of today's young people would not 'own' campfire songs, though some would. I will digress slightly for a moment to recount an episode I regret. For a few years after forsaking school teaching for university work I ran the local village mixed-gender scout group 'to keep in touch with young people'. I recall a campfire on a classic perfect evening with the stars in the sky. Somebody suggested singing. As leader, I can only say I 'wimped out'. I did not take the cue and get them all singing. I was mindful of something a Y7 boy had said to me during some research I had undertaken for the City Council's arts and culture department:

> In primary school they made us do crazy things like sing little campfire songs.

The next day, I learned that some of the boys had been disappointed that there had been no singing. I bear to this day the shame of letting them down. That is one of the personal experiences that motivates me to write about strong leadership in singing.

To return to the main theme, context is perhaps all. Boys will sing Byrd motets in a church choir at the weekend but never admit this to their school peers. Equally, some at least might sing campfire songs at the weekend but not admit that to school peers either. The context we are working with here is the lower secondary school, attended in some form through compulsion by almost all boys and girls. Again, quite a lot has been said about that in previous chapters but it is worth reiterating now that within that context there are at least two further sub-contexts, the compulsory curriculum music lesson for all and the voluntary extracurricular vocal programme. There is the further complication that, as we discussed earlier, there is little to no equivalent in the UK of the curriculum choral programme of the American junior high school.

To which of these contexts is cambiata suited, either or both? Here we need to revisit earlier discussion of the difference between 'choral' and 'vocal'. 'Choral' is a particular and highly developed genre of vocal music that appeals to a limited number of children and requires extensive commitment and rehearsal. 'Vocal' is a broader term that includes, among other things, singing to develop musical skill through the class chorus. With this in mind we need also to consider what has been said during the book about the pedagogical function of singing in the lower secondary school. Choral work is certainly not 'just singing'. It is the preparation for performance of choral music, usually in several parts and very likely including students of different ages from different parts of the school. Vocal work, too, is not 'just singing'. The class chorus is a continuous, linked, and developmental programme to internalize musical sounds and concepts through linking listening and the voice. It may well also contribute quite significantly to developing musical literacy and learning notation. Unlike choral work, the class chorus of course comprises students in one year group only. This, we shall shortly see, is highly significant.

The reference standard for cambiata music is undoubtedly that set by the Cambiata Vocal Institute of America (CVIA). CVIA was founded by Don Collins, a graduate student of Cooper's, in order to maintain and develop the cambiata concept after Cooper's death in 1971. Associated with CVIA is the Cambiata Press, which is uniquely dedicated to publishing arrangements that properly follow cambiata principles. Cambiata, then, is an American concept. In adapting something conceived in one country's education system for use in another we have to consider whether there are any contextual factors that need to be taken into account—and there are. There is the difference in age-range and therefore pubertal vocal status between the English middle or lower secondary school and the American middle or junior high school. There is the absence in the UK of elective programmes of choral instruction that take place during the time-tabled curriculum. Both these differences are of considerable significance.

Cambiata and treble

Cambiata has its roots in American junior high schools. It may be recalled from Chapter 1 that the age range for these is most commonly grade 7 to grade 9, that is age 12–13 to age 14–15 (UK Y8–Y10). This is the age range that works best with cambiata music. Most boys in US G7 or UK Y8 will begin with higher cambiata voices and progress during junior high school to emerging baritone. The dominant sound of an ensemble with such voices is quite unlike the treble sound of a class of 11–12-year-olds, as in the English Y7. It is lower and darker—more like a youthful 'male voice choir' voiced from high tenor to bass.

Advancing the age range by a year, as in US middle schools for G6–G8 (age 11–12 to 13–14) will have the potential effect of introducing a higher proportion of voices that are unchanged or only just beginning to change, but this is still some way from the English middle school with its age range of 9–10 to 12–13. An English middle-school choral ensemble would be dominated by

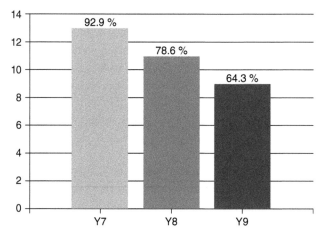

Figure 10.1 Response of the practitioner group to the question 'Does singing take place regularly as part of the timetabled curriculum for all pupils in any of the following groups?'

treble voices. The few emerging baritones that might be found would be a small minority, quite lacking the robust solidarity of the lower voices of a US junior high school ensemble. Middle schools are rare in the UK, though. The real issue confronting the much more common lower secondary school with its age range of 11–12 to 13–14 is shown in Figure 10.1.

Here we see a pattern that largely defines the approach currently taken in English lower secondary schools. Y7 is the most important year for singing, and there is progressively less use made of singing, particularly in chorus, as Y9 is approached. To be fair, this is an approach I have to some degree commended in what I have said about Y7 being the crowning year when all the primary school singing reaches its apotheosis. For the majority of boy choristers, Y7 is the 'golden year' when their treble voices reach their peak. It is the top year of the Scottish primary school. It is all these things and more but it is not cambiata. Use of cambiata might show in columns of more equal height as the decline toward Y9 should be diminished. Little of real value will be gained by dipping into cambiata once or twice during a lower-school scheme of work. It should be part of a programme of continuous vocal and musical development as it can be in the US-style choral programme.

The above graph assumes that *vocal work* is taking place in school year groups, in which case one is not looking to create *choral* parts such as SATB, one is looking to create part-singing that will accommodate the different voices found in one particular year group, and to accommodate the changes that occur within the class year on year. The vocal parts are thus likely to be closer

Table 10.1 Two-part voicing for boys

	Comfortable tessitura	Full range
Cambiata	G3–E4	F#3–F#4
Baritone	D3–A3	A2–C4

Table 10.2 Three-part voicing for boys

	Comfortable tessitura	Full range
Cambiata I	A3–F4	F#3–G4
Cambiata II	G3–D4	E3–E4
Baritone	D3–A3	A2–C4

together and fewer than in four-part choral work. For example, classes of 12–13-year olds would be well served by two- or three-part music with parts in the ranges shown in Tables 10.1 and 10.2 and currently recommended by CVIA. Y8 boys will all be accommodated within the cambiata ranges given unless they are advanced in puberty for their age, in which case they can take the baritone part. There will obviously be more baritones in a Y9 class than a Y8 class and the tone will darken.

It will be noted that these tables do not mention treble voices. Treble voices do not mix well with cambiata voices, and trebles and cambiate are best kept apart in my view, though a scheme of voicing for treble/cambiata I/cambiata II/baritone is suggested in the book by Barham & Nelson (1991), *The boy's changing voice: new solutions for today's choral teacher*. The inclusion of 'choral teacher' in the title of this American publication is not without significance. The way schooling is organized in the majority of English state schools does indeed present interesting challenges and dilemmas here. The treble voices of Y7 are something different and might still be treated in effect as the end of primary school (not that one would present it to the students in that way, of course). A Y7 treble chorus is both possible and desirable, but for other reasons we shall discuss shortly, it does not really belong with the cambiate. Y8 is the best time for boys (most boys, an inevitable compromise) to be taught explicitly about what puberty does to their voices and perhaps relaunch their singing careers as cambiate.

English music teachers, even some of those in schools where the singing is strong, may thus need to reappraise their practice if they are to capture what Irvine Cooper set out to achieve—junior high school boys participating enthusiastically in the singing class. There needs to be a positive focus on the changing voice with explicit teaching about puberty. The attitude that Y7 is where we do most of the singing needs to change—if, that is, it is thought important to keep boys singing and develop the sound of young male teenagers and young men singing in chorus.

Why to avoid SAB music

The main exception to cambiata/baritone voicing will be, not if there are boy trebles present, but if the class is mixed gender and there are girls present. Most who work with changing adolescent voices are agreed that mixed-gender work is far from ideal, but it is the reality most teachers have to work with during curriculum time. If we are going to develop cambiata work with mixed-gender classes in Y8 and Y9 (grade 7 and 8) we need to remember that girls' voices change as well as boys'. The important work of Lynne Gackle (e.g. Gackle 2011) was reviewed in Chapter 5. In cambiata, girls as well as boys should sing in a limited range until later adolescence when work can begin on developing the adult soprano or alto voice. Gackle advises a full range of B3–C5 with a tessitura of B3–G4 for girls at the climax of voice change. This can be expanded to A3–G5 once the mutational climax has passed and adult vocal qualities can begin to develop.

A single upper voice part with two lower parts sounds superficially like the SAB voicing that is popular for choirs of limited means (i.e. not many boys or men). Irvine Cooper was strongly against unison singing, for perhaps obvious reasons, but reserved his strongest objection for this kind for SAB voicing. SAB voicing has seen something of a growth in the UK, largely in response to the massive gender imbalance that has been allowed to develop in choral singing. The concept of SAB is that the majority of voices will be female and therefore soprano or alto. This is the first mistake because it runs contrary to much expert opinion that is against premature classification of girls' voices. It is better practice to adhere to the unclassified pubescent female ranges specified by Gackle, monitoring where the different registers of each individual girl's voice are beginning to develop. Cooper himself believed that adolescent girls should not be classified as sopranos and altos, calling them 'blues' and 'greens' to distinguish different parts of equal voices.

In SAB music there may be a few token men or boys, and these might be accommodated somewhere. If their voices have not 'broken' they can sing with the girls. If they have—well, they have their own 'men's' part. I write with some passion and conviction here because I made the mistake of using some SAB arrangements when I worked with the National Youth Choir on the original 'Boys Keep Singing' project. Given what I have said earlier about stereotyping boys' vocal music as inevitably about football and sport, it may or may not have been a mistake to fall back on 'You'll Never Walk Alone' and 'Swing Low, Sweet Chariot'.[2] It undoubtedly *was* a mistake to use a published SAB arrangement.

The boys brought it off, just. They did so only because they were experienced and accomplished singers under the direction of an exceptionally good conductor. Even so, they only just managed it and it did not bring out the best in their voices. For the average secondary school developing cambiata work, it would have been a complete disaster. I relate this story amongst other reasons to underline the strength of conviction one needs to have when confronting composers, arrangers and publishers with the unsuitability of SAB material for adolescent boys. Needless to say, I take full responsibility for doing this to the National Youth Choir!

Here is why we only narrowly averted disaster. First and worst, the soprano part was far too high and too wide in range for boy trebles who had begun puberty. All boys in the choir were of secondary school age and though at least one of them was still a cathedral chorister, there were too many moments when the tone was strained or forced. This really should be no surprise. Cooksey is quite clear that once a boy has begun puberty, he begins to lose the top of his range, which becomes 'breathy and strained'. The safest assumption is that all boys in the lower secondary school are in puberty, even if up to half of the Y7s are not.

An arrangement with cambiata I as the top part would have been far more suitable as the basis of keeping boys singing during adolescence. Alternatively an arrangement to show off the beauty of some unchanged Y7 voices would have been quite possible, even desirable. The mistake is in mixing the two. Cambiata and treble, as we have said, are best kept apart. Substituting girls for boy trebles during the time of female voice change, however, is not an answer. The soprano part is still too high and wide-ranging for girls undergoing voice change. Girls may be forced to develop too high an upper register that will not be the right one for them as adults. Neither is it advised that the girls sing alto as it may be too low for them, encouraging all sorts of bad habits such as larynx

---

[2] In the UK 'You'll Never Walk Alone' is associated with Liverpool Football Club and 'Swing Low, Sweet Chariot' with the England rugby team.

depression and failing to maintain the upper register that the girls will need if they are to begin properly to develop their adult voices.

For the boys, a generic, general-purpose 'men's' part is completely unsuitable. In the arrangement we used this part was, exactly as Cooper predicted, pitched with too high a tessitura for newly emerging baritone voices. The relatively mature and experienced young male voices of the National Youth Choir were able to cope, but newly emerging baritones in a Y9 class would not. They would be singing for too long in the upper extremities of their range when what is needed is to secure the lower tessitura in a relaxed way. The comfortable tessitura for newly emergent baritones given above is D3–A3, yet the tessitura of the 'men's' part of 'You'll Never Walk Alone' was F3–D4. Tension, strain, and an ultimate dissatisfaction will be almost inevitable if Y9 baritones are subjected to this.

For cambiata boys, it is a complete non-starter. Their voices just do not fit anywhere. The comfortable tessitura is G3–E4 with an extreme range of F♯3–F♯4. The tessitura of the given alto part in 'You'll Never Walk Alone' was C4–G4 with an extreme range of C4–C5. Too high and too wide-ranging! Neither can these boys sing the baritone part, because it goes down to C3, which is at least two notes below the bottom of their extreme range. This is why Cooper 'adamantly discouraged choosing soprano, alto, baritone (SAB) music for ... young singers because ... there was no part for the cambiatas [sic] to sing'.

If we truly understand young adolescent voices, we have to be resolute in the face of unsuitable published material. SAB arrangements are the least suitable of all for any ensemble that might be formed of 12–14-year-old boys and girls. The problem is that there is very little published material that *is* suitable. Until teachers and conductors with a good understanding of young adolescent voices start demanding it from publishers in the UK, this is likely to remain the case. Until then, there is much to be said for unison songs for baritones, cambiate, and girls separately. A well-disciplined Y9 class should be quite capable of group work, perhaps in break-out rooms if available. The resourceful teacher will devise ways for the young people to learn the songs, perhaps with a student with keyboard skills leading, or with a prerecorded rehearsal track.

Much more success was achieved when recording with the National Youth Choir for the 'Boys Keep Singing' project with the Sting song 'Fields of Gold'. For this we kept trebles and cambiate separate. We recorded it twice, once in the key of B♭ major to show off the beauty of some unchanged Y7 voices, then again in the key of F major to show off the equal but entirely different beauty of Y8 and Y9 voices that had descended to cambiata. The bottom note of F3 was four semitones below the average pitch at which these boys spoke, so it was a very specific and deliberate choice of key. F3 was the lowest clearly resonant note all the boys could produce and a semitone higher than the bottom of the suggested range for cambiata II. The top note of F4 was admittedly a semitone higher than the extended range for this part, but the boys being experienced and well-trained singers managed this easily. The sound that was produced was true cambiata—very different from either treble, alto, or even the sound of a cambiata/baritone group dominated by darker voices. There is much to be said for beautiful singing by one part alone to get the best out of voices. Part songs for adolescents are very difficult without some degree of compromise.

Finding cambiata music

Finding cambiata music that will appeal to young people in the UK is, at the time of writing, an extremely difficult task. There is almost no music at all arranged for the combination of changing-voice girls with cambiata and baritone boys. Perhaps the place to start is where the biggest problem lies, which in many UK schools is still with engaging boys. Although almost no music is currently available from UK publishers for cambiata, there is a quite extensive catalogue available in the US from the Cambiata Press. No one who has heard boys perform Cambiata Press music can doubt for a minute that it is highly appropriate, not only for the physical attributes of the boys' voices, but at least equally for their vocal identity. It makes the boys sound like exactly what they are—teenage boys and young men engaging in disciplined vocal work. It does so in a way that is truly honouring and authentic.

However, there are two considerations that the English conductor or teacher will want to think through before ordering from the Cambiata Press catalogue. First, the Cambiata Press is (understandably) heavily biased towards US culture. Only a small proportion of their catalogue is likely to appeal to teachers in the UK. This in itself is interesting. There is little in the way of pop arrangements that UK teachers, even those who engage in classical choral work outside school, tend to favour for classroom work. This is one quite significant reason for my describing a difference between vocal work and choral work. The term 'choral programme' is very much part of the language of CVIA and we are now well aware that this is not a familiar concept in UK schools. It was suggested that the term 'vocal work' has a wider meaning that is more applicable to the curriculum music lesson, with 'choral' being reserved for extracurricular work that boys and girls who enjoy choral singing undertake voluntarily.

When working in the UK, the best approach is to employ the cambiata principle when arranging songs for class use (see Chapter 7). Such songs need to be straightforward and can certainly be in unison or for one part only. The teacher need not pay undue attention to ill-informed calls for 'progression' that imply difficult part-singing. The aim must be for progression in accuracy that is possible when parts are properly limited to the compass of the voice. In all likelihood this will never have been achieved by classes brought up on 'just singing'. Boys who can be persuaded to join an extracurricular cambiata group will then be able to progress and tackle music designated as being for a 'choral programme'. Part and parcel of this is the way the arrangements are geared to teaching children how to read music and develop their sight-singing ability. This was discussed at some length in Chapters 7 and 8, so there is no need to repeat that discussion here. It is, though, worth reiterating that there needs to be some consideration given to the match between reading ability and reper-toire if vocal work is ever to progress beyond a call and response to 'just singing'. Given the average starting point for Y7 classes in English schools, a lot of progress needs to be made rapidly during Y7 to bring the majority of children up to the standard where they could attempt even the simplest of repertoire conceived with a 'choral programme' in mind. The difference between 'just singing' and choral accuracy can never be underestimated. Ideally, this is perhaps where we would want the students to be by the beginning of Y8, which is when cambiata work can really start.

Although there are very good reasons for gender segregation in lower secondary school singing, this is relatively unlikely to be the practice in class music. The best voicing for developing class cambiata work from Y8 upwards is probably three-part arrangements for girls, cambiata boys, and baritone boys. For advanced work, girls can be divided into two or more equally voiced parts, but not into alto/soprano. Boys could be split into a higher and lower cambiata as show in Table 10.3, but three-part work, let alone four or five, would be challenging for the majority of English secondary school classes.

Table 10.3 Three-part mixed-gender voicing during mid-puberty (Y8/grade 7)

	Comfortable tessitura	Full range
Girls	B3–G4	B3–C5
Cambiata boys	G3–E4	F♯3–F♯4
Baritone boys	D3–A3	A2–C4

Example 10.1 Assessing the suitability of music for cambiata voices.

This is more readily taken on board when represented in notation (Example 10.1). The first bar represents the safe range where the part should be pitched most of the time. The second bar represents how far the part can extend for more limited periods. When assessing the suitability of a piece of music, draw these notes in at the beginning of the score. Successively line a ruler up with these notes and run the edge along each vocal staff to make an assessment of whether the parts lie within these ranges and, if not, how often they exceed them. The odd note is probably acceptable but as a rough guide, if more than about 60% of the part is outside the tessitura and more than 5% of it outside the full range, it is not going to get the best out of the pubertal voices of untrained singers.

In this way, it is sometimes possible to select an SAB arrangement, especially if transposition is used. An example that I have seen boys in an elective cambiata group enjoy recently was 'N'kosi Sikeleii Africa' (Weeping) by Dan Heymann, arranged by Alexander L'Estrange (Example 10.2). This can be made to work for changing voices by transposing it down a tone, which approximately converts the alto part into a cambiata part and brings the soprano part into the range of changing-voice girls. The 'men's' part is also conveniently brought into the range of emerging baritones (albeit the very top). Without transposition, however, the repeated D4 in the baritone is too high for good tone and sound technical development in new baritone voices, and the soprano part also goes above the recommended C5 for girls. Should this part be sung by mid-pubertal boys, it will be just at that awkward point where some may need to flip to falsetto and the tone of those that do not may be strained and often unpleasant.

Some teachers who have developed a clear understanding of cambiata have been resourceful in scouring published work to spot pieces that might be adapted with a little simple ingenuity. Patrick Allen's 'Only You' (V. Clarke/ Flying Pickets; Example 10.3) from Singing Matters was made to work very

Example 10.2 'N'kosi Sikeleii Africa'. From L'Estrange (1998) *Songs of a Rainbow Nation* (Choral Basics), Faber.

Example 10.3 'Only You'. From Allen (1997) *Singing Matters,* Heinemann.

well for cambiata boys. The top part is in the A3–F4 tessitura that is ideal for early-stage cambiata boys and does not take them to the dangerous lift point around B4/D5 that occurs in the untransposed 'Weeping'. The other part was ingeniously performed in octaves, accommodating other boys comfortably within an upper or lower octave tessitura.

Example 10.4 'Scarborough Fair'. From Cambiata Press (1976): Sound of Singing Boys Choral Series

If the desire is truly for safe cambiata voicing rather than the SAB that is suitable for older singers, the choice is between ingenious adaptation, original teacher-created arrangements as described in Chapter 7, or purchasing music specifically arranged for cambiata. The extract of 'Scarborough Fair' (Example 10.4) is an example of an English folk song arrangement in the Cambiata Press catalogue. The parts lie perfectly within the specified ranges, as we might expect. All who heard a performance by some English cambiata boys agreed that it undoubtedly brought out the best in their voices. However, there is no girls' part and it cannot be said that the boys thought it the 'coolest' item in their concert. 'Scarborough Fair' was sung with compliance, 'Only You' with enthusiasm. At the same time, while the boys worked very hard at 'Scarborough Fair', the end result lacked the accuracy, precision, and finesse necessary to qualify as 'choral'.

This only goes to show, in my view, the considerable gulf between vocal work and choral work. Choral work has to begin with musical children well below lower secondary age, and be worked at intensively with those children as they progress into and through the lower secondary phase. Perhaps here there is a difference of expectation between the UK and the US? Finding music for *all* children to sing in chorus during the lower secondary phase that is more than 'just singing' pop yet occupies the territory of 'mutually acceptable repertoire' for challenging and useful learning is truly the greatest difficulty facing any composer, arranger or teacher. In the words of the Coldplay song, 'Nobody said it was easy, no one ever said it would be this hard'.

Summary

♦ The lower secondary years are a unique life phase when voices do not comfortably fit the conventional parts of SATB.

- The cambiata system of alternative voicing was devised to reflect the principle that the song should be made to fit the voice, not the voice the song.
- Cambiata is most suited in English schools to voices from Y8, Y9, and Y10. Treble voicing is still the best option for Y7. Beyond Y10, students can begin to work on their adult voices.
- Girls' voices change and operate outside SATB as well as boys' voices. It is possible and desirable to create mixed-gender voicing that reflects this.
- Cambiata voicing is not the same as SAB voicing. SAB arrangements are more suitable for adult ensembles or older students of sixth-form age.
- There is a difference in expectation and possibility between the elective US-style choral programme and the inclusive, compulsory music class for Y8 and Y9 students.
- The best approach to developing the system in the UK is to introduce simple cambiata-inspired arrangements in class, with then opportunity of progression to extracurricular choral work.

Further reading

Barham, T. & Nelson, D. (1991) *The boy's changing voice: new solutions for today's choral teacher*. Van Nuys, CA: Alfred Publishing.
Freer, P. (2009) *Getting started with middle school chorus*. Lanham, MD: Rowman & Littlefield.

Bibliography

Alexander, R. (2004) 'Still no pedagogy? Principles, pragmatism and compliance in primary education', *Cambridge Journal of Education*, 34 (1): 7–33.

Alexiadou, N. & Brock, C. (2013) *Education around the world: a comparative introduction*. London: Bloomsbury.

Ashley, M. (2002a) 'Singing, gender and health: perspectives from boys singing in a church choir', *Health Education* 102 (4): 180–7.

Ashley, M. (2002b) 'The spiritual, the cultural and the religious: what can we learn from a study of boy choristers?', *International Journal of Children's Spirituality* 7 (3): 258–72.

Ashley, M. (2006) *The Creative Education Project: arts enrichment in the Opportunity Network*. Bristol: Bristol City Council Arts Service.

Ashley, M. (2008a) 'Boyhood melancholia and the vocal projection of masculinity', *THYMOS: Journal of Boyhood Studies* 2 (1): 26–39.

Ashley, M. (2008b) *Teaching singing to boys and teenagers: The young male voice and the problem of masculinity*. Lampeter: Mellen.

Ashley, M. (2009a) *How high should boys sing? Gender, authenticity and credibility in the young male voice*. Aldershot: Ashgate.

Ashley, M. (2009b) 'Time to confront Willis's lads with a ballet class? A case study of educational orthodoxy and white working class boys', *British Journal of Sociology of Education* 30 (2): 179–91.

Ashley, M. (2010a) '"Real boys" don't sing, but real boys do: the challenge of constructing and communicating acceptable boyhood', *THYMOS: Journal of Boyhood Studies* 4 (1): 54–69.

Ashley, M. (2010b) '"Slappers who gouge your eyes": vocal performance as exemplification of disturbing inertia in gender equality', *Gender and Education* 22 (1): 47–62.

Ashley, M. (2010c) 'Technique or testosterone? an empirical report on changes in the longevity of boy singers', *Journal of Singing* 67 (2): 137–45.

Ashley, M. (2011) 'The perpetuation of male power and the loss of boyhood innocence: case studies from the music industry', *Journal of Youth Studies* 14 (1): 59–76.

Ashley, M. (2013) 'Broken voices or a broken curriculum? the impact of research on UK school choral practice with boys', *British Journal of Music Education*, 30 (3): 311–27.

Ashley, M. (2014) *Contemporary choral work with boys*. Abingdon: Compton.

Ashley, M. and Howard, D. (2009) *Boys keep singing*. Filmed material, directed by Tom Blackham. Liverpool: River Media.

Ashley, M. & Mecke A-C. (2013) Boyes are apt to change their voices at about fourteene yeares of age: an historical background to the debate about longevity in boy treble singers. *Reviews of Research in Human Learning and Music*, 1. Available at: <http://rrhlm.org/index.php/RRHLM/article/view/13>.

Baldy, C. (2010) *The student voice: An introduction to developing the singing voice*. Edinburgh: Dunedin.

Barham, T. & Nelson, D. (1991) *The boy's changing voice: New solutions for today's choral teacher*. New York: Alfred.

Barrett, M. (2010) 'On being and becoming a cathedral chorister: a cultural psychology account of the acquisition of early musical experience'. In *A Cultural Psychology of Music Education*, ed. M. Barrett, 259–87. Oxford: Oxford University Press.

Beadle, P. & Murphy, J. (2013) *Why are you shouting at us?: The dos and don'ts of behaviour management*. London: Bloomsbury.

Bennett, A. (2000) *Popular music and youth culture: Music, identity and place*. Basingstoke: Macmillan.

Bentley, A. (1966) *Musical ability in children and its measurement*. London: Harrap.

Bobetsky, V. (2009) *The magic of middle school musicals: Inspire your students to learn, grow, and succeed*. Lanham, MD: Rowman & Littlefield.

Bourdieu, P. (1984) *Distinction: A social critique of the judgment of taste*. London: RKP.

Bourdieu, P. (1986) 'The forms of capital'. In *Handbook of theory and research for the sociology of education*, ed. J. Richardson. New York: Greenwood Press.

Bridcut, J. (2006) *Britten's children*. London: Faber & Faber.

Button, S. (2009) 'Key Stage 3 pupils' perception of music', *Music Education Research* 8 (3): 417–31.

Carr, M. & Pauwels, A. (2006) *Boys and foreign language learning: Real boys don't do languages*. Basingstoke: Palgrave MacMillan.

Chaplain, R. (2003) *Teaching without disruption in secondary schools: A model for managing behaviour*. London: Routledge Falmer.

Connell, R. (2005) *Masculinities*. Cambridge: Polity.

Connell, R. & Messerschmidt, J. (2005) 'Hegemonic masculinity: rethinking the concept', *Gender and Society* 19 (6): 829–59.

Cooksey, J. (1993) 'Do adolescent voices "break" or do they "transform"'? *Voice*, 2 (1): 15–39.

Cooksey, J. (1999) *Working with adolescent voices*. St Louis, MO: Concordia.

Cooksey, J. (1977) 'A facet-factorial approach to rating high school choral music performance', *Journal of Research in Music Education*, 25 (2): 100–14.

Cooksey, J. (2000) 'Voice transformation in male adolescents'. In *Bodymind and voice—foundations of voice education* , ed. L. Thurman & G. Welch, 718–38. Iowa City, IA: The VoiceCare Network.

Cooksey, J. & Welch, G. (1998) 'Adolescence, singing development and national curricula design', *British Journal of Music Education*, 15 (1), 99–119.

Cooper, I. (1964) 'A study of boys' changing voices in Great Britain', *Music Educators Journal*, 51 (5): 110–18.

Cooper, I. & Wikstrom, T. (1962) 'Changing voices', *Music Educators Journal*, 48 (4): 148–51.

Crabbe, S. (2005) Giving boys a voice. <http://www.onlineopinion.com.au/view.asp?article=3385>.

Daily Telegraph (2008) 'National Song-book project falls flat' 04 May 2008 <http://www.telegraph.co.uk/news/1925329/National-Song-book-project-falls-flat.html>.

DCMS (2011) *The importance of music: a national plan for music education* [The Henley Report]. DFE-00086-2011 (<http://publications.education.gov.uk/>).

Dreger, R. M. & Aiken, L. R. (1957) 'The identification of number anxiety in a college population', *Journal of Educational Psychology*, 48: 344–51.

Durrant, C. (2003) *Choral conducting: Philosophy and practice*. London: Routledge.

Dweck, C. (2006) *Mindset: the new psychology of success*. New York: Ballantine.

Elorriaga, A. (2011) 'The construction of male gender identity through choir singing at a Spanish secondary school', *International Journal of Music Education* 29 (4): 318–32.

Emmons, S. & Chase, C. (2006) *Prescriptions for choral excellence*. New York: Oxford University Press.

Epstein, D., Elwood, J., Hey, V., & Maw, J. (1998) *Failing boys?* Buckingham: Open University Press.

Francis, B. (2010) 'Re/theorising gender: Female masculinity and male femininity in the classroom', *Gender and Education* 22 (5): 477–90.

Freer, P. (2009) 'Boys' descriptions of their experiences in choral music', *Research Studies in Music Education*, 31 (2): 142–60.

Freer, P. (2009) *Getting started with middle school chorus*. Lanham, MD: Rowman & Littlefield.

Freer, P. (2010) 'Two decades of research on possible selves and the "missing males" problem in choral music', *International Journal of Music Education* 28 (1): 17–30.

Freer, P. (2012) 'From boys to men: male choral singing in the United States', In *Perspectives on males and singing*, ed. S. Harrison *et al.* London: Springer.

Frosh, S., Phoenix, A., & Pattman, R. (2002) *Young masculinities*. Basingstoke: Palgrave.

Gackle, L. (2011) *Finding Ophelia's voice, opening Ophelia's heart: Nurturing the adolescent female voice: An exploration of the physiological, psychological, and music*. Dayton OH: Heritage Music Press.

Gardner, H. (1983) *Frames of mind: the theory of multiple intelligences*. Philadelphia, PA: Perseus Books.

Gaul, S. (2006) 'Boys singing their hearts out', *The Boys in Schools Bulletin*, 9: 25–8.

Gordon, E. (1986) *Intermediate measures of music audiation (grade 1-6) on CD-ROM*. Chicago, IL: GIA Publications. Available at <https://www.giamusic.com/search_details.cfm?title_id=9096>.

Gordon, E. (2007) *Learning sequences in music: a contemporary music learning theory*. Chicago, IL: GIA Publications.

Green, L. (1997) *Music, gender, education*. Cambridge: Cambridge University Press.

Green, L. (2002) *How popular musicians learn: A way ahead for music education*. Aldershot: Ashgate.

Green, L. (2008) *Music, informal learning and the school: A new classroom pedagogy*. Aldershot: Ashgate.

Green, L. (n.d.) *Musical futures, informal learning*. Video gallery at <http://www.musicalfutures.org/resources/c/informallearning>.

Green, L. & Walmsley, A. (2006) *Classroom resources for informal music learning at Key Stage 3*. Paul Hamlyn Foundation Special Project. Available at <http://www.webarchive.nationalarchives.gov.uk/20130401151715/http://www.education.gov.uk/publications/eOrderingDownload/0478-2006PDF-EN-03.pdf>.

Hanley, B. (1998) 'Gender in secondary music education in British Columbia', *British Journal of Music Education* 15 (1): 51–69.

Harrison, S. (2009) *Male voices: Stories of boys learning through making music.* Camberwell, VIC: ACER Press.

Henley, D. (2011) *Music education in England: A review for the Department for Education and the Department for Culture, Media and Sport.* DfE-00011-2011.

Houlahan, M. & Tacka, P. (2008*) Kodály today: A cognitive approach to elementary music education.* Oxford: Oxford University Press.

Jackson, C. (2003) 'Motives for "laddishness" at school: fear of failure and fear of the "feminine"', *British Educational Research Journal,* 29(4): 583–98.

Jackson, C. (2006) *Lads and ladettes in school.* Maidenhead: Open University Press.

Jarman-Ivens, F. (ed) (2007) *Oh boy! Masculinities and popular music.* London: Routledge.

Joyce, H. (2005) *The effects of sex, age and environment on attitudes to singing in Key Stage Two.* Master's dissertation, Institute of Education, University of London.

Juchniewicz, J. (2010) 'The influence of social intelligence on effective music teaching', *Journal of Research in Music Education,* 58 (3): 276–93.

Kehily, M. (2002) *Sexuality, gender and schooling: Shifting agendas in social learning.* London: Routledge Falmer.

Kehily, M. (2007) *Understanding youth: Perspectives, identities and practices.* London: Sage.

Kindlon, D. & Thompson, M. (2000) *Raising Cain: Protecting the emotional life of boys.* New York: Ballantine.

Koza, J. (1992) 'The missing males and other gender related issues in music education, 1914-1924', *Journal of Research in Music Education* 41 (3): 212–32.

Leck, H. (2009) 'The boy's ~~changing~~ expanding voice: take the high road', *Choral Journal,* 49 (11): 49–60.

Legg, R. (2013) Reviewing the situation: a narrative exploration of singing and gender in secondary schools, *Music Education Research,* 15(2): 168–79.

Lingard, B., Martino, W., & Mills, M. (2009) *Boys and schooling: Beyond structural reform.* Basingstoke: Palgrave Macmillan.

Love, R. with Frazier, D. (1999) *Set your voice free; how to get the singing or speaking voice you want.* New York, NY: Little, Brown.

Mac an Ghaill, M. (2002) Keynote address, expert symposium, Centre for Research in Education and Democracy, UWE, Bristol, 17 October.

Mac an Ghaill, M. & Haywood, C. (2006) *Gender, culture and society: Contemporary femininities and masculinities.* London: Palgrave McMillan.

MacGregor, H. & Chadwick, S. (2005) *Roald Dahl's Goldilocks and the Three Bears.* London: A&C Black.

Martin, A. & Marsh, H. (2009) 'Academic resilience and academic buoyancy: multidimensional and hierarchical conceptual framing of causes, correlates and cognate constructs', *Oxford Review of Education* 35 (3): 353–70.

Martino, W. & Meyenn, B. (2002) '"War, guns and cool, tough things": interrogating single-sex classes as a strategy for engaging boys in English,' *Cambridge Journal of Education,* 32 (2): 303–24.

Martino, W. & Pallotta-Chiarolli, M. (2003) *So what's a boy? Addressing issues of masculinity and schooling.* Maidenhead: Open University Press.

McCormack, M. & Anderson, E. (2010) '"It's just not acceptable any more": the erosion of homophobia and the softening of masculinity at an English sixth form', *Sociology,* 44 (5), 843–59.

McPhersen, G. (2006) *The child as musician: A handbook of musical development.* Oxford: Oxford University Press.

Mills, J. (2005) *Music in the school.* Oxford: Oxford University Press.

Mills, M. & Keddie, A. (2007) 'Teaching boys and gender justice', *International Journal of Inclusive Education* 11 (3): 335–54.

Neall, L. (2002) *Bringing the best out in boys: Communication strategies for teachers.* Stroud: Hawthorn Press.

OFSTED (2009) *Making more of music: An evaluation of music in schools*, Office for Standards in Education report 2005/08, 080235. London: DCSF.

OFSTED (2012) *Music in schools, wider still and wider: Quality and inequality in music education 2008-2011.* Office for Standards in Education report 110158. Manchester: DfE.

OFSTED (2013) *Music in schools: Promoting good practice.* Manchester: Office for Standards in Education.

OFSTED (2013) *Music in schools: What hubs must do.* Office for Standards in Education report 130231. Manchester: DfE.

Paechter, C. (2006) 'Masculine feminities/feminine masculinities: power, identities and gender', *Gender and Education*, 18 (3): 253–63.

Paechter, C. (2012) 'Bodies, identities and performances: reconfiguring the language of gender and schooling', *Gender and Education*, 24 (2): 229–41.

Parry, C. H. (1899) Inaugural address. *Journal of the Folk-Song Society*, l (1), 1–2.

Phillips, K. (2003) 'Creating a safe environment for singing', *Choral Journal*, 43: 41–3.

Phillips, K. (2013) *Teaching kids to sing.* (2nd edn.) New York: Schirmer Books.

Pitts, S. (2012) *Chances and choices: Exploring the impact of music education.* Oxford: Oxford University Press.

Pollack, W. (1999) *Real boys: Rescuing our sons from the myths of boyhood.* New York: Henry Holt.

Regueiro, P. (2000) 'An analysis of gender in a Spanish music text book', *Music Education Research*, 2 (1): 57–73.

Rich, A. (1980) 'Compulsory heterosexuality and lesbian existence', *Signs* 5 (4): 631–60.

Roberts, R. & Christenson, P. (1997) *It's not only rock and roll: Popular music in the lives of adolescents.* Cresskill, NJ: Hampton Press.

Roberts, S. (2012) '"I just got on with it": the educational experience of ordinary yet overlooked boys', *British Journal of Sociology of Education* 33 (2): 203–21.

Roulston, K. & Mills, M. (2000) 'Male teachers in feminised areas: marching to the beat of the men's movement drums?' *Oxford Review of Education* 26 (2): 221–37.

Rudolph, T. & Frankel, J. (2009) *YouTube in music education.* Milwaukee, MI: Hal Leonard.

Rutkowski, J. (2010) 'The measurement and evaluation of children's singing voice development', *Visions of Research in Music Education*, 16 (1): 81–95.

Sassi, S. (2009) *Effects of vocal registration training on the vocal range and perceived comfort of the adolescent male singer.* Doctoral thesis, State University of New Jersey.

Savage, M. (2006) 'The musical field', *Cultural Trends* 15 (2/3): 159–74.

Schwartz, K. & Fouts, G. (2003) 'Music preference, personality, style and developmental issues of adolescents', *Journal of Youth and Adolescence*, 32 (3): 205–13.

Scott-Bennetts, K. (2013) 'Boys' music? School context and middle school boys' musical choices', *Music Education Research*, 15 (2): 214–30.

Skelton, C. (2001) *Schooling the boys*. Buckingham: Open University Press.

Skelton, C. & Francis, B. (2010) 'The "renaissance child": high achievement and gender in late modernity', *International Journal of Inclusive Education*, 16 (4): 441–59.

Suin, R. & Edwards, R. (1982) 'The measurement of mathematics anxiety: the mathematics anxiety rating scale for adolescents—MARS A', *Journal of Clinical Psychology*, 38 (3): 576–80.

Swain, J. (2002) 'The right stuff: fashioning an identity through clothing in a junior school', *Gender and Education* 14 (1): 53–69.

Swanson, F. (1961) The proper care and feeding of changing voices. *Music Educators Journal*, 48 (2): 63–67.

Swanson, F. (1977) *The male singing voice ages eight to eighteen*. Cedar Rapids, LA: Laurance Press.

Teaching Music (2014) <http://www.teachingmusic.org.uk/>. Accessed July 2014.

Viggiano, F. (1941) 'Reaching the adolescent who thinks it's sissy to sing', *Music Educators Journal*, 27: 62–3.

Walker, B. & Kushner, S. (1999) The building site: an educational approach to masculine identities. *Journal of Youth Studies*, 2 (1): 45–8.

Warin, J. (2010) *Stories of self: Tracking children's identity and wellbeing through the school years*. Stoke-on-Trent: Trentham.

Welch, G. (2006) 'Singing and vocal development'. In *The child as musician: A handbook of musical development*. ed. G. McPherson, 311–29. Oxford: Oxford University Press.

Welch, G. (2009) Evidence of the development of vocal pitch matching in children, *Japanese Journal of Music Education Research*, 1–13. Available at <http://imerc.org/papers/nsp/welch2009.pdf>.

Welch, G., Himonides, E., Papageorgi, J., Saunders, T., Rinta, C., Stewart, C., Preti, J., Lani, M. V., & Hill, J. (2009a) The National Singing Programme for primary schools in England: an initial baseline study, *Music Education Research*, 11 (1): 1–22.

Welch, G., Papageorgi, I., Vraka, M., Himonides, E., & Saunders, J. (2009b) *The Chorister Outreach programme: a research evaluation 2008–2009*. London: IMERC/Institute of Education.

Whiteley, S. (2005) *Too much too young: Popular music, age and gender*. Abingdon: Routledge.

Williams, J. (2012) *Teaching singing to children and young adults*. Abingdon: Compton.

Willis, E. & Kenny, D. (2008) 'Effect of voice change on singing pitch accuracy in young male singers', *Journal of Interdisciplinary Music Studies*, 2 (1&2): 111–19.

Wing Chan, T. & Goldthorpe, J. (2007) 'The social stratification of cultural consumption: some policy implications of a research project', *Cultural Trends*, 16 (4): 373–83.

Wiseman, H. (1967) *The singing class*. Oxford: Pergamon.

Younger, M., Warrington, W., Gray, J., Ruddick, J., McClellan, R., Bearne, E. Kershner, R., & Bricheno, P. (2005) *Raising boys' achievement*. Research report 636. London: DfE.

Zyngier, D. (2009) 'Doing it to (for) boys (again): do we really need more books telling us there is a problem with boys' underachievement in education?' *Gender and Education*, 29 (1): 111–18.

Index